TRANSGENDER STUDENTS
IN ELEMENTARY SCHOOL

Youth Development *and* **Education Series**

Series edited by Michael Sadowski

OTHER BOOKS IN THIS SERIES

TRANSGENDER STUDENTS IN ELEMENTARY SCHOOL

*Creating an Affirming
and Inclusive
School Culture*

MELINDA M. MANGIN

HARVARD EDUCATION PRESS
Cambridge, Massachusetts

Paperback ISBN 978-1-68253-525-7
Library Edition ISBN 978-1-68253-526-4

Library of Congress Cataloging-in-Publication data is on file.

Published by Harvard Education Press,
an imprint of the Harvard Education Publishing Group

Harvard Education Press
8 Story Street
Cambridge, MA 02138

Cover Design: Ciano Design
Cover Image: Ekaterina kkch/Shutterstock.com

The typefaces in this book are Adobe Garamond Pro and Futura Standard.

*To queerlings everywhere
and to my favorite gender warriors:
Tavish, Dragon, and Tenzin.
You are my greatest joy.*

Contents

Foreword

Growing up as a transgender youth in an extremely under-resourced environment, I never had a vocabulary to talk about my feelings. There wasn't anyone I could look to and see my experiences and feelings reflected back at me. There was no discussion about gender outside the strict and binary norms that we were all expected to adhere to. These conversations don't happen for a lot of reasons. Ignorance, intolerance, apathy. But one big reason these conversations don't happen is that there isn't enough education or resources to help guide caretakers, educators, and cisgender peers.

When I came out as a boy to my mother in 2014, the closest support group was nearly two hours away. There were very few books; there were even very few websites. And what could be found often still used antiquated language, or perpetuated bad or outdated information on transitioning as a minor.

Just when I finally got over the anxiety and urgency of early transition and had begun to happily settle in to myself, I was thrust into a terrible situation by my school system. I was banned from using the boys' bathroom for being transgender, and so began a legal battle that has spanned four years and counting. The American Civil Liberties Union filed suit on my behalf, arguing that the school's bathroom policy is unconstitutional under the Fourteenth Amendment and violates Title IX, a federal law prohibiting sex discrimination by schools. The case was granted cert at the Supreme Court before eventually moving back down into the lower courts again. In 2019, the US District Court for the Eastern District of Virginia ruled that the school had violated my rights.[1]

cisgender: denoting or relating to someone whose sense of personal identity corresponds with gender assigned to them at birth.

At every stage where I suffered harm, from the mistakes my mother made early in my transition to the discrimination and public humiliation I faced at the hands of my school board, quality information was desperately lacking. Some information was out there, but very little in the way of helping schools and educators navigate the experience of having a trans student. Nothing showed the humanity of trans people while also outlining how we can best support them in an educational environment.

Melinda Mangin's book *Transgender Students in Elementary School* bridges that gap in a way that is accessible and actionable. Using real-world examples, Mangin introduces you to the perspectives and lives of transgender children and the educators who lead them. She also connects these examples to guided questions, to better frame information that may well be entirely new to many people. She begins with the concept of what it means to be transgender, and goes on to show how we all can use this knowledge to create an equitable space for everyone.

Importantly, Mangin talks about these things in the context of intersectionality, describing the ways in which our backgrounds affect our experiences. She examines power structures and privilege, highlighting the ways that these strict and binary gender expectations harm us all.

I think it is more than fair to say that if a book like this existed in 2014 when I came out, I may well have had a safer and less traumatic transition. The people in my life and in my school system may have better known how to support me and the other trans kids who are in that school or who one day will be.

A single book alone will not eliminate all of these inequalities, but *Transgender Students in Elementary School* provides a baseline for a dialogue that we can all build from. The necessary societal, cultural, legislative, and educational changes all must work together to liberate trans and gender-nonconforming people, and the largest part of that starts with education. If the culture and language in the classrooms that are shaping young minds are changed fundamentally, then the world will quickly become a place where discrimination or pain because of who you are is a thing of the shameful past. Children will be exposed to far fewer instances of rigid gender norms being forced upon them, resulting in less shame, less pain, and fewer restrictions on happiness.

Mangin's book does not just start the conversation, it offers the tools to keep it going. While I transitioned several years before its publication, I remain excited to see how this book and other important resources like it can help change the landscape both within our educational system and within our society. *Transgender Students in Elementary School* will undoubtedly be a valuable and powerful tool in the hands of people who want to build a better world for the trans and gender-nonconforming people living in it.

—Gavin Grimm

CHAPTER 1

"Are You a Boy or a Girl?"

Teaching preK for so long, I have found it very interesting how early and quickly kids pick up gender and what they can and can't do based on their gender. Also, when they are given an option or their idea is challenged, it's interesting how quickly they can shift. I think of this particularly with colors. Kids say, "Pink is for girls, pink is for girls," and I say, "No, I like pink and I'm a boy. Boys can use pink." After a couple of conversations, a number of the boys say, "I want to use pink, I want to use pink," and they just feel free where initially they said "no" to pink. All they really needed was someone to challenge the idea that it doesn't have to be the way things are.

Even though they seem very set, I can read them a book and talk about another child's experience, saying, "This is another idea, another way to be." A lot of the books I read with trans or gender-nonconforming characters are about treating each other fairly. Seeing a kid get treated badly and cry because they were made fun of, my students really connect with that. Then they say, "Well, that's just who they want to be." Some kids are very self-defined saying, "No, boys don't do that" or "I can't do that." So, we talk about it in a way that says, "Everyone decides for themselves what they want to be. You can be a boy and you don't have to like pink, but you can't tell other people what they can or can't be. You have to respect them."

—**DANNY CARVER**, PS 25 Kindergarten Teacher

In second grade, on the bus, a kid came up to her and said,
"Are you a boy or a girl? I'm going to find out."

—MEREDITH'S MOM

"Are you a boy or a girl?" is a common question heard on playgrounds and in parks, wherever children interact and, especially, when children transgress social norms for boys and girls. On the surface, "Are you a boy or a girl?" sounds like a request for factual information, but underneath, this question demonstrates how gender is policed, even among young children, and underscores the problematic nature of gender in our society and in our schools. The question frames gender as a binary concept and reinforces the idea that gender should be easy to discern based on external indicators. Not being discernably boy or girl is construed as a problem that requires investigation. Therefore, asking whether someone is a boy or a girl is not an innocent question. It is both an accusation and an insult. It demands and threatens exposure. In this instance, the follow-up statement, "I'm going to find out," also threatens violence. For transgender and gender-expansive children, being asked "Are you a boy or a girl?" can evoke feelings of shame and humiliation. This sets the context for transgender students' school experiences.

wow! *

Schools today are more likely than ever to enroll transgender students. These students may openly identify as transgender, or they may be nondisclosed, preferring not to share their gender identity. Some may fit gender norms for girls and boys, whereas others may be gender expansive, defying traditional gender expectations. The public has been quick to focus on challenges associated with transgender students when, in reality, these children present schools with a unique and valuable opportunity. Transgender students remind us that gender is complex, and gender norms are constraining. The limits imposed by traditional notions of gender inhibit development and reinforce inequity. Transgender students present us with an opportunity to envision and create schools that truly reflect the educational ideal of equity.

This book presents the experiences of elementary-level educators who support transgender and gender-expansive students. It is both an introduction to transgender identities and a guide for educators who want to create learning environments that facilitate all students' sense of belonging and reduce the constraints inherent in binary gender norms. The examples come from practicing educators working in a range of elementary school contexts including public, private, charter, and religious schools. The educators' stories demonstrate both the successes and challenges of creating affirming school environments for transgender and gender-expansive students. As such, readers will find real stories of imperfect practice meant to convey possibility. Through this book, educators can deepen their understandings about *why* we need to make schools gender inclusive and *how* to make it happen. In this way, the book is designed to be a useful tool for practicing educators who can use the examples to inform their own practice.

For many educators, the topic of transgender students is new and unfamiliar territory. Educators seldom receive formal training related to gender or the needs of gender-diverse students.[1] This lack of training makes teachers, principals, and other educators uncertain about what it means to be transgender and how to support transgender students, and also concerned that support could lead to backlash from the school community.[2] Consequently, many educators fail to take any proactive steps to affirm transgender students. While some educators may be intentionally unsupportive and even transphobic, most educators want to help their students. What appears to be a lack of support for transgender students may stem from a lack of know-how, fear of reprisals, or worries about getting it right.[3] Educators need opportunities to learn about gender and how to support students with a wide range of gender identities. For transgender and gender-expansive children, educators' support can, quite literally, make the difference between life and death.

Some educators may question whether their limited time should be spent learning about transgender children. This thinking misses the real problem, which is not transgender children, but rather, gender norms. Traditional gender norms are expressed as two mutually exclusive categories—boy and girl—whereby the activities and behaviors considered appropriate for one are deemed unacceptable for the other. In the past, these so-called sex-role differences between men and women were believed to be natural, biological differences; however, comparisons over time and across cultures clearly show that gender norms result from learned societal expectations, not our biology. Rigid enforcement of binary gender norms has a direct adverse effect on everyone because gender norms limit who we can be and what we can do. Moreover, gender norms reinforce and perpetuate inequity. Consider, for example, how gendered career expectations impede women's earning potential or how gendered parenting norms reduce fathers' opportunity to nurture their children.

While gender norms constrain everyone, they are especially harmful to gender-nonconforming people who are subjected to strict gender policing, the enforcement of gender norms. Gender policing involves subtle and not-so-subtle messaging about the "right" way to be a boy or girl. In the process, gender policing also conveys that more expansive forms of gender expression are deviant or bad, leading many gender-nonconforming people to feel shame and self-hatred. The stigma associated with gender nonconformity can prompt families to rigorously enforce gender norms, sometimes in an attempt to deflect shame or, paradoxically, to protect their children from ridicule and harassment. Some children are subjected to harmful "reparative" therapy, which includes punishments for nonconforming behaviors. Tragically, children who do not conform to gender norms commonly face mistreatment and even abuse.[4]

Schools are common sites for gender policing and surveillance. Students whose gender expression does not conform to societal norms are often met with pathological levels of intolerance, including harassment and bullying. As a result, gender-expansive students are at heightened risk for social exclusion, emotional distress, and disrupted learning.[5] The 2015 US Transgender Survey reported:

> Fifty-four percent (54%) of those who were out or perceived as transgender in K–12 were verbally harassed, nearly one-quarter (24%) were physically attacked, and 13% were sexually assaulted in K–12 because of being transgender. . . . Seventeen percent (17%) faced such severe mistreatment as a transgender person that they left a K–12 school.[6]

For students with additional marginalized identities based on race, ethnicity, language, religion, class, citizenship, ability, etc., the adverse effects of intolerance are even greater.[7] The prevalence of gender policing suggests that schools may not be sites for growth and learning for gender-expansive students, but rather, our educational institutions may be toxic. Whereas gender norms are limiting for everyone, for gender-expansive children the dehumanizing effects of gender norms can be life threatening. Education scholar Harper B. Keenan brings this idea into stark reality stating, "In classrooms I was *taught* to hate my genderqueerness. I was *taught* to hate myself."[8]

However, as Danny Carver said in the opening vignette, "It doesn't have to be the way things are." Most educators enter the profession to make a positive difference in the lives of children. The realization that schools are toxic for some students should serve as a catalyst to change our educational practices. That said, meaningful change is not achieved easily, particularly when it upsets existing power structures.[9] Inequity in the United States did not happen by chance. Our institutions are intentionally designed to reproduce and maintain systems of inequality that disproportionately advantage some (historically speaking, White males) and restrict access to opportunity for others. Institutionalization of inequity in our economic, social, legal, political, and educational systems reinforces beliefs about inequity as natural and justified. On this basis, schools can be understood as intentionally reinforcing inequity, including gender inequity.

Educators who want to improve schools for transgender and gender-expansive students may be uncertain about what is allowable under the law. Courts are increasingly defending transgender students' rights. As of 2019, nine legal rulings in seven states upheld existing protections for transgender students.[10] Collectively, these rulings indicate that, under Title IX of the Education Amendments of 1972 and the Equal Protection Clause of the US Constitution, schools must allow equal access to restrooms for transgender students; school policies that protect transgender students do not violate others' rights; and discrimination against transgender students is sex discrimination. These rulings reinforce federal civil rights protections for transgender students and suggest that educators should feel confident about pressing for more supportive educational practices. Some districts and state departments of education are developing policies aimed at supporting transgender students and educators.[11] At the same time, absent opportunities to learn about transgender identities and how to support transgender students and educators, policy mandates alone are unlikely to facilitate change.[12] Deeply entrenched gender bias can impede policy implementation, and fear of reprisal can dissuade educators from speaking up about inequity.

Even when educators are willing, change is difficult and changing gender norms in schools is a formidable task. Meaningful change requires a multidimensional approach that includes changing individuals' beliefs in addition to policy, practice, and school culture. This book features schools and educators who demonstrate that change is possible. Schools do not have to be sites for gender policing. At the same time, these schools also show that sustaining change is difficult. This effort requires more than the good will of individual teachers, but rather, meaningful shifts in the shared norms that constitute school culture. Cultural change happens when educators collaboratively shift the status quo of what is acceptable and advocate for policies and practices that dismantle gender inequity in our schools. Meaningful cultural change can begin with individual educators who are willing to rethink the role of gender in schools and make changes to their practice so that schools can become sites of belonging for all students, regardless of gender identity.

If making this type of change seems like a near-impossible task, remember that beliefs about gender are changing in the United States. Increased visibility has brought greater awareness about gender in general and transgender identities in particular. Most people don't have to look beyond their own experience to realize that gender is complex and in flux. As individuals, our gender identity evolves over time with new experiences and in response to cultural and social trends.[13] At any given point in time, we can express ourselves in ways that are both "masculine" and "feminine." We increasingly understand that there are no "boy things" and "girl things" and that anyone can like any activity, toy, color, hobby, etc. In short, there is no one way to be a boy or a girl, and there are many gender identities other than girl or boy. You might even conclude that there are as many different gender identities as there are people because everyone's gender identity is unique. Now, more than ever, we understand that gender identity is complex. If anything, our schools lag behind shifting societal trends.

As we take up the challenge of making schools sites of gender equity, we need to think beyond equality for girls and boys. Schools are designed to maintain and reinforce gender inequity through structures and practices that constrain all children's identities to traditional gender norms that situate boys and girls as mutually exclusive. Gender equity requires that we trouble binary notions of gender and affirm transgender and gender-expansive identities. Transgender children are not a problem to be fixed; rather, our schools constrain gender development in ways that restrict learning and hurt children. The goal, then, should be to create school cultures where every child's gender identity is nurtured and affirmed.

THIS BOOK

This book is designed to be a useful tool for educators who can use the examples to inform their own practice. At the same time, it is impossible to present every possible scenario, and, more importantly, responses to difficult educational challenges cannot be neatly articulated in a playbook. Prescriptive or formulaic dictates that attempt to standardize procedures are unlikely to yield real, meaningful changes to practice. Similarly, the guidelines that emerge from legal rulings and policy mandates are also limited in their capacity to effect change. As blunt instruments for reform, policies can provide general parameters for action but lack the nuance required to solve complex problems. For these reasons, educators who aim to support transgender and gender-expansive students must be reflective practitioners, capable of critically examining, questioning, and deliberating around difficult matters and committed to dismantling systems of gender inequity that reinforce and reproduce oppression. The examples presented in this volume provide readers with an opportunity to begin to engage in the kind of reflective practice needed to do this work.

The target audience for this book is educators who are new to the topic of transgender identities. The content can be incorporated into teacher education courses that introduce preservice teachers to historically marginalized student populations and the educational practices that promote students' sense of belonging. Experienced teachers who want to deepen their commitment to gender equity in the classroom can also use this book to explore new pedagogical practices and gender-neutral ways to organize their classrooms. Other educational stakeholders such as school board members and district-level administrators can turn to this book to strengthen their understanding of how transgender children experience school settings and how to develop policies that make schools more gender inclusive. The stories from this book can also inform parents about the kinds of gender-equitable practices they can ask for in their children's classrooms and schools. Proactive school districts can feature this book as part of a communitywide book study or smaller book study groups, as a way to build understanding within the larger school community.

To protect the privacy of the study participants, all names of people, schools, and school districts are pseudonyms—with one exception. Afsaneh Moradian is not a pseudonym but rather the actual author of *Jamie Is Jamie*. Moradian's name is used intentionally, with permission.

Terms and Language

The language in this book is intended to be accessible to people who are new to the topic of gender and gender identities other than girl and boy. The use of plain speech facilitates application of the practices and ideas that the educators describe. A glossary of transgender-related terms is included at the end of this volume to aid clarification.

Writing about transgender identities presents a linguistic challenge because language is always evolving. Terms that were previously acceptable may become less favorable, or even derogatory. In some instances, terms that were once derisive, like *queer*, are reclaimed as a way to assert agency. Historically, many of the terms used to describe transgender identities came from the fields of medicine and psychology, fields that pathologized transgender people as mentally ill and even dangerous. Some terms have always been derogatory, such as *tranny*, which is short for *transvestite* and extremely demeaning. Other terms that remain common are being increasingly critiqued, including *gender variant, gender nonconforming* (GNC), *FTM* (female to male), and *MTF* (male to female). Generational, cultural, and contextual differences can influence the appropriateness of terms.[14] There is no singular transgender community, and not everyone agrees on terminology. The best approach is to respect the terms that transgender people use for themselves.

Throughout this book, I use the adjectives *transgender* and *gender expansive*.[15] When I use *transgender* to describe gender identity, I am including all gender identities other than *cisgender*, which is an adjective to describe people whose identity aligns with the legal sex category assigned to them at birth. Transgender people commonly use even more precise terms to describe their gender identity including, but not limited to, *agender, bigender, gender expansive, gender fabulous, gender fluid, genderqueer, nonbinary* (sometimes ENBY or nb), *transfeminine, transmasculine,* among many others. The use of so many varied terms reflects the highly personal nature of gender. My use of the term *transgender* is, therefore, an imprecise umbrella term that says very little about the gendered experiences of individuals. It is important not to make assumptions about another person's gender based on a term that can have different meanings to different people.

I also use the term *gender expansive* to explicitly refer to gender identities or forms of expression that challenge binary gender norms for boys and girls. Some transgender people feel a strong gender identity that aligns with binary gender norms, albeit for a gender/sex that is "opposite" from the one they were assigned at birth. However, many more people feel a sense of gender identity that defies conventional gender norms. They may identify as somewhere in the middle of the boy-girl continuum, or they may feel equally boy and girl. Some gender-expansive people experience shifting gender identities, feeling one way some days and different on another day. Although gender-expansive identities may be dynamic, they do not indicate gender confusion. Rather, gender-expansive identities remind us that gender norms are limiting and that everyone's identities shift in both subtle and significant ways. By using the term *gender expansive*, I want to explicitly highlight gender identities that challenge us to think beyond the gender binary.

When quoting the educators and families featured in this book, I have retained the substantive meaning of their speech while removing filler sounds and words such as *um, like,* and *you know.* This helps increase readability without distorting the speaker's meaning. Sometimes the featured speakers use a child's deadname, their name prior to social transition, or pronouns that are no longer appropriate.[16] This usually happens when the speaker is referring to a previous time when those pronouns and/or name were the terms in use. In those instances, I have used *[sic]* to note the erroneous language.

The Educators, Schools, and Families in This Study

The stories in this book are the result of qualitative research. Generally speaking, qualitative research is a way to intentionally document and attempt to explain people's experiences, thoughts, and feelings. When designing a research study, researchers make decisions about what to research and why, how to identify participants, and how to ethically elicit accurate and detailed information. Here, I briefly describe how I collected stories from educators and families. More detailed information about the research methodologies can be found in appendix A.

I initiated this study with one overarching question: How do elementary-level educators create supportive environments for transgender and gender-expansive students? I was specifically interested in the elementary level because adults often describe children in early grades as being too young to learn about gender. I was curious about how educators in elementary schools were handling this potentially controversial topic. Rather than randomly select participants, I wanted to learn from educators who were actively engaged in supporting transgender and gender-expansive students. But how to find these educators? I turned to parents who had sought guidance and services for their transgender and gender-expansive children. Three organizations assisted me in making connections with parents: PFLAG, GLSEN, and Camp Aranu'tiq.[17] Via email, I asked parents who were affiliated with these groups to nominate elementary principals they perceived as having been supportive of their child. Parents provided me with the names of twenty principals from six states, all of whom agreed to be interviewed.

After interviewing the principals, I wanted to know more about how teachers and other school-level educators created supportive environments for transgender children. Five of the principals invited me to their schools to conduct observations and interviews with educators in their school. At each of these case study schools, I spoke with approximately ten educators, all of whom had worked with the transgender child who served as the entry point for this study. The teachers, principals, and support staff shared their experiences and insights, giving rise to detailed stories about their successes and challenges. To round out my understanding, I also interviewed eight parents. Six were mothers who recommended principals for this study. Two were mothers of gender-expansive and transgender children, whom

I met while interacting with educators at the case study schools. In all, I conducted seventy-five formal interviews and had many more informal interactions with a wide range of school personnel. The end result is a set of rich narratives that detail educators' personal stories and demonstrate the potential for changing how we handle gender in our schools.

The educators whose stories are presented in this book are fairly typical of other elementary-level educators in the United States. All identified as cisgender, and nearly all described themselves as heterosexual and White. Few had any specialized knowledge about gender, and even fewer had experience with transgender adults. None of the educators had any prior experiences working with openly transgender students, although some recalled having students who departed from gender norms. These educators were also typical in their lack of gender-related training. If they received any training, it was only after their school knowingly enrolled a transgender or gender-expansive student. As fairly typical educators, they shared experiences that may generalize to a larger population of teachers.

The schools presented in this book represent a variety of contexts. They are located across six different states: Delaware, Massachusetts, New Jersey, New York, Pennsylvania, and Rhode Island. They reflect a range of school settings including public, private, charter, and religious schools. They also reflect a range of socioeconomic and demographic contexts. This variety can help readers see themselves in the stories. Too often, when educators are asked to change their practice, they lack adequate examples for *how* to change, or the examples come from educators in ideal circumstances, with extended learning opportunities, special supports, and access to high-quality resources. Such exemplars can leave educators feeling as though the proposed changes are unrealistic and prompt them to conclude, "Not at my school, not with my kids." In contrast, the schools featured in this book represent a variety of contexts, making it more likely that readers may be able to imagine themselves applying the ideas from this book in their own schools.

It is also important to note the ways in which the educators, schools, and families in this book may not be typical or generalizable. Foremost, all of the principals were characterized as being "supportive" by the families that recommended them for participation. Moreover, the families themselves were supportive of their gender-expansive and transgender children. This twofold source of supports—principals and parents—may be significantly different from other contexts where principals and parents may be reluctant to learn about gender or even hostile toward transgender people. With regard to the schools, although they represent a range of contexts, they tilt toward wealthier and predominantly White communities. Similarly, the families who recommended their child's principal also skew wealthy, White, and educated. As such, the families had a high level of social capital and privilege that likely contributed to their ability to successfully advocate for their children.

The Children

This book is not specifically about transgender and gender-expansive children; rather, it is about the practices that cisgender educators used to support and affirm them. After careful deliberation, I chose not to interview the children because, even with the best intentions, interviews can sometimes cause harm. First, there is a delicate line between giving voice to marginalized people and treating them as objects of curiosity, which contributes to their dehumanization. This challenge may be exacerbated for children who may not have the language to fully convey their experience. Second, transgender children face relentless scrutiny as they are continually asked to justify their very being, which can cause them to feel self-doubt, shame, and even trauma. Interviews can reproduce this sense of being scrutinized. Interviews can also revive unpleasant memories and make children feel uncomfortable or unsafe. Third, even when the intention is to "give voice to the voiceless," the interviewee inevitably relinquishes some control over their own story, which is interpreted by the interviewer. This reality amplifies the inherent lack of control that children have over their own life experiences. Given these considerations, I was not 100 percent certain that interviews would not pose a risk to the children's emotional well-being. As a result, the stories in this book focus primarily on the adults' experiences.[18]

Eighteen children served as introductory entry points for this study, acting as the connection between the adult interviewees and me. Looking across the eighteen students, ten were assigned female at birth, and eight were assigned male at birth. Based on the adults' reports, it seems that all eighteen ultimately claimed binary gender identities, conforming to gender norms; however, some experienced extended periods (sometimes years) of more expansive or nonconforming gender expression. Nearly all of the eighteen students used traditional pronouns—*she/her/hers* and *he/him/his*—as opposed to singular *they/them/their/theirs* or other less common pronouns such as *ze/zir/zirs*. Five of the eighteen were children of color, four of whom were transracial adoptees.[19] In their interviews, adults reference these eighteen children as well as other transgender and gender-expansive students, when they describe how they worked to create supportive school environments.

The five children from the case study schools are featured more prominently than the other children in this study due to the larger number of educators interviewed at their schools, which allowed me to develop a more detailed understanding of the students' experiences and the practices intended to support them. In contrast, at the non–case study schools I interviewed only the principal, which precludes me from corroborating the content of their interview. Here I provide brief descriptions of the children from the five case study schools and basic demographic information about their school setting.

Meredith attended elementary school at Mercer Elementary, a K–5 school that is located in a small city in Massachusetts with a population of 68,000. Meredith, who was assigned male at birth, is White and lives with her mother, father, and younger sister. The city is racially/ethnically diverse with a population that is 65% White (non-Latinx), 13% Latinx (any race), 6% Black, and 6% Asian. The median income is $100,000. Meredith was in fifth grade at Mercer when this study began. For much of her time at Mercer Elementary, Meredith presented as a gender-expansive boy and used her birthname. Meredith's social transition spanned several years as Meredith gradually shifted to using the girls' bathroom, *she/her/hers* pronouns, and eventually her new name.[20]

Jacob lives with his mother who adopted him from China as an infant. Jacob, who was assigned female at birth, lives in Greater Prospect School District, an exurb of a large Pennsylvania city. The community has a population of 58,000 people who are 81% White (non-Latinx), 7% Asian, 5% Black, and 3% Latinx (any race). Greater Prospect is known as a wealthy community with a median income of $115,000; however, Jacob's small family would be best characterized as middle class. Jacob was in fourth grade at Jefferson Elementary School when this study began. Jacob socially transitioned over the summer prior to first grade, after consistently asserting his identity as a boy. Jacob's stereotypical "boy" interests prompted others to describe him as having a gender-conforming, masculine gender expression.

Natalia, a Latina transracial adoptee with White parents, attended Northstar Charter School, a K–8 school in Rhode Island. Natalia's small town of 19,000 supports numerous blue-collar industries; however, both Natalia's parents are professionals with advanced degrees. The town population is 64% Latinx (any race), 20% White (non-Latinx), and 14% Black. The median income is $26,000. Natalia attended Northstar for kindergarten through eighth grade. Natalia had recently graduated when this study began; however, her younger brother remained a student at Northstar. Natalia, who was assigned male at birth, enrolled at Northstar as a boy and presented as gender expansive for much of elementary school. In fifth grade Natalia began to grow out her hair, and in sixth grade she changed her name and pronouns and identified as a girl.

Sophie, a White student who was assigned male at birth, enrolled at Pacificus Learning Collaboratory as a fifth-grade girl. Pacificus, a private K–8 school, is located in a college town in Delaware with a median income of $75,000. The town population is 72% White (non-Latinx), 10% Black, 9% Asian, and 7% Latinx (any race); however, the eighty students enrolled at Pacificus are more predominantly White than the larger population. Prior to attending Pacificus, Sophie had attended a public school where her decision to socially transition in fourth grade lacked adequate support. As a result, Sophie's parents enrolled her at Pacificus, where she opted not to disclose her transgender identity to her classmates, instead identifying as "just a girl." Sophie had recently graduated from Pacificus when this study began.

Leo, a White transgender boy who was assigned female at birth, enrolled at Rosa Parks Public School (PS 25) in New York City as a kindergartener. PS 25 is located in a gentrifying neighborhood where the median income is $45,000, and the borough population is 35% White (non-Latinx), 35% Black, 19% Latinx (any race), and 11% Asian. This racial and ethnic diversity is similarly represented at PS 25. Leo was in first grade when this study began. As a kindergartener, Leo had already claimed his new name and pronouns, and proudly identified as a transgender boy to his friends and classmates. Leo had the full support of his parents and two older siblings. The educators describe how Leo's openness created opportunities for conversation among educators and in classrooms with young children.

Together, these children present an array of gender identities, expressions, and school experiences. Through conversations with their parents, teachers, principals, and other educational staff, we learn how schools can provide the supports that transgender children need to have a positive school experience.

CHAPTER OVERVIEW

Beyond this introductory chapter, subsequent chapters are organized by topic. Each chapter includes detailed examples drawn from varied school contexts that provide readers with concrete information about how to create a supportive school environment for transgender and gender-expansive students.

Chapter 2, "Transgender and Gender-Expansive Children," provides background information needed to better understand the experiences of the educators, children, and families whose stories are featured in this volume. The chapter starts with a vignette depicting one health educator's journey toward gender equity. Brief historical information and recent statistics underscore the heightened levels of discrimination, harassment, and assault that transgender people face in the United States. Sex, gender, and sexual orientation are explained in a way that demonstrates how these distinct concepts are often conflated and misunderstood. The chapter concludes with descriptions of social, legal, and medical transition.

Chapter 3, "The Role of Supportive Principals," situates principals as pivotal actors who can directly influence a school's response to transgender children. The chapter begins with a vignette from a charter school with a social justice mission and a proactive principal. Subsequent sections describe three key characteristics that distinguish supportive principals. First, they serve as lead learner, modeling a learning stance for their staff. Second, they employ a child-centered approach, focusing on each student's individual needs. Third, supportive principals foster strong school-family collaboration. Combined, these three characteristics increase principals' capacity to meet transgender children's needs. The chapter concludes with a discussion of how principals can support a student whose gender identity is not accepted by their family.

Chapter 4, "Leveraging Learning in the School Community," emphasizes the importance of building knowledge and understanding about gender and transgender identities. The opening vignette depicts a training session provided to educators in one district. The chapter goes on to respond to the question, "Who needs to know what and why?" Subsequent sections detail the kinds of educational experiences available to a wide range of school actors including teachers, support staff, and the larger school community. Through the examples in this chapter, readers gain a better understanding of the learning content, formats, and resources that can help schools build capacity for supporting transgender and gender-expansive students. The chapter concludes with a discussion of missed learning opportunities, underscoring the role that communication plays in building understanding and changing school culture.

Chapter 5, "Gender-Inclusive Classroom Practices," responds to the question, "How can teachers create classrooms where transgender and gender-expansive students experience affirmation and belonging?" The opening vignette portrays real-life author Afsaneh Moradian reading from her children's picture book. Subsequent sections draw on the experiences of more than thirty teachers to describe three main principles for creating gender-inclusive classrooms. First, teachers reduce gendered classroom management strategies such as gendered bathroom passes and seating arrangements. Second, teachers increase discussions about gender, adding books to their libraries and designing activities that create opportunities for students to examine and discuss gendered social norms. Third, teachers affirm transgender and gender-expansive children. Detailed examples of these practices provide readers with strategies they can use in elementary classrooms.

Chapter 6, "What to Do About Gendered School Spaces?," discusses the ubiquitous nature of gender in schools and how cisnormative spaces harm children. The vignette provides an example of how one district worked to develop supportive policies and equitable practices to support transgender students. Drawing on data from across all twenty schools, the chapter examines three approaches to gendered spaces, their benefits, and drawbacks. The first two, accommodating and assimilating students, help children navigate gendered spaces but make few actual changes to those spaces. The third, modifying school spaces for universal accessibility, requires more significant change on the part of schools and offers potentially more positive outcomes for a broader range of students. The chapter concludes with a brief discussion of change efforts and the challenge of achieving breadth, depth, and sustainability.

Chapter 7, "Reculturing Schools for Gender Equity," reviews the lessons learned from across the chapters, underscoring the positive outcomes that result when educators support and affirm transgender and gender-expansive students. This chapter also examines the limitations inherent in a child-centered approach, noting that changes to practice were limited in scope and sustainability. In response, this chapter explains the need for a two-pronged approach that includes changing school cultures in addition to meeting individual children's needs. Subsequent sections call on educators to be proactive and reculture schools for gender equity. This effort includes making space for transgender and gender-expansive identities, inviting difficult conversations about gender, and developing formal policies and written curriculum.

The book concludes with two appendixes. Appendix A provides detailed information about the research methodologies. Appendix B provides resources for schools including literature, organizations, and websites that can further support educators' efforts to create a supportive school environment for transgender and gender-expansive students.

CHAPTER 2

Transgender and Gender-Expansive Children

Everything about Mickie Cullen conveys dynamic energy: her springy hair, fast-paced walk, and seamless chatter. Even after twenty years in education, Mickie still has the stamina to outlast the most energetic elementary students. Mickie's exuberance is vital for her work as a districtwide health educator. In a given week she teaches every fifth grader in the district for half an hour, 700–750 students across eight elementary schools. Fifth grade is the first year the students have formal health education, and Mickie's curriculum covers four topics: nutrition, drugs and alcohol, diseases, and puberty.

A few years ago, a parent came to Mickie with concerns about their child, who had been assigned male at birth but increasingly preferred clothing typically associated with girls. Gradually, the child came to identify as a girl and socially transitioned in the second grade, prompting Mickie to rethink her health education curriculum. Seated at a desk in a fifth-grade classroom, Mickie shared her thoughts about the puberty curriculum and why she altered it from the traditional girl-boy presentation to become more gender inclusive. She started by describing the negative effects a traditional puberty education curriculum could have on transgender and gender-expansive students and explained the thought process that led Mickie to change her instructional practice.

I'm embarrassed because, as a health educator, I felt I should always be on the forefront, the most supportive being on the planet. I never realized how often I said "girls and boys," and what that does to their being, to their soul, their existence as a person. It was a lot, for me, reflecting. I swear, I just sat there and thought about the words that I said. [Asking myself,] "How can I say this in a way that is more inclusive?" I feel sort of bad about it at times. How was I not inclusive before? I didn't realize that I wasn't being inclusive, until I realized I'm not being inclusive. But it wasn't purposeful. I wasn't purposely saying I'm not going to include transgender children, because I never had a student that was transgender.

It was almost like the first time I had a student whose parent died of cancer, and thinking, "How do I teach? I have to pretend in my mind that everybody in here has a parent that died of cancer so that I am being inclusive." But I never even thought about it [with regard to being transgender]. I thought about it with disease and cancer. I've had many children, far too many children, that have been raped. I have never not had a fifth grader that hasn't been sexually assaulted, ever, since I started teaching twenty years ago, every year. So, when I teach the puberty unit, and I'm showing pictures of a penis and a vagina on the board, I have to think, "How is that child, that child who has been abused, how do I teach this in a way that they feel comfortable?" Because they need to know about the body but in a way that they're not scared or having flashbacks. When I teach nutrition, I just think about any possible problem. Maybe someone has an eating disorder or there's someone in this classroom that is obese. When I talk about obesity, how is that child going to feel when everyone's eyes turn on them? It's hard, because you still have to teach about obesity, but you never want a child to be the one that everyone stares and looks at.

So, what words am I going to use [to discuss puberty]? Just being mindful, I guess. That was what I thought about. How am I mindful of the fact that Rosa has a penis? So before, when I put up the diagram of a penis, I would have written on top "male anatomy." Then, really thinking, well, is it male? Who says it's male? Who decides you are male or female? Do I just need to let that heading go? And just show a penis on the board or just a vagina? It was a lot of reflecting. Then I'm like, oh my gosh, I am spending this much time thinking about a heading. I need to be thinking about how this child, or any child, is going to be feeling inside. I used to say, "Girls, when you get your period. . . ." Rosa is not getting her period, so I can't say that anymore.

It took me awhile, and I was so afraid that I was going to slip up. I had to practice. What's awesome is that I did the exact same lesson forty times a week. It was constant practice. I only teach fifth grade, so when I was teaching my fifth graders and Rosa was in fourth grade, I was just working on it. I literally would write a note. I would have, like, a little Post-it, and I would just jot down a little word. And I would feel it as soon as I said it. "Oh, shit, I messed that one up." Then I was aware of it. Before I would always say "girls and boys." "Boys, when your penis gets hard. Boys, when you get an erection." And then it was, "Why am I saying this? I don't need to say that." So now I'm like, "If you have a penis," you know what I mean?

I'm very animated when I'm teaching; I'm just, like, all cuckoo bananas at times. I'm like "You have to know what you got going on!" But also, this is the first time any of these kids are learning about parts, so it's also about making everybody feel safe, because they're learning something that all of their lives is something private. Some are understanding "My body is changing, so I need to hear this, but I still feel like I'm a kid and I don't want to hear it." And there's the kid that has been assaulted that already knows way too much about this. And the child that's like "Oh, God, I have this penis and I hate this penis." You know? And maybe there's other thoughts that kids are having in their head that I haven't even thought of yet. Oh, God, I don't want to do wrong by children. You know what I mean? But it's hard, because, like, with Rosa, I never thought about it [being transgender]. I just never even thought about it, until the situation came where I'm like "I need to think about this." And then it made me better.

Educators across the United States are having experiences like Mickie Cullen and asking themselves: What does it mean to have a transgender student? How should I change my practice to better meet their needs? Mickie's capacity to imagine how her students experience health education helps her see that a gendered approach to sex education can cause distress for a student whose gender identity does not conform to their sex assigned at birth. Unless educators see transgender identities as legitimate, they will remain unmotivated to change their educational practice. This chapter introduces readers to transgender and gender-expansive identities, including historical and sociopolitical background information that sets the context for the school-specific content presented in subsequent chapters. This new knowledge can help educators understand the legitimacy and importance of supporting transgender students. Additional suggested resources are provided in appendix B, and the glossary serves as a quick reference to an expanded list of terms.

TRANSGENDER AND GENDER-EXPANSIVE CHILDREN

Two common misconceptions about transgender children predominate: first, that transgender identities are rare, and second, that only adults are transgender. For educators in our K–12 schools, the inaccuracy of these statements has become increasingly clear. Schools nationwide are experiencing significant growth in the number of students who openly identify as transgender, and there is little doubt that many more transgender students are enrolled but remain nondisclosed. Increased awareness of transgender and gender-expansive identities creates an opportunity for educators to develop greater understanding of gender and how to create more gender-inclusive classrooms. At the same time, transgender students present a learning challenge for schools. Meeting transgender students' needs is not just a matter of creating new supports but also dismantling existing systems that harm transgender and gender-expansive children as well as cisgender and gender-conforming children.

The term *transgender* can be confusing because it is defined and applied in multiple ways. Generally, it is an adjective that refers to people whose gender identity differs from the gender expectations associated with the sex assigned to them at birth. That said, the degree to which someone's gender differs from gender norms can vary quite dramatically. When interpreted narrowly, transgender describes people whose gender identity conforms to binary social norms, albeit for the gender that is "opposite" from their natal sex. When interpreted more broadly, transgender can describe people whose gender identity does not conform to social norms for either girls/

women or boys/men. This latter definition includes a broad array of people who may use terms other than *transgender* to describe their gender identity, such as *gender nonconforming, genderqueer, nonbinary, gender fluid,* or *gender expansive,* the term used throughout this volume to signal to gender identities or forms of expression that challenge binary gender norms for boys and girls. As an umbrella term, *transgender* includes everyone whose gender identity is not *cisgender,* the term used for people whose gender identity conforms to the gender norms associated with their sex assigned at birth.[1] As an adjective, it is appropriate to say, for example, "transgender woman," just as you might say "smart woman." It is not correct to say "transgendered woman," just as you would not say "smarted woman."

There is a growing effort by researchers to calculate the number of transgender people in the United States. Until recently, few surveys asked questions about gender identity. While no conclusive gender identity data are available for children under the age of thirteen, a growing body of information is available on teenagers. Results from one study that used a narrow definition of transgender found that 0.7 percent of teenagers identify as transgender.[2] In contrast, a study of California teens asked about gender nonconformity more broadly and found that 27 percent of teens ages twelve to seventeen identify as gender nonconforming, with 6.2 percent characterized as highly gender nonconforming and 20.8 percent as androgynous, or equally feminine and equally masculine.[3] Other studies that focused on measuring transgender identity found variations that indicate between 1.3 to 3.2 percent of teens identify as transgender.[4] Although these studies have not been replicated in younger children, the information learned from teenagers, combined with reports from practicing educators, makes it clear that transgender children, broadly defined, are enrolled in our schools, and they are becoming more visible.

This chapter provides background information needed to better understand the experiences of the children, families, and educators whose stories are featured in this volume. Three questions guide this discussion:

- What does being transgender mean?
- What is the difference between sex, gender, and sexual orientation?
- What does transitioning mean?

Having a better understanding of transgender children can help educators see transgender students positively and may increase educators' motivation and capacity to create gender-inclusive environments that benefit all children.

WHAT DOES BEING TRANSGENDER MEAN?

The notion that some people are transgender remains a new concept to many Americans even though gender variation has been documented across cultural contexts for centuries.[5] In recent decades, increased visibility of transgender people has prompted many to wonder whether there are more transgender people than in the past. Experts from a range of fields—medicine, psychology, sociology, and history—generally agree that the perceived increase in gender diversity does not reflect growth in numbers but, rather, greater visibility due to improved connectivity. New technologies, such as the internet, enable us to more easily share information and create new language to describe our experiences. Learning new terms like *transgender, cisgender, gender nonconforming,* or *genderqueer* can help people of all ages understand their gender identity more fully. New and affirming language is fueled by and contributes to increased visibility for people with transgender identities.

Although gender-diverse people have always existed, how people understand and express their gender has shifted in ways that depend on cultural and historical contexts. Historian and director of the Stonewall Center at the University of Massachusetts Amherst, Genny Beemyn explains the complex task of preserving historical context while simultaneously recognizing gender diversity over time:

> While it is problematic that historians have often failed to acknowledge or accept individuals who cross-dressed or live as a gender different from the one assigned to them at birth, it would also be inappropriate to assume that "trans people," as we currently understand the term, existed throughout history. Given that "trans" is a contemporary concept, individuals in past centuries who might appear to have been trans or gender nonconforming from our vantage point would quite likely not have conceptualized their lives in such a way. But at the same time limiting trans history to people

who lived at a place and time when the concept of "trans" was available and used by the individuals in question would deny the experiences of many people who would have been perceived as gender nonconforming in their eras and cultures.[6]

In our contemporary context, it is important to respect the terms and language that individuals use for themselves, regardless of how they look, dress, or behave. Gender is first and foremost a personal and self-defined identity, not superimposed using externally derived criteria. For example, a child with a crew cut hairstyle may not identify as a boy, even though traditional gender norms in the United States associate short hair with boys. Therefore, it is important to believe and honor the gender identity that people claim, regardless of appearance or behavior.

It wasn't until the 1950s that the concept of transgender identity began to take on some of the meaning that we see today.[7] One factor that increased transgender people's visibility and legitimacy in this time period was medical science, which made it possible for so-called transsexuals to undergo what was known as "sex-reassignment surgery."[8] Perhaps the most well-known transgender figure of that era was Christine Jorgensen, who made a public transition "from GI Joe to blonde bombshell," attracting the curiosity and astonishment of the American public.[9] This attention, however, was not synonymous with acceptance or even tolerance. Anyone who transgressed social norms for men and women was subject to persecution and criminalization. Gradually, this mistreatment gave rise to civic organizing, and activists in urban centers began to speak out. Many of these activists were transgender Women of Color, for whom the intersection of race and gender served as a catalyst for especially violent oppression. Today, transgender Women of Color, including Miss Major Griffin-Gracy, Sylvia Rivera, and Marsha P. Johnson, are recognized as playing a key role in the fight for LGBTQ civil rights. For example, Johnson, a Black transgender woman, is often credited with "throwing the first brick" during the Stonewall Riots that took place in New York City in 1969, an uprising that invigorated the queer rights movement.[10]

Tragically, the violent oppression that transgender activists were protesting during the Stonewall Riots is not an artifact of history. Today, transgender and gender-expansive people in the United States are subjected to higher rates of discrimination, harassment, and assault. They have lower rates of employment and medical care. These factors place transgender people at higher risk for drug and alcohol abuse, homelessness, incarceration, lethal violence, and death by suicide. The negative societal impacts are greatest for transgender people who face multiple forms of discrimination. For example, the 2015 U.S. Transgender Survey reports 29 percent of transgender people were living in poverty, compared with 14 percent of the general population, while transgender People of Color faced even higher rates: 43 percent of Latinx, 41 percent of American Indian, 40 percent of multiracial, and 38 percent of Black transgender survey respondents lived in poverty.[11] The survey results further show that transgender people who are undocumented and those with disabilities also faced higher rates of economic instability, mistreatment, violence, and discrimination than the general population of transgender individuals.

The higher rates of discrimination and violence inflicted on transgender people are exacerbated by a lack of adequate legal and legislative protections.[12] Although some states and localities do have laws that ban discrimination on the basis of gender identity, currently no federal laws specifically protect the rights of transgender individuals. Therefore, transgender people depend on other legal protections such as the Equal Protection Clause in the Fourteenth amendment to the US Constitution; Title VII of the Civil Rights Act of 1964, which prohibits employment discrimination based on sex; or the Fair Housing Act of 1968, which prohibits housing discrimination based on sex. The challenge, however, is that courts have interpretive latitude to decide whether anti-sex discrimination protections apply to transgender people, resulting in uneven outcomes that often hinge on the knowledge and decision-making capacity of individual judges. Even when legal rulings favor the rights of transgender people, they are not always enforced. Taken together, this confusing and chaotic legal backdrop creates a hostile environment for transgender people.

Transgender people's exclusion from basic human and civil rights is a result of our society's historic efforts to dehumanize transgender people. This dehumanization creates a context where transphobic discrimination and civil rights abuses are justified and accepted. Our task, then, is to vigorously humanize transgender and gender-expansive people by centering their experiences and honoring their lives. Schools, as social institutions, are key contexts where this work needs to take place. In addition to their educational mission, schools also socialize children into accepted societal norms. To promote gender norms that humanize and affirm transgender people, educators need a solid understanding of what it means to be transgender. The following two sections provide factual information that can help educators develop a better understanding of what it means to be transgender and, as a result, more effectively legitimize and affirm transgender identities at school and in the classroom.

WHAT IS THE DIFFERENCE BETWEEN SEX, GENDER, AND SEXUAL ORIENTATION?

In the United States, society has become more open to transgender identities. The early 2000s marked a sharp increase in the number of mainstream media outlets featuring transgender people. Some celebrities and high-profile figures underwent public transitions (e.g., Chaz Bono, Caitlyn Jenner, Kristen Beck, and Chelsea Manning), and others disclosed their transgender or nonbinary identities (e.g., Janet Mock, Laverne Cox, Ruby Rose, and Sam Smith). Human interest stories followed transgender children and their families through the process of social transition, providing new opportunities to learn about a topic long considered taboo.[13] Teen icon Jazz Jennings documented her medical transition in the fifth season of her reality television show. Transgender people even appeared on the political front. In November 2017, Danica Roem was elected to the Virginia House of Delegates, making her the first openly transgender person serving in any US state legislature. In the 2018 midterm elections, fifty-one openly transgender people ran for public office, nine of whom ran for congressional seats.[14] While none had successful election campaigns, this increased visibility reflects growing openness toward transgender identities.

People today are more likely than ever to know someone who identifies as transgender.[15] Even so, confusion about gender and what it means to be transgender remains high. This confusion is compounded by the conflation of sex, gender, and sexual orientation, which are three distinct concepts.

Factual information about these key concepts and how they differ can help educators better understand and support their transgender students and create an educational environment where all gender identities are affirmed.

Sex

The predominant view of biological sex in the United States emphasizes two binary categories, male and female, which are commonly conveyed as mutually exclusive, stable, and easily identified based on external genitalia. From a scientific standpoint, however, biological sex is actually a combination of multiple physiological characteristics including hormones, chromosomes, and anatomy. While external genitalia may provide some indication of sex, genitalia alone tell only part of the story. A complete biological profile of the components that constitute sex would require genetic and chromosome karyotype testing as well as endocrine and physiological evaluations. In the absence of health problems, few people undergo the expensive procedures needed to fully understand all the components of biological sex. As such, even medical professionals commonly use external genitalia as an imperfect indicator for binary sex.[16]

Given the physiological complexity of biological sex, it is little surprise that sex can be manifested in an array of subtle and not-so-subtle variations across people.[17] People with physiological differences that do not align neatly with the biology generally associated with males and females are known as intersex, a condition that is sometimes mistakenly and derisively referred to as hermaphroditism.[18] Intersex is a broad category that includes people with ambiguous genitalia, chromosomal anomalies, and hormonal anomalies. Some of these variations are evident in utero, whereas others may not be detected until later in life, often when puberty or conception do not progress as expected. The rate of occurrence varies across the different conditions, but collectively, intersex people account for approximately 1.7 to 2 percent of live births, similar to the percentage of redheads.[19] Ultimately, what counts as intersex is not a precise science; rather, people make subjective determinations, influenced by societal norms, about the physiological traits required to be characterized as intersex, female, or male.

Historically, intersex conditions have been treated as secret and shameful; however, the topic of intersex rights is slowly gaining visibility. It has been common practice to perform surgical "corrections" on infants born with ambiguous genitalia based on a physician's judgment and usually without regard for the child's gender identity or chromosomal or hormonal make-up. Information about intersex conditions and related surgeries is often withheld from patients "for their own good" even into adulthood.[20] Increasingly, intersex advocates have raised awareness of the negative effects of medical interventions in infancy, which can include painful scarring and loss of sensation; it also can include being raised to conform to societal expectations that may not align with the individual's physiology or gender.[21] Advocates contend that any surgical modifications should be delayed until children can contribute to the decision-making process. Intersex rights have gained further attention in response to several high-profile intersex athletes, whose bodies defy the simple binary constructs that dominate our society and competitive sports.[22]

Our cultural fixation on binary sex, despite the real variations that occur across humans, has led us to define sex in medico-legal terms. That is, sex takes on both medical and legal aspects that are regulated by federal and state-level government entities. As a medico-legal category, the criteria used to define and determine sex can differ based on legal context and not solely on the basis of biology or medical expertise. One example is the case of Dana Zzyym, an intersex Navy veteran who was denied a passport because they were unable to mark their sex on the passport application, which allowed only for male and female designations. In 2016 the US District Court of Colorado agreed that the US State Department discriminated against Zzyym. The State Department has continued to require either F (female) or M (male) markers on US passports, prompting additional rulings in favor of Zzyym in 2017 and 2019.[23] Zzyym's case demonstrates the intersection between medicine, law, and governmental regulations that gives rise to medico-legal definitions of sex.

Schools regularly record information about students' sex, typically asking whether a child is male or female. School administrators consider such information an important part of ensuring that girls and boys have access to equitable educational opportunities, as mandated under Title IX of the Education Amendments of 1972. Growing public awareness about intersex rights and our increased understanding that gender is not a binary and does not always align with sex are prompting schools to rethink the kinds of data being collected, their purpose, and utility. Many schools are shifting their language to focus on gender rather than sex. In the section that follows, we examine what is meant by the term *gender* and its role in society and in schools.

Gender

Gender is an internal sense of identity and, like sex, it is commonly understood as a binary—girl/woman or boy/man. When an infant's sex is assigned at birth, gender norms are also presumed. It is generally expected that babies assigned male at birth will develop gender identities as boys and men. Babies assigned female at birth are expected to develop identities as girls and women. People who experience congruence between their sex assigned at birth and their gender are known as cisgender. The prefix *cis* means "adjacent" or "on this side of" and is commonly used in chemistry, along with the prefix *trans*, to describe the arrangement of atoms in organic compounds. Someone whose gender identity (e.g., "I am a girl") matches the gender norms for their sex assigned at birth (e.g., "I was assigned female at birth") is a cisgender girl. Sometimes the term *cis* is used as shorthand for *cisgender*. Many cisgender people do not explicitly identify as cisgender or even realize there is a term to describe their gender. This speaks to the privilege inherent in cisgender identity. In our cisnormative society, cisgender identities are centered as normative, and other gender identities are situated as non-normative. For example, in schools, children are not referred to as cisgender boys or cisgender girls. The unstated assumption is that all children are cisgender.

People who experience incongruence between their sex and gender are broadly understood as transgender. The prefix *trans* means "across" or "on the other side of." *Transgender* is an umbrella term and is sometimes written as *trans* or *trans**, whereby the asterisk corresponds to the wildcard in a database search to convey the expansive nature of transgender identities. Even without the asterisk, *transgender* is an adjective that refers to a wide variety of gender identities and expressions. Some transgender people conform to binary gender norms albeit for a different sex from the one they were assigned at birth. Some transgender individuals defy gender norms, pushing on the boundaries of what is commonly accepted or expected. Transgender people refer to themselves using a wide range of terms, including but not limited to *AFAB* (assigned female at birth), *AMAB* (assigned male at birth), *enby, nonbinary, gender fluid, genderqueer, agender, transmasculine, transfeminine, gender nonconforming, gender expansive,* or simply *boy/man* or *girl/woman.*[24] The language people use to represent their gender identity is highly personal. Recent research suggests that 0.6 percent of adults in the United States identify as transgender.[25]

Gender expression refers to the ways that gender is outwardly presented through behaviors and appearance such as clothing, hairstyle, adornments, or mannerisms. We often make assumptions about someone's gender identity based on gender expression; however, it is important to remember that gender identity is an internal sense of self that can be expressed in a wide variety of ways. There is no singular way to express gender. For example, a child with long hair who wears dresses or plays with dolls may not identify as a girl, even though we commonly associate such outward expressions as specific to girls. Narrow cultural expectations about how boys and girls should express their gender are gender stereotypes, and they constrain or limit authentic expression for both cisgender and transgender people. Reinforcement of gender stereotypes is also known as gender policing, and it is a common part of children's socialization in schools. Gender policing subtly and overtly aims to force conformity with deeply engrained cultural norms. For example, girls might be ridiculed, by peers and adults alike, for being active, being loud, or playing sports, traits associated with and valued in boys. Gender policing in schools preserves and reproduces long-standing social inequities between girls and boys as well as the erasure of transgender identities.

Culture and societal expectations have a strong influence on how we make sense of and treat gender. Gender expectations are context dependent and change over time. For example, in the Western world up until the early 1900s, it was culturally acceptable to dress boys in clothing that today we would use exclusively for girls.[26] One image frequently circulated online shows Franklin Delano Roosevelt, former US president from 1933 to 1945, as a child in 1884. Young Franklin's hair flows past his shoulders, and he is wearing a ruffled gown and thin-strapped Mary Jane shoes and holds a plumed hat in his lap. As evidenced in this photograph, it was common for boys to be "unbreeched," or without trousers, until between the ages of four to eight. It was only later in the century that sex differences and sex-specific clothing came to be emphasized and differentiated in infancy. Because gender expectations change in relationship to cultural context, gender is often described as a social construct or a performance, rather than an innate or essential biological category.[27] Researchers' efforts to explain gender identity development increasingly include both social and biological components. As such, we currently understand gender identity as a composite of the physical body, self-expression, erotic attraction, and cultural context. All of these components contribute to an individual's sense of self and gender identity.

Developmental psychologists contend that children's core gender identity develops by the age of two or three for both transgender and cisgender children and continues to develop through young adulthood.[28] This does not necessarily mean that transgender children will articulate their gender identity at this early age, although some do. A person's ability to articulate their gender identity depends, in part, on access to adequate language to describe their experience. Children are immersed in binary language related to boys and girls. They have fewer opportunities to access and make sense of themselves using more expansive language that might be used to describe nonbinary gender identities. Social pressures can also constrain gender identity development, and many transgender people self-censor, hiding their authentic identity in deference to others or in fear of rejection. Ultimately, like gender itself, the path that gender identity development takes is highly individualized. Transgender and gender-expansive people can come out, or share their gender identity, at any age. Transgender identities are no less real if they are disclosed late in life, during early childhood, or at any point in between.

Contrary to common perception, gender identity development does not depend on physical anatomy. That is, having a penis does not automatically make someone a boy/man, and having a clitoris does not necessarily make someone a girl/woman. The presumed congruence between anatomy and gender often leads people to remark that transgender people are "born in the wrong body." While some transgender people do feel dysphoria in relationship to their body, other transgender people reject this characterization, which presumes that something is inherently wrong with their body. An alternate narrative situates gender as primary, such that if someone identifies as a boy, then they have a boy body, regardless of their anatomy. Following this logic, it can be said that some boys have a clitoris, and some girls have a penis. Anatomy does not make anyone more or less a boy or girl. Such statements create a liberatory narrative where gender is not dictated by sex. This notion of gender as an internal sense of self and distinct from one's physiology is reflected in the opening vignette and health educator Mickie Cullen's efforts to remove gender from her discussion of anatomy.

The fields of medicine and psychology have significantly, and often negatively, influenced how we understand gender in the United States. In 1980, the American Psychiatric Association added *gender identity disorder* to the *Diagnostic and Statistical Manual of Mental Disorders* (DSM) adding to the misperception that being transgender is a mental illness. In the current edition, the DSM-5, which was released in 2013, *gender identity disorder* was replaced with *gender dysphoria*. Despite this linguistic shift away from the concept of "disorder," including gender identity in a manual of mental disorders continues to perpetuate false beliefs about transgender identities as pathological. Paradoxically, even though many transgender people decry the use of pathologizing labels, access to transition-related services is often dependent on a diagnosis of gender dysphoria (more on transition later). As such, the fields of medicine and psychology act as gatekeepers, capable of invalidating gender identity and restricting access to gender-related services. In contrast, in 2019 the World Health Organization released a statement indicating that the term *transsexualism* would be replaced with *gender incongruence* and would be defined as part of sexual health and not mental or behavioral disorders.[29] In the United States, our failure to locate transgender identities within the realm of health contributes to transphobia—the negative attitudes, behaviors, and even violence directed at transgender people.

Sexual Orientation

Sexual orientation refers to patterns of romantic, emotional, and physical attraction that contribute to sexual identity.[30] In a discussion about sexual orientation, the terms *sex* and *gender* are often conflated or confused, or they overlap. Who we are attracted to often depends on how we "read" another person or interpret their gender expression, not necessarily based on how they self-identify or their biological sex. Coupled with the inadequacy of language to accurately convey experience, our efforts to categorize, sort, and label people leaves us struggling to describe sexual orientation in meaningful ways. Moreover, gender and sex are not the only variables that determine sexual attraction. Someone might be attracted to people who are, for example, tall, fat, quiet, bold, erudite, easy-going, or tattooed. The endless variables that influence sexual attraction likely preclude any definitive categorization. Nevertheless, legal and sociopolitical realities situate some sexual identities as privileged, whereas others are pathologized and criminalized. Thus, categorizing sexual orientation can help us identify patterns of injustice and, hopefully, make changes to our social systems to reduce bias and discrimination.

In the United States, some common terms used to describe sexual orientation include *gay* (G), *lesbian* (L), *bisexual* (B), and *straight*. The term *gay* describes someone who is attracted to people of the same sex/gender. This accepted term can be used for both men and women; however, sometimes women prefer the term *lesbian*. *Gay* can also be used as an insult to ridicule a person, idea, or even an inanimate object. This usage is not always linked to actual sexual orientation; however, it perpetuates negative connotations related to gay sexual identity, and using the term as an insult is considered hurtful to gay people even when it is not directed at gay people. The use of *homosexual* for gay people is increasingly understood as derogatory and should be avoided because of its linkage to homophobic ideologies and efforts to pathologize and criminalize gay people. *Bisexual* refers to individuals who are attracted to both men and women. It is common to see the initials *LGB* linked together because people with these sexual orientations have a common history of marginalization and oppression. For similar reasons, *transgender* (T) is often included in this grouping even though it refers to gender and not sexual orientation—and transgender people can be any sexual orientation. *Straight* refers to someone who is attracted to people whose sex/gender differs from their own. This is formally known as heterosexuality, and some straight people describe themselves using the term *het*.

Straight people benefit from societal norms that privilege heterosexuality above all other sexual orientations.

In addition to LGB, other more nuanced terms are increasingly being used, especially among younger generations. The growth in language related to sexual identities reflects new understandings that binary representations of sex and gender fail to convey the richness of human experience. For example, *pansexual* describes someone who is attracted to the entire array of people regardless of their sex or gender identity. *Polysexual* people are attracted to multiple genders but not all genders. *Demisexual* refers to someone who experiences sexual attraction only to people with whom they have an emotional connection. *Asexual* describes a person who is not sexually attracted to other people but may still have a sexual libido. Perhaps the most widespread, and one that is often added to LGBT, is *queer* (Q). Originally, *queer* was a synonym for "peculiar" but was commonly used as a slur for gay people throughout the twentieth century. In the 1980s LGB activists deliberately began to use *queer* to describe people with sexual and/or gender identities that challenge heteronormative and cisnormative identities.[31] Reclaiming words that were once pejorative is a way for marginalized groups to assert sociopolitical agency.[32] Another way that oppressed groups can build social, political, and legal influence is to form alliances. This is why LGBTQ identities are commonly grouped together, despite their differences. Sometimes this abbreviation also includes *intersex* (I), *agender* (A), *asexual* (A), *two-spirit* (2S), *questioning* (Q), and the addition symbol (+), which conveys the expansiveness of queer people.[33]

The United States is commonly described as a heterosexist or heteronormative society, meaning that straight or heterosexual identities are privileged while queer identities are disadvantaged. Heteronormative ideals are evident in our legal and justice systems as well as medical and educational institutions.[34] As a result, people who are perceived as gay are often subjected to homophobia—negative attitudes, behaviors, and even violence directed at LGBQ people.

Despite pervasive discrimination, the twenty-first century has brought some significant advances for LGBTQ people. For example, a series of successful state-level legal decisions, beginning in 2008, made it possible for same-sex couples to legally marry in multiple states, including

Massachusetts, Connecticut, and Iowa. In 2013, in *United States v Windsor*, the Supreme Court ruled that the 1996 federal Defense of Marriage Act (DOMA), which banned federal recognition of same-sex marriages, was unconstitutional. In 2015, the United States Supreme Court ruled in *Obergefell v Hodges*, making same-sex marriage legal and protected under federal law in all states. This ruling reflects a monumental shift in societal attitudes about lesbian, gay, and bisexual (LGB) people and their right to equal opportunities under the law.

If we look across these three concepts and the various ways they intersect, it is no surprise that sex, gender, and sexual orientation are confusing for many people. Following are some key points to remember:

- Sex is a medico-legal construct and not strictly biological.
- Biological sex is a composite of hormones, chromosomes, and anatomy and is not strictly binary.
- Transgender people are assigned a sex at birth that does not align with their gender identity.
- Gender identity is an internal sense of self that is influenced by one's cultural context and social norms.
- Gender is not limited to "boy/man" and "girl/woman."
- Transgender people may conform to or challenge gender norms.
- Transgender people can be any sexual orientation.

Sex, gender, and sexual orientation are complex concepts that challenge simplistic binary thinking. Increased understanding about each can facilitate greater acceptance and support for transgender identities.

WHAT DOES TRANSITIONING MEAN?

For some transgender people, incongruence between sex and gender can cause distress, which the medical field refers to as "dysphoria." Unsupportive social contexts and interactions can exacerbate dysphoria. Not all transgender people experience dysphoria, but for those who do, it can lead to feelings of inadequacy, humiliation, self-hatred, and depression. To decrease dysphoria, many transgender people transition and live as their affirmed gender.

Transition refers to the process by which transgender people begin to express and live as their affirmed gender rather than conform to expectations for their sex assigned at birth. For transgender people who identify and express their affirmed gender early in childhood, the concept of transition may not be central to their experience. For others who may have lived a portion of their lives conforming to societal expectations, transition can be a significant milestone. There is no standard transition, and each individual transitions in accord with their own needs; however, many transgender people experience external barriers that limit their ability to transition. Transition can be relatively simple. It can also be complicated, time consuming, and expensive. The three primary aspects of transition are social, legal, and medical. Not all transgender people want to transition along all three dimensions, and many do not have the opportunity.

Social transition can happen at any age and generally refers to changes in gender expression that are externally visible, such as hair and clothing as well as pronouns and name. For transgender children, the social transition process may be complete prior to enrolling in school, or children may transition during the school year. Some children boldly orchestrate their own social transition, leading and teaching adults. Children may transition gradually, sometimes trying out their affirmed gender identity at home before sharing their gender identity with a broader public. Or, in the context of a less-supportive home, children may first identify as their affirmed gender at school. Educators in schools increasingly find themselves helping children navigate how and when to transition socially. Sometimes this is a straightforward process with clear endpoints, but more often transition involves twists and turns as children's gender identity develops gradually over time. All aspects of social transition are reversible. Research shows that socially transitioned transgender children have low levels of depression and anxiety in comparison to children who experience dysphoria yet are unable to socially transition.[35] Given these benefits, it is important that educators develop mechanisms to ensure that children are supported in their transition.

Legal transition is the process of amending identity documents to align with gender identity. This may involve changing one's legal name and/ or sex/gender marker on a wide variety of documents. States govern the amendment procedures for names, birth certificates, and driver licenses, and, as a result, requirements and accessibility vary widely by state.[36] Restrictive state laws may require gender confirmation surgery as a condition to be met prior to amending identity documents. Moderately restrictive laws may require certification or proof of gender identity from a professional, usually a health-care provider. There is also variation in the number of sex/gender options available. The majority of states continue to offer two binary options: female (F) or male (M); however, in recent years more states have added a nonbinary option, usually indicated by X, on driver licenses and birth certificates. In addition to state-based identity documents, transgender people may also seek to amend federal documents such as passports and social security cards in addition to identity documents associated with bank accounts, insurance policies, and other legally binding records.

School records are another type of documentation that commonly include students' sex/gender and name. State departments of education and individual school districts are increasingly developing policies and procedures intended to support students' transition prior to the finalization of legal documentation. The most supportive policies allow schools to change a child's name and gender marker in their data system without legal documentation. These policies help ensure that children will not be deadnamed or misgendered. Educators are often unaware of all the places and ways students' names and/or gender markers are on display. For example, rosters are commonly distributed to substitute teachers, the librarian, the nurse, cafeteria servers, bus drivers, class parents, and chaperones. Some children confront their deadnames each time they sign in to the school's computer system. It is important for educators to know how their district supports transition and whether more proactive supports are needed given that many children are not in a position to change their legal documents.

Medical transition refers to physiological changes that can be made to the body to reduce dsyphoria.[37] Adults who have completed puberty as their sex assigned at birth may seek a range of medical procedures intended to better align their bodies with their gender identity. Some transgender adults take hormone replacement therapy, and/or they may elect to have any number of surgical procedures including facial feminization or masculinization, chest reconstruction, and gender confirmation surgeries to alter their genitals. Adults do not always medically transition. For many, it is cost prohibitive. Some may have health conditions that preclude medical transition. Some transgender adults may not experience levels of dysphoria that make medical transition necessary. The goals of medical transition vary with the individual. Not all transgender people aim for a body that allows them to pass as male or female. Some may seek to alter particular features that create the most dysphoria. For example, they may seek only chest reconstruction and forgo hormone replacement therapy or vice versa. It is important to remember that bodies are private, and it is inappropriate to ask about or offer unsolicited opinions regarding someone's medical transition.

Medical transition for transgender children is different from adults' transition in several ways. First, prepubescent children do not medically transition. Medical transition for children begins with the first signs of puberty. Children who demonstrate consistent, persistent, and insistent transgender identity may take hormone suppressant medication, sometimes called "blockers," at the first sign of puberty. Hormone suppressants pause and delay puberty, allowing the child time to mature and more fully understand the implications of medical transition. If children do decide to go through puberty as their affirmed gender, they would begin to take hormone replacements: testosterone or estrogen. Hormone replacement therapy for children typically begins between the ages of thirteen and fifteen. Generally speaking, for transgender girls, blockers impede the development of secondary sex characteristics, and estrogen facilitates breast development. For transgender boys, testosterone facilitates masculinization of physical features, including growth of facial hair, larynx enlargement, broadening of shoulders, deepened voice, heavier bone structure, and increased muscle mass. Later in puberty transgender teens may seek affirmation surgeries that alter the genitals. For children, medical transition is highly dependent on supportive parents, access to information, and adequate financial resources.

Unfortunately, transgender people experience many barriers to transition. In addition to the societal stigma associated with transgender identities, fear of rejection from family and friends can delay or inhibit transition. Economic factors can also impede transition. Not only are the associated legal and medical costs high, but transition can result in discrimination and loss of employment for adults. Parents of transgender children may worry about the risk of prolonged medications, possible infertility, and the prospect of being rejected by extended family, friends, and even their community. Access to information and counseling from professionals who are knowledgeable about transgender identities can help ease the transition process. Support and affirmation from educators are equally important and can help ensure the continuity of transgender children's social transition.

CONCLUSION

Transgender and gender-expansive people experience higher rates of discrimination and violence across all facets of society. Tragically, our schools mirror many of these same injustices. Building our factual knowledge about what it means to be transgender can help legitimize transgender identities and, hopefully, lead to increased access to basic human and civil rights within and outside our educational institutions.

Learning about transgender identities begins with basic information about the differences between sex, gender, and sexual orientation. These distinct concepts are regularly conflated and treated as interchangeable. Medical forms may ask about a patient's gender when information about physiology is needed. Families ascribe gender to infants based on genitalia and before infants can express gender identity. Elementary schools avoid talking about gender, mistakenly believing that gender is synonymous with sexuality and sexual activity. Paradoxically, despite our failure to accurately distinguish between sex, gender, and sexual orientation, our society works overtime to emphasize and reinforce binary distinctions within each of these categories. Extraordinary emphasis is placed on the differences between men and women, males and females, and gay and straight people in an effort to construct sex, gender, and sexuality as binary, mutually exclusive, stable categories. In the end, these false binaries reproduce norms that limit everyone.

The chapters that follow present insights from practicing educators with experience supporting transgender and gender-expansive students. The educators' stories demonstrate both the successes and challenges of creating affirming school environments. Moreover, their compelling descriptions of transgender students' school experiences demonstrate *why* we need to make schools gender-inclusive and *how* to make it happen.

CHAPTER 3

The Role of Supportive Principals

The lobby of Northstar Charter School feels almost like a neighborhood café. Big windows let in morning light. A side table holds a carafe of fresh coffee and an assortment of creamers. One corner hosts a small children's library with books for all ages, a brightly colored carpet, and cushioned benches. Professional artwork and student creations enliven the space. Adults from the community, including parents and neighbors, occupy each of the four tables. They chat in Spanish and sip coffee as small children toddle around with board books and big smiles. An older gentleman greets the teachers by name and, although his own children are long grown, he is a daily visitor to the Northstar lobby.

The welcoming atmosphere in the lobby reflects Northstar's commitment to creating a supportive environment for students and the larger community. Northstar serves grades kindergarten through eight. It is located in a town of nineteen thousand residents that might be characterized as working class, situated along a river rimmed with windowless factories. The median family income is $26,000. In recent decades the population has become increasingly Latinx, which is reflected in the Spanish-language shop signs around town and in the student population at Northstar, where 78 percent identify as Latinx, 15 percent as Black, and 5 percent as White. Moreover, 32 percent are English language learners, and 83 percent of Northstar's students qualify for free or reduced-price lunch, a proxy for poverty.

When Northstar received its charter from Rhode Island in 2004, it included a mission statement focused on social justice. Principal Rebecca

Neumann, one of the school's founders, described the mission as guiding all facets of their school operations and, in particular, her leadership. As part of this social justice mission, Principal Neuman was committed to creating a supportive environment for Natalia, the first transgender student to socially transition at Northstar. Principal Neumann described her experience:

> We have always had this mission around social justice. It is "literacy empowers each individual to have a voice, assume community responsibility, and take social action." We had focused a lot on the voice part and kids really would identify, "Yes, I have a voice, and yes, I'm responsible for my community." We hadn't really, at that time, gotten to the social action part, and even as adults we hadn't really figured out what that meant.
>
> So right when the Natalia experience was happening was when we were finally wrapping our heads around what we needed to do [with regard to social action]. . . . For me, the biggest learning that came from that experience was taking values from a theoretical place to a really immediate human place. It was a very powerful experience, and I think it helped us figure out what we mean by social action.
>
> The child entered our school in kindergarten as a boy, adopted from Guatemala with two White parents, and was with us all the way through eighth grade. So, for nine years I got to know this child. In mid-elementary school he [sic] started to express himself [sic] more in a less gender-conforming way. In fifth grade he [sic] started to grow his [sic] hair out and grow his [sic] nails out and had a lot of anxiety at that time [that we addressed with] social emotional support.
>
> Sixth grade was really when Nicolás [sic] told his [sic] parents that he [sic] wanted to identify as a girl and changed his [sic] name to Natalia. They immediately reached out to me. I have a close relationship with them. We have close relationships with our families here in general. We really just talked through the experience that they're going through, thinking about what her experience was going to be like here at school. They're really wonderful people, and they were immediately

very supportive of her choice and her experience and sought out resources right away and asked for my support, which obviously we did.

I worked with the family to say, "Listen, we will do whatever you need as a school," and because Natalia was in conversation with [her parents] and not with us at that time, I said, "You're going to have to let us know what she wants us to do in terms of when we switch pronouns if we do or if she wants us to keep using the male pronoun and wait until she goes to high school. So, let's let her take the lead and tell us what we need to do."

Principal Neumann drew upon Northstar's mission to create a supportive school environment for Natalia; however, not all schools emphasize the importance of social justice. How, then, can school leaders, without the benefit of a social justice mission, create a positive elementary school experience for gender-expansive and transgender students? This chapter examines three leadership characteristics that facilitated principals' capacity to support gender-expansive and transgender children across a variety of school contexts.[1]

THE ROLE OF SUPPORTIVE PRINCIPALS

Principals have a tremendous influence on nearly every aspect of schools, including school climate, teacher satisfaction, and student learning outcomes.[2] Not surprisingly, principals also play a crucial role in the development of inclusive schools.[3] Principals' actions, as well as their inaction, affect school practices and culture in ways that directly and indirectly influence transgender students' school experience. Unfortunately, educational leaders do not typically receive training related to gender or transgender youth.[4] As a result, they lack factual knowledge about transgender identities and practical knowledge about how to support transgender and gender-expansive students. Many educators express fear that actions they take in response to a transgender student could result in community backlash.[5] Lack of information increases the likelihood that leaders' actions could be hasty, ill conceived, or poorly executed and thus result in backlash from the school community. While large-scale community backlash is rare, educators' fears are not entirely unfounded. Some high-profile legal cases involving transgender students have included vitriolic community protests and media coverage.

The story of the Maines family is documented in *Becoming Nicole: The Transformation of an American Family*.[6] In that case, the Orono School District was uncertain about transgender students' rights or their own legal responsibilities. As a result, Orono first extended, and then withdrew, support for Nicole Maines, a transgender student. The case played out publicly in the media and in the courtroom. The school district experienced picketing, hate speech, and angry board meetings. The level of animosity aimed at the Maines family forced them from their home and community. Ultimately, Maine's Superior Court ruled in favor of the Maines family and found that the Orono School District had discriminated against Nicole when they failed to allow her to use facilities associated with her gender identity, specifically, the girl's bathroom. This high-profile case resulted in new legal protections for transgender students.[7] And, while the ruling in favor of the Maines family was the first of its kind, eight additional rulings in seven states provide protections to transgender students, further decreasing the potential that schools will experience community backlash, particularly if they are upholding the law.[8]

Despite legal mandates supporting transgender students' rights, educators continue to have limited opportunities to learn about transgender students and how to support them. As a result, many administrators struggle to implement supportive practices for transgender and gender-expansive students. One study of six principals who implemented trans-affirming policies found that, despite the principals' willingness, they struggled to sustain the work over time, shift cultural norms, and create opportunities for the parent community to engage in deep conversations about gender and gender-inclusive practices.[9] Thus, educators' failure to support transgender students may not reflect a lack of motivation but, rather, a lack of know-how.

How then, in the absence of training and know-how, did supportive principals create positive experiences for transgender and gender-expansive students? Despite their divergent educational contexts and lack of experience with transgender children, the principals in this study converged around three interrelated characteristics that contributed to their success. Supportive principals do the following:

- serve as lead learners
- employ a child-centered approach
- foster strong school-family collaboration

Regardless of the school setting or their personal background, these characteristics facilitated principals' capacity to create a positive school experience for transgender students. In turn, supportive principals described working with transgender and gender-expansive students as some of the most rewarding work they had experienced, both professionally and personally.

SERVING AS LEAD LEARNERS: "I DIDN'T HAVE ENOUGH INFORMATION."

First and foremost, supportive principals approached the topic of transgender students as a learning opportunity. As one Pennsylvania principal stated, "Anything that life gives you becomes a teachable moment, and either you listen and learn or you don't." This willingness to be a learner was common across all of the principals.

While all the principals positioned themselves similarly, as learners, they varied in their initial level of knowledge and comfort with the topic of transgender identities. Some principals identified as lesbian, gay, or bisexual, or had direct connections to queer communities; however, none felt they had sufficient expertise. As a result, even principals with some background knowledge approached the experience of having a transgender student as a learning opportunity. For example, Principal Neumann, from the opening vignette, had a comparatively high level of LGBTQ connections but still lacked knowledge about transgender children. She explained:

This was my first personal experience with a transgender child. I have friends who are transgender, and I experienced school myself as a bisexual person growing up in a hetero-normative world. I wasn't out [as bisexual] until after college, but I saw a lot of mistreatment of peers who were gender nonconforming. That was a very different environment that I grew up in than what we've created here, I hope.

Even principals with exposure to transgender identities lacked adequate knowledge related to transgender children. This led all of the principals to position themselves as learners, which, in turn, enabled them to develop the know-how they needed to create a supportive environment.

While none of the principals expressed overtly anti-trans views, some shared that they had started from a place of bias or misinformation. Principals attributed their lack of understanding to the absence of opportunities to meet and learn about transgender people. Even though transgender people are not an insignificant portion of society—0.6 percent of adults or approximately 1 in every 140 people is transgender—the majority of Americans are unaware of having ever met or known a transgender person.[10] This is due, in part, to stigma and risks associated with being openly transgender. As a result, transgender people often live low-profile lives, and many are never able to transition and live as their true selves.

The principal at Quail Road Elementary, a public school in a small, wealthy Massachusetts town, explained how her lack of exposure led her to misunderstand what it means to be transgender:

I really didn't understand. I hadn't had a personal experience close enough to provoke or probe my thinking. I was of the old way of thinking, and I hope not in a judgmental way, but I didn't have enough information. I knew that if I went to [a certain restaurant] on Tuesday nights a group of transvestites met there. I had some very surface impressions based on old terminology. I looked at things through the sexual identity lens. I didn't appreciate that gender identity was something real that didn't have ties to sexual preference.

This principal was aware of different gender identities and expressions, but she lacked the vocabulary needed to adequately and respectfully engage the topic. After being introduced to a transgender child and learning about their experiences, she recognized the misconceptions in her own thinking. Many of the principals reported shifting their personal convictions and overcoming their initial disbelief that a young child could know their gender identity.

Principal Daniel Tavoli at Talbot Elementary, a wealthy suburban school, introduced himself saying, "I like to describe myself as the poster child for someone who can't deal with this, who is a White, Catholic, male, straight, over-sixty person." Despite his traditional background, Principal Tavoli went on to describe the learning stance he had assumed with regard to transgender children:

> Probably my biggest goal is just to educate myself. I think if it were happening to one of my colleagues, I probably would not have been very open minded. I have to be honest. So, I've been trying hard to fight that intellectual instinct and emotional instinct and just be open and try to learn.

Statements like this demonstrate that principals did not need to have specialized knowledge or prior experience with LGBTQ matters to be supportive. According to the Transgender Training Institute, approximately 60–80 percent of people can be characterized as the "movable middle," that is, folks who are willing to learn in spite of their limited understanding.[11]

Other principals started out with moderate, but limited, information. Several had peripheral exposure to transgender adults—a distant cousin, the parent of a student, a friend from college—but no in-depth knowledge. The principal at Ovid Preparatory, a religious private school, shared:

> I have a transgender distant cousin who transitioned fully with surgery when I was young. We didn't spend a lot of time together, so it wasn't so present [in my life], but it was sort of matter-of-fact, and everybody still loved him and that was the thing. But I don't have a lot of super personal experience with it.

Principals who had some general awareness of transgender people were quick to point out that their knowledge and acceptance were not easily transferable to the school context. That is, having a friend or relative who is transgender does not prepare principals to support transgender students. And, knowing one transgender person does not provide adequate insight into the wide variety of transgender identities and experiences. Principals and other educators wanted more specific, school-level information about the kinds of practices that need to be in place, ways to implement those practices, and possible stumbling blocks. Without school-specific knowledge, principals remained uncertain about how to "get it right" and intimidated by the prospect of messing up, especially when transgender children's well-being is at stake. As the principal at Ovid Preparatory remarked, "I have been terrified of something going terribly wrong."

Even a high level of knowledge related to transgender adults was insufficient for supporting a transgender elementary student. One such principal was Jackie Kendall at Kirby Learning Center, an independent progressive school in Massachusetts with 140 students. Like Principal Neumann, Principal Kendall had thought extensively about gender and transgender identities and self-identified as queer. Principal Kendall had been drawn to Kirby's social justice mission and the school's open acceptance of queer families. Kendall described how the culture at Kirby attracted a dynamic community of gender-diverse individuals:

> When I came to this school as a teacher in 2007, for a school of our size, we had a significant number of lesbian parents with children in the school. Some of those parents did not adhere to gender norms in terms of their expression and would probably be identified as androgynous or butch. So, there was definitely an openness to exploring gender, and the school did not have a prescribed expectation of what people should look like or how they express [their gender], which was great for me because I'm queer. I have a wife and my wife definitely identifies as androgynous, so that felt like a very comfortable setting for me.

At the time of our conversation, the Kirby Learning Center had five transgender or gender-expansive children enrolled, and some parents and staff also identified as transgender or genderqueer. Even in this progressive, affirming context, Principal Kendall explained that a lot of learning still needed to take place at Kirby, and she described herself as a learner:

> I don't have to be the sort of administrator who knows everything . . . we're in this together. I see myself as a learner and as a facilitator and as a person who's willing, very willing, to continue to take other people's advice.

The principal at Dixon Primary School cautioned that it is a mistake to presume that LGB-identified educators have adequate knowledge to support transgender students. He explained: "I made it clear right away that I don't have more expertise because I'm a gay male."

While it is tempting to presume that all principals would naturally assume a learning stance when faced with new challenges, school leaders commonly face both external and internalized pressure to "know all the answers." The past two decades of education reforms have emphasized accountability and raised the stakes associated with outcome measures such as standardized test scores and teacher evaluations. Such accountability pressures can decrease educators' willingness to acknowledge areas of weakness or limited know-how.[12]

Moreover, the topic of transgender students presents unique challenges for educators. Despite clear legal rulings upholding the rights of transgender students, some entities in the United States have worked to delegitimize transgender people and bar their access to civil rights granted to all American citizens. For example, at the time of this study, the Trump administration attempted to define sex as exclusively male/female and determined by genitalia, which would have the political effect of barring transgender and intersex people from equal access protections under Title IX of the Education Amendments of 1972. Such political moves create the perception that being transgender may not be real or that the decision to accept or reject transgender people is somehow a matter of personal preference.[13] In this context, school administrators can feel trapped in the cross-hairs of competing narratives and reticent to appear political or side with one faction over another. As such, school leaders may try to avoid the topic of transgender identities rather than embrace a new learning opportunity.

In contrast, supportive principals' willingness to assume a learning stance helped them develop a clearer understanding of the science behind sex and gender, the validity of being transgender, even in childhood, and increased awareness of transgender people's legal rights. Rather than getting caught up in subjective arguments about morality, these principals experienced greater certainty that their role as educators demanded that they support their transgender student, first and foremost, regardless of others' discomfort or opposition. For principals and other school leaders who aim to support gender-expansive and transgender students, learning about transgender identities is the first step to creating a supportive school environment.

EMPLOYING A CHILD-CENTERED APPROACH: "WE NEED TO TAKE CARE OF THIS PERSON."

The second characteristic that all principals exhibited was employing a child-centered approach to transgender students. Taking a child-centered approach means making decisions on a case-by-case basis in line with a child's needs, rather than applying rules in the absence of contextual information. Canadian scholar Hélène Frohard-Dourlent describes this as a "student in charge" approach to decision-making that has potential to disrupt cisnormativity in schools.[14] Principals commonly described themselves as "following the child's lead" to determine how to best support transgender and gender-expansive children. In the words of Principal Tavoli at Talbot Elementary School, "We deal with every child, as much as we can, as an individual, with whatever they bring to the table." Supportive, child-centered principals described the importance of meeting students' unique needs and addressing children's social-emotional well-being.

Unique Individuals

A child-centered approach to transgender students rejects generalized procedures or a one-size-fits-all perspective in favor of individuation. Some supportive principals described using a child-centered approach with all the students in their school, not just transgender or gender-expansive students. The principal at Harborside Cooperative School, a public school situated in a large, dense city, explained:

> First and foremost in our minds was, "We need to take care of this person." That's always first on my mind when I think about all the kids in our school. Hope is one unique kid, but we have lots of unique kids that are unique for other reasons, and they are also quite vulnerable in different ways. We have kids with special needs. We have kids living in poverty, kids living in shelters and in temporary housing. Everyone has got a story, and some of them are quite intense. So, I think for all of the adults in the school, that was always first and foremost in our minds.

This view of children as unique individuals with their own stories stands in contrast to educational approaches that ask students to leave their problems at the school door and ask administrators to standardize their procedures. A child-centered approach places children at the core of educational practice and considers all facets of their well-being.

The expectation that school leaders should attend to students' needs may seem intuitive; however, transgender people's needs are often portrayed as being at odds with the cisnormative interests of larger society. One reason for this perception is zero-sum thinking, or a belief that gains for one group equal losses for other groups. Zero-sum thinking makes dominant populations reluctant to share power and contributes to pervasive inequities. In schools zero-sum thinking leads people to mistakenly believe that increasing transgender students' access to facilities and programs will reduce access for cisgender people.[15]

It is true that the distribution of finite resources can produce demonstrable winners and losers; however, this logic does not hold when making decisions about human or civil rights. Human rights are fundamental; that is, they are not distributed but rather are "inalienable." Human rights may be protected in laws as civil rights. In the United States we have a long history of restricting the civil rights of marginalized peoples. This is true despite the fact that human and civil rights can be extended without reducing or compromising the rights of others. For example, allowing transgender people to use the bathroom that matches their gender identity does not preclude cisgender people from accessing the bathroom. This notion is sometimes expressed by the retort "It's not pie," meaning that human rights are not finite in the same way that a pie must be divided and shared, wherein more for some means less for others. Human rights are not a zero-sum matter; everyone can get what they need.

In some legal cases, opponents of transgender rights have argued that extending civil rights to transgender students, such as access to bathrooms or locker rooms, compromises the civil rights of cisgender students. Federal courts have consistently ruled that inclusive policies for transgender people do not violate others' rights.[16] Even if people are uncomfortable in the presence of transgender people, freedom from discomfort is not a civil right. On the contrary, transgender people do have the right to expression, education, equal protections, and freedom from discrimination under existing civil rights legislation. Based on legal rulings, transgender people have the same rights as cisgender people. Unfortunately, even when the law is on the side of transgender people, school leaders feel pressured to reconcile stakeholders' conflicting needs.

Taking a child-centered approach reduces zero-sum thinking and seems to alleviate some of the pressure principals feel to prioritize some students over others. Instead, principals stayed focused on the needs of each student. Principals were less likely to be swayed by the suggestion that one student's discomfort should negate another student's civil rights. The Griffin principal, who previously worked at Mercer Elementary when Meredith was in grades kindergarten through third, presented one example:

> A parent called me and was out of her mind saying, "What are we supposed to do? That's a boy using a girl's bathroom. He [sic] shouldn't be allowed to do that. My daughter doesn't feel comfortable." . . . I said to her, "Your child is welcome to use the nurse's bathroom." It came to me naturally. Why should [Meredith] be treated any differently? . . . I believe I also said to the mom, "Everybody here deserves what they need. Equal doesn't necessarily mean fair. Here we give everyone what they need and that's what [Meredith] needed." And the other child did not choose to use the nurse's bathroom, which is how I knew it was a

parent issue and not a student issue. After that one conversation, it never went anywhere else.

In this example, the principal employed a child-centered approach that preserved Meredith's right to use the bathroom corresponding to her gender identity while simultaneously meeting another student's espoused need. The principal's child-centered response facilitated her ability to create a supportive and affirming school environment for the transgender student.

Social-emotional Well-being

A child-centered approach also involves attending to students' social-emotional well-being, an aspect of student growth that some schools avoid. Under pressure to produce measurable student learning gains, educators may believe that attention to matters other than academic content undermines children's opportunities to learn. Moreover, social-emotional well-being is commonly understood as the purview of the school counselor and a distraction from teachers' time on task. Principal Tavoli at Talbot Elementary, who described himself as the "poster child for someone who can't deal with this," conveyed his beliefs about social-emotional well-being when he described his educational priorities:

> Touchy-feely is not naturally my greatest strength. I come from a place where school is academic. . . . If you had asked me ten years ago what my top ten priorities were in education, "kids' feelings" probably wouldn't have been in there.

Like Principal Tavoli, many educators prioritize the core technologies of schooling—teaching and learning—and turn their attention to students' social-emotional well-being only in response to heightened behavioral problems. This logic overlooks the fact that attending to students' social-emotional well-being may preempt behavioral problems.

However, educational priorities can change. Principal Tavoli's perspective on so-called touchy-feely topics began to shift in response to the anticipated enrollment of a transgender child. Principal Tavoli had been notified a year in advance that Jamie, a transgender kindergartener would enroll the following September, providing him with time to prepare. Together with the guidance counselor and school psychologist, he began to learn about transgender children, which altered his perspective on the educational priorities at Talbot Elementary. He explained:

> It quickly became evident that there are probably other Jamies in our school whose parents aren't as proactive or maybe they haven't fully realized or can't articulate [their gender identity] as clearly as Jamie had. So, we just felt like we needed to notch up our whole game in terms of making everybody feel validated and welcomed for who they are. . . . My feelings have changed even more in the last year as we get more and more into this. It just became so evident how many other kinds of challenges kids face that we just aren't as attuned to as we probably should be.

Principal Tavoli's stance as a learner and his child-centered approach enabled him to develop new understandings about the importance of children's social-emotional well-being and the need to incorporate it into their educational goals. Equally important, Principal Tavoli understood that all students would benefit, not just the incoming transgender child.

Transgender children are at higher risk than cisgender children for social and emotional distress in schools. Multiple components contribute to the problem. Foremost, schools are organized to reinforce cisnormative gender expectations and portray gender-nonconforming behaviors as bad or shameful. In some cases, adults and/or peers may criticize a child's gender expression, thereby creating an overt climate of animosity. Cisnormative school cultures can lead children to self-censor their behavior and feel internalized self-hatred and emotional distress. Even seemingly innocent questions from curious children can cause distress for gender-expansive and transgender children, including questions such as "Are you a girl or a boy?" "Why are you wearing that shirt?" or "Didn't you used to be a girl?" Invasive questions are difficult to handle at any age.[17] Children may perceive such questions as judgments. Children may not know how to articulate or explain their emotions. Or, they may feel responsible for putting others at ease. All of these factors, and more, can combine to decrease children's sense of belonging and safety and increase the level of risk for transgender and gender-expansive students.

Supportive principals understood that transgender children are at risk because of their environment, not because of any inherent deficit associated with their gender identity. Being aware of this increased risk led supportive principals to pay greater attention to transgender students' well-being. For example, the principal at Aberdeen Academy, a private independent school, understood the obstacles that transgender and gender-expansive children face. As a result, she made a commitment to making the school a safe and affirming environment. She explained:

> The goal has been to make sure we get it right. We don't want to put up any roadblocks because these kids have enough roadblocks. Some of them are internal, and they're certainly going to have external road-blocks because not every environment is going to be like [Aberdeen]. So, it's just making sure that we don't put up the roadblocks.

All of the principals expressed a desire to "get it right," or as one principal bluntly stated, "I just don't want to f--- it up!"

A child-centered approach helped supportive principals "get it right." By attending to students' unique needs and social-emotional well-being, these principals were able to provide vital support to transgender students, even when they started with limited understanding. As the principal from Crescent Elementary, explained, "I'm really here for the students, and what is best for students, and so in every situation [I ask], 'What are we doing for the student at hand?' … Keeping that focus is really what my goal is, to keep kid focused and centered." Particularly in the context of stakeholders' conflicting needs, a child-centered approach can help school leaders maintain and reinforce a focus on students' rights and well-being.

FOSTERING STRONG SCHOOL-FAMILY COLLABORATION: "IT'S ALL ABOUT RELATIONSHIP BUILDING."

The third characteristic that supportive principals exhibited was fostering strong school-family collaboration. Having a positive relationship with the student's family created the context for open communication and shared understandings. Moreover, families served as a resource to the principals, helping them learn about supportive practices for transgender children. As the principal at Aberdeen Academy stated, "I draw on the preference of the parent and the child and follow their lead." Providing adequate supports to transgender students was dependent, in part, on having a strong relationship with the student's family.

The importance of meaningful school-family collaboration is well documented. Authentic partnerships can have a positive effect on students' academic, social, and emotional learning.[18] Dr. David Farnsworth, the principal at Forrest School, explained the importance of school-family collaboration for meeting students' needs:

> It's all about relationship building, and I can have a transgender student, or a special education student, or a regular education student who is not thriving for some reason, and our job is to find out what is going on and how do we help make them successful. So regardless of what you need, we're going to try very hard to provide that for you. That's just our culture, and it works tremendously well.

As this principal explained, all students can benefit from strong school-family collaboration; however, a positive relationship may be especially important for gender-expansive and transgender students, who may experience bullying, emotional distress, and social disengagement in the absence of adequate support. In their study of six principals, researchers Bethy Leonardi and Sara Staley found that a good relationship with parents increased principals' ability to create a positive school experience for transgender students.[19]

Principal Farnsworth's commitment to school-family collaboration enabled him to create a positive school experience for Bek, a gender-expansive, "school-phobic" student who enrolled in second grade at Forrest School in 2007. In the following extended excerpt, Principal Farnsworth describes his experience working with Bek, who was assigned female at birth, and the positive relationship he cultivated with Bek's parents.

> Mom and Dad were newly divorced or separated, and Mom was moving, so she went to each of the schools and talked with the principals

and learned that we had a very good approach to bullying . . . so she decided to send her second-grade daughter [sic] to Forrest. Mom wasn't quite sure what she was dealing with, but this child was adamant [about being a boy] from the time I met him. But Mom and Dad had a difference in how they wanted to treat it.

Bek moved from a Catholic school where everything was boy and girl, really separated. And because of those experiences in the Catholic school, Bek was very school-phobic and spent a lot of time ill, avoiding school. In second grade, Bek, which are his initials, was going by Bailey, which is one of those names that can be either/or. . . . If Bek came from her [sic] dad's house, she [sic] came with very feminine clothes, because that was all Dad would let her [sic] wear. So, all the kids identified her [sic] as a girl. But it would come up in PE, and the bathroom became an issue very soon. By fourth grade Bek no longer felt comfortable being referred to as "she" at all and wanted to use the boys' bathroom. Nobody knew what to do, so that is where the relationship with the parents came along, and Bek.

The best thing that happened was the parents and I developed a very close relationship. Mom and I probably met monthly, or more frequently than that, and I would meet separately with Dad, and sometimes we would all meet together. There were special education issues as well that we dealt with, so there were times when we all had to meet together. That relationship building with the parents meant really listening and letting them know that no matter what was happening at home or no matter what was happening here, we were going to do what was necessary to help Bek make all of the educational milestones, and to feel comfortable in what we were doing.

There were a lot of times when I wish I had anticipated something, rather than had to be reactive. That's where the relationship with the parent became really important because Bek would go home and say, "I had this experience today and it was awful," and luckily Mom would call me, not in an accusatory way, but to say, "I just want you to know this is what happened today." So, I would say build a close relationship, an open door, open communication with the family, first and foremost. But expect to make mistakes, and then own them. Say to the parents, say to the child, "I am so sorry. You have to know that we didn't anticipate this happening. We're going to try to make it right, and we won't make that mistake again."

In this example we see the challenges that parents may face, trying to make sense of their child's gender identity development. We also see the difficulties that Bek experienced as a second grader who was already exhibiting school-avoidance behaviors. And finally, we see the principal's willingness to learn and his child-centered approach. Open communication between Principal Farnsworth and Bek's parents allowed them to develop a shared understanding about how to best support Bek. In fact, Principal Farnsworth continued to stay in touch with Bek, even after Bek left Forrest School, and he had plans to attend Bek's high school graduation. Their continued relationship demonstrates the value of school-family collaboration.

Together, the three key characteristics of supportive principals—serving as a lead learner, employing a child-centered approach, and fostering strong school-family collaboration—were mutually reinforcing. Having a collaborative school-family relationship reinforced the principals' capacity to be lead learners and to be child-centered. Principals overwhelmingly described families as their primary source of information about transgender children. Therefore, a positive relationship and open communication with the family helped principals stay informed. And, a positive school-family relationship facilitated principals' child-centered approach, enabling principals to develop shared understandings with the families and provide individualized supports at each stage of the child's development. As the principal at Quail Road Elementary explained, "Having a relationship with the family perpetuated deeper, more honest communication, and [helped] educators put their best selves forward."

SCHOOL SUPPORT IN THE ABSENCE OF FAMILY SUPPORT

Unfortunately, some families do not accept their child's gender identity. How, then, can a principal provide the necessary supports?

Findings from research make a clear case for supporting transgender children. Kristina Olson, a developmental psychologist, explains that transgender adolescents and adults suffer elevated risk of anxiety, depression, and suicidality as a result of rejection, stigma, prejudice, and discrimination. Similarly, children with gender dysphoria demonstrate some of these same outcomes, particularly, elevated anxiety and depression in comparison to their peers. In contrast, in a study that included seventy-three transgender children and two control groups, Olson found that "socially transitioned, prepubescent transgender children showed typical rates of depression and only slightly elevated rates of anxiety symptoms compared with population averages."[20] These results confirm the importance of affirming and supporting transgender children.

In the absence of parental support, schools may be uncertain what role to play. Some states, including Massachusetts, New Jersey, and Rhode Island, have policies to guide educators' practice regardless of whether the parents accept their child's gender identity.[21] These states take a student-centered approach that aligns with research. For example, the policy developed by the New Jersey Department of Education is as follows:

> A school district shall accept a student's asserted gender identity: parental consent is not required. Further, a student need not meet any threshold diagnosis or treatment requirements to have his or her gender identity recognized and respected by the district, school or school personnel. Nor is a legal or court-ordered name change required. There is no affirmative duty for any school district personnel to notify a student's parent or guardian of the student's gender identity or expression.[22]

Supportive policies, like New Jersey's, make clear that educators should believe children when they express a gender identity other than the one assigned to them at birth and act in ways that affirm and support their development and well-being.

States and districts that lack policy guidelines leave leaders guessing about their responsibility to transgender students. From a legal standpoint, it seems clear that school and district administrators should act in accord with case law. Litigation in eight states has repeatedly clarified that transgender and gender-expansive students should be treated in a manner consistent with their gender identity, under Title IX of the Education

Amendments of 1972. However, educators are not attorneys, and case law established in other states can feel too removed from their daily reality to guide leadership practice. The situation may be most difficult for those principals who lack know-how, policy guidance, and the support of affirming parents. However, in the absence of strong school-family collaboration, principals can utilize the first two characteristics, being a lead learner and being child-centered, to guide their actions.

Foremost, even in the absence of parental support, principals can take ownership of their learning and work to develop a knowledge base related to gender-expansive and transgender children. Even though school districts may not provide training opportunities, organizations like Gender Spectrum, GLSEN, and Welcoming Schools, a program created by the Human Rights Campaign, have developed tools that educators can use to support and guide their practice. When parents are not prepared to support their children, much less educate principals, then it is the principals' responsibility to educate themselves. In our information age, high-quality resources are available digitally and for free. Appendix B provides a list of some resources available to educators.

Second, principals have an ethical obligation to do no harm and provide supports that will keep students safe. To help meet this obligation, principals can take a child-centered approach, consulting directly with the student, even when parents decline to offer their support. Research demonstrates that student involvement in decision-making can increase agency, belonging, and competence.[23] For gender-expansive and transgender students who lack parental support, principals' efforts to collaborate directly with students and take a student-centered approach can help meet students' individual needs. Providing students with increased opportunity to have a voice may also help them feel affirmed and support their emotional well-being.

The tragic reality is that not all gender-expansive and transgender children are accepted by their families. Having supportive parents is a privilege. In fact, some parents reject and even punish or abuse their children for exhibiting gender-nonconforming behavior.[24] In the absence of clear guidelines, principals walk a fine line when it comes to supporting children whose parents reject their gender identity. The school's role, in loco parentis, demands that principals affirm children and create a school environment where they can succeed. At the same time, principals may worry that their actions could place children at risk outside the school, when they are at home with their families and caregivers. This impossible balancing act points to the absolute necessity of clear guidelines and procedures, which can be developed by individual districts where states have failed to provide adequate guidance. It is not an overstatement to say that children's lives depend on educators' actions.

SUPPORTIVE PRINCIPALS' REFLECTIONS

School leaders commonly express fear that actions they take in response to a transgender student could result in community backlash. Principals worry about calls from angry stakeholders, contentious meetings, and even the possibility that controversial decisions could jeopardize their careers. In contrast, supportive principals described their experience working with transgender students and their families in almost exclusively positive terms, characterizing it as both professionally and personally beneficial. The language they used to describe their experience included "humbling," "powerful," "enlightening," an "honor," "exciting learning opportunity," "emotional experience," and "transformative." These responses stood in stark contrast to the negative assumptions that school leaders commonly hold about how school communities would react to a transgender student.

Supportive principals explained that having a transgender student presented a growth opportunity. Not only did principals learn factual information about gender and transgender identities, but the situation also challenged them and their school community to grow in unanticipated ways. The principal at Quail Road Elementary explained:

> It was one of the most powerful learning experiences I've ever gone through professionally, and I suspect for others. Intellectually, we had a lot to learn about [being] transgender. Emotionally, it helped us remember to be open-minded and compassionate and empathic in ways that [are] implied as part of our professional community, but spending

concerted time to consider a student's feelings, the family's feelings, the community impact, it was really powerful. It was a really powerful growing opportunity for all of us.

Having a transgender or gender-expansive student challenged school communities to act in ways that would reflect their professional beliefs and values. The depth and intensity of these experiences were also remarkable. Some supportive principals got choked up or were moved to tears when describing their experiences. The principal at Crescent Elementary stammered:

You're going to make me cry, sorry. . . . I'm sorry, I'm sorry. I think it is an emotional experience, and that's why I'm crying, because you want what's best for the kids and the families, and you can feel from meeting with them and talking to them that there is so much going on in the background that you want this to be their safety net. You don't want this to become the problem. You want this to be the solution to whatever else is going on.

Learning about the difficulties that transgender people face and realizing that the school context can, quite literally, mean the difference between life and death were profound experiences for many supportive principals.

In fact, some principals referred to their experience working with a transgender student as one of the most significant experiences in their career. The principal at Lincoln School was nearing retirement when one of her students socially transitioned. She described the impact of that experience on her career as an educator and principal:

If I were to phase out my career with just what I had done, I don't know that I would be happy. It would be okay, but I wouldn't have done anything meaningful really that changed people's lives in the way that is obvious. I know people say, "Of course you change children's lives. You do things every day." Yes, but this was so evident that what I experienced was transformative for me as a person and as a leader. I really did something meaningful, and it just rejuvenated me as a leader.

Her positive experience supporting a transgender student prompted this principal to delay retirement. In addition to staying on as principal, she began to counsel other principals on how to support transgender students and shared her experience at a regional conference. While the Lincoln School principal's experience stands out as especially transformational, all of the principals resoundingly described their experience working with a transgender student as a positive growth opportunity for themselves and their school community.

CONCLUSION

The three key characteristics of supportive principals are serving as a lead learner, employing a child-centered approach, and fostering strong school-family collaboration. The principals' stories demonstrate how these mutually reinforcing characteristics increased their capacity to create positive school experiences for transgender and gender-expansive students. Identifying these three key characteristics makes it more likely that schools and districts can intentionally develop these skills and create more supportive school environments. Ultimately, having a transgender student was a positive learning experience for the entire school community.

At the same time, we should not underestimate the depth and breadth of work involved. To truly support transgender and gender-expansive students, we must fundamentally change the cisnormative culture of schools and the ways that schools are organized to reinforce cisnormativity. We must change our beliefs about gender and gender identity. This kind of change cannot be accomplished with a checklist. It isn't achieved with mandatory professional training. Real change demands that principals, their colleagues, and entire educational communities engage difficult questions, challenge deeply held beliefs, and dismantle implicit gender bias. This is the work of a lifetime. It demands that we make ourselves uncomfortable and vulnerable to critique. It demands emotional commitment and sustained attention.

More than anything, it is incumbent on people with cisgender identities to take up this work. Cisgender people have privileged positions of power and, thus, a platform for challenging gender bias in schools, developing new norms, and shifting the status quo. To make schools sites of belonging for everyone, regardless of gender identity, we have to engage this work proactively. The following chapters provide additional insights from supportive educators who have begun to ask, "How can I make my school a supportive environment for transgender students?"

CHAPTER 4

Leveraging Learning
in the School Community

The meeting room has all the markers of a traditional professional learning environment: ten round tables, a projection screen, a podium, and a side table displaying books. If not for the full-size rainbow flag and LGBTQ book titles, a casual observer might presume this is a typical corporate training. Rather, Mark Palermo will be presenting an interactive three-hour professional development session titled "Supporting Transgender and Gender-Nonconforming Students." The participants include thirty educators from a single school district—a mixture of classroom teachers, paraprofessionals, and counselors. As they walk in the door, each participant receives a folder with an agenda, resource list, and learning outcomes that state

Participants will:
- be able to articulate and use correct LGBTQ terms and definitions
- understand the experiences of LGBTQ students and families
- have reviewed laws and policy guidance as it relates to supporting transgender students and families
- be aware of the research on the factors that promote resilience and positive outcomes for LGBTQ students
- increase their comfort and confidence in talking about gender identity, expression, sexual orientation, and school climate, and responding to bias-based language
- have a plan to use the content learned

Mark, a cisgender gay man, starts the session by saying, "I don't expect you to know anything about this topic. We are all learners, and this is a place where you can ask any and all questions." Mark is an experienced presenter. In his role as LGBTQ Safe Schools Program Director for the Department of Education, Mark makes dozens of presentations annually, all aimed at increasing school inclusivity. Mark's extensive experience has taught him not to make any assumptions, and he carefully reviews definitions for each of the letters: L, G, B, T, and Q. The "T," Mark explains, "represents some of the most vulnerable children in our schools and the identity that most people know least about." Without missing a beat, Mark turns to the young man to his left and introduces River, a local college student and transgender activist.

The educators keep their eyes fixed on River as he describes the role teachers played in his life. At thirteen, River was depressed and suicidal. His immigrant mother worried that their move to the United States had corrupted her child, and she prayed for God to make River more feminine. It was his teachers, River explained, who accepted and supported him. "My teachers taught me to accept myself." It was teachers' caring and love that allowed River to persevere, transition to his authentic self, and enroll in college.[1] Later, when Mark invites the educators to respond to River's message, many share their own stories. One teacher recalls, "I will never forget in 1985, when Vincent Gianni had me open the dictionary to 'homosexuality' and asked me if I wanted him to leave. Instead, I gave him a hug." Building on these stories of compassion, Mark emphasizes that children know, from small gestures and subtle language, which teachers are accepting. "Queer kids are able to name the people who created safe space for them." Some educators share how they have used stickers, books, and posters to signal that they are LGBTQ allies. Mark explains how these microaffirmations can have a positive cumulative effect that can counteract some of the microaggressions LGBTQ children experience daily.

As the session progresses, more participants speak up, raising their concerns and expressing uncertainties. Mark uses anecdotes and examples to acknowledge the educators' anxieties while simultaneously challenging them to move beyond their discomfort:

There was a time, if you picked up the USA Today sports section, there were zero women. I once counted up all the pictures in the [newspaper]. There were eighty-four pictures, zero women. I was told, "There's no market for it." But this is a message about who is valued and who is privileged. It is a point of privilege that everyone gets my pronouns right. That isn't true for everyone. For people who are gender fluid or nonbinary, their pronouns are *they, them, theirs*. People tell me, "I just don't want to make a mistake." Don't avoid pronouns because you are afraid. In education we need to value mistakes as a way to learn and grow. The default for animals is always male. If you want to get better at pronouns, try rereading books with animal characters using *they/them/their/theirs*. Practice makes perfect. Yes, you may feel uncomfortable, but that's an opportunity. Discomfort cannot be used as a reason to treat people unequally.

Through his examples, Mark creates a narrative that situates educators as privileged and, therefore, capable of disrupting discriminatory practices in schools. To conclude and cement the day's learning, Mark asks the participants to add their ideas to five posters that are hung around the room. The noise level in the room rises as the educators travel to each of the posters, reading others' contributions and adding their own. The posters ask:

How have you and your school district supported LGBTQ students?

What are some ways you can support and educate parents regarding sexual orientation and gender identity?

What are some ways to support transgender students?

What are some questions you have in regard to supporting transgender students?

What resources can help you and your school support LGBTQ students and families?

For Mark Palermo, teaching about transgender identities is both a profession and a personal passion. He knows that educators can have a powerful influence on their students and colleagues. The challenge, then, is getting educators to understand the gravity of the situation for transgender students as well as the relevance of learning about transgender identities and the potential benefits for all students. This chapter reviews the kinds of learning opportunities available to educators and how they could be improved.

LEVERAGING LEARNING IN THE SCHOOL COMMUNITY

The education profession demands continual learning. Teachers need to stay informed about new curriculum standards, instructional strategies, and the changing needs of their student populations. Principals must stay up to date on new laws, policies, and administrative procedures. It seems possible, then, that the learning stance required to be a highly skilled educator might be leveraged to mobilize opportunities to learn about gender identities. Educators who are committed to life-long professional learning might embrace the growing visibility of transgender students as a potential learning opportunity.

When transgender students enroll or transition, educators are presented with an opportunity to assess whether they have adequate knowledge to support the student and what they might need to learn. One first-grade teacher from PS 25 described the learning stance her school and colleagues assumed in response to Leo, a transgender kindergartener. "Everybody was just so happy to have this family in the school and to use it as an opportunity to teach more about gender fluidity, not necessarily sexuality, but more about gender roles." She went on to explain:

> He really changed things in the school. Just this one little kid who came in as a four- or five-year-old made this school go, "We need to get on board with this. We need to educate our teachers. We need to educate ourselves about this situation because he's going to come through the years, and everyone is going to be in contact with him somehow. How are we going to do this as a school?"

Having an openly identified transgender student can be a catalyst for learning about transgender identities. It can also be an opportunity for cisgender educators to critically examine their own gender identity and beliefs about gender.

Although having an openly identified transgender student can compel educators to learn and change their educational practice, relying on individual children to be the impetus for learning about transgender identities can come at a cost: it places transgender children and their parents in a position of great responsibility and vulnerability. Education scholar Elizabeth Meyer and her colleagues raise this point of concern and describe these students as potential "sacrificial lambs," explaining that they may lose their right to privacy by being the catalyst for learning.[2] One teacher worried that the amount of attention placed on the openly transgender student at her school made the student a "poster child" and placed undue emphasis on one aspect of the student's identity. This notion of a poster child situates the transgender child as representative of an entire complex community.[3] The child is also situated as being responsible for others' learning.[4] In this way, visible transgender students and their families unfairly shoulder the burden of educating cisgender adults and leading the change effort.

Unfortunately, in the absence of an openly identified transgender or gender-expansive student, school districts may not support professional learning related to gender or transgender children. Administrators may be reluctant to initiate discussions about topics that are perceived as controversial or political. They may also question the relevance of learning about transgender identities and the benefits such learning can have for the larger school population.[5] Avoiding the topic of gender until a specific issue arises or a transgender child enrolls almost guarantees that schools will struggle to provide adequate support to transgender students. A proactive approach can enable districts to structure productive dialogue and avert problems before conflict occurs.

Educators generally agreed that knowledge and learning could facilitate a positive school experience for transgender elementary students; however, they struggled to answer: *Who needs to know what, and why?* This chapter describes educators' responses to these questions and the kinds of learning opportunities that were available to adults, including the following:

- learning for teachers and staff
- learning for the school community
- missed learning opportunities

Generally, supportive principals leveraged learning as a way to build support for transgender and gender-expansive students. At the same time, principals also missed learning opportunities, particularly when they perceived transgender identities and experiences as having only narrow, rather than broad, relevance.

LEARNING FOR EDUCATORS: "EVERYTHING ALL OF A SUDDEN CLICKED."

As supportive principals planned how to create a positive environment for their transgender students, they considered who would need information and how best to provide professional learning. All of the schools identified teachers as needing opportunities to learn about transgender identities. Being knowledgeable about gender-expansive and transgender students could help teachers create gender-inclusive classrooms and facilitate students' sense of belonging. Here, we focus on the kinds of professional learning opportunities that schools implemented and the educators they targeted. By far, the most common recipients of transgender education were teachers in direct contact with the student whom they knew to be transgender. Schools were less likely to provide professional learning to noncertified staff such as lunch monitors, recess aides, or bus drivers.

Learning for Teachers

Teachers were the most common recipients of professional learning related to transgender students. They typically participated in a single information session, presented during a faculty meeting or perhaps on a designated professional development day. These sessions usually included factual information about the difference between sex, gender, and sexual orientation and a basic introduction to transgender children. A fifth-grade teacher from Mercer Elementary described her experience as follows:

> That's when I fully really understood everything. Everything all of a sudden clicked, and it was like, I know this; I understand the difference between sexuality and gender and orientation and sex. I understand all of this now, and I feel like I am so much better prepared to handle

anything that comes up, any conversations I have with parents or kids, or even in my adult life, with my friends and my family. I have a lot more knowledge.

One-time learning sessions were a way to introduce teachers to key concepts and correct common misconceptions about gender being associated with sexuality or children being too young to know about gender. Teachers and administrators typically participated together in these learning sessions, developing some shared understandings about gender.

In some cases, principals started with a small group of teachers, usually those teachers in direct contact with the student whom they knew to be transgender. In the absence of adequate financial resources, targeting a limited number of teachers can reduce the cost of professional learning while ensuring that key teachers receive needed information. According to the principal at Griffin Elementary, a turn-key approach, with teachers teaching one another, may lead to greater receptivity. She explained:

> There may be a smaller group of teachers you want to start with, the ones that have the most impact at the given time, and then, have them be ambassadors for what they learned at that professional development. . . . I feel like teachers hearing from teachers is sometimes the best pathway, as opposed to me saying, "This is the way we're going to do things." Sometimes people are more accepting when they hear from their colleagues.

While a targeted approach to professional learning may be better than none, relying on turn-key strategies can result in misinformation or uneven understandings across the school. In contrast, providing professional learning to all teachers sends a clear message that all teachers are expected to support transgender students, and it increases the likelihood that teachers will have shared understandings about gender and transgender identities.

Access to financial and human resources for professional learning varied across schools and states. Massachusetts had a state-level educator dedicated to providing LGBTQ-related professional development throughout the state. This was also true for New York City, which includes the two school districts where Harborside Cooperative and PS 25 were located. Even with a dedicated liaison, educators wished information were more readily available. A teacher from PS 25 complained, "There's one LGBT liaison for all of New York City. There should be one for each district at least, going to every school, and giving every staff training." Limited in-district resources meant that many schools sought professional learning from external organizations or consultants and, sometimes, from the transgender student's family.

Educators described their deep appreciation for the expert knowledge that organizations and presenters brought to their schools. For example, at Pacificus Learning Collaboratory, a nonprofit organization provided training during a professional learning day in August, in anticipation of enrolling their first known transgender student:

> The Transgender Alliance came and did a workshop with us that was really wonderful. The first question they asked us was, "When did you decide you were a girl or a boy?" I thought that question was so great because nobody decides. They just know. Everybody says, "I just knew," and so I thought that was a great way to frame it. That was our first introduction to how to think about transgender students.

Organizations with expertise in providing transgender-related professional learning worked to grow educators' knowledge and develop positive perceptions about transgender students and the learning opportunities they bring to schools. The principal at Ovid Preparatory, a private religious school, invited a speaker to work with the teachers for a 1.5-hour session. She shared:

> He himself was transgender, but he didn't talk about that until the end, which I thought was really interesting. He went through what transgender is and defined a lot of important terms. Then he talked about the implications at school, like bathrooms and locker rooms and when boys and girls get divided up into lines. He helped my staff think about "What's the language I use? Do I say, 'hey, guys' or 'hey, girls?'" So, paying attention to language and also paying attention to the moments

that might be particularly challenging for a transgender child and [asking] how are we helping that piece in the process?

Having an expert present information relieved some of the pressure supportive principals felt to be a source of information. As such, most of the principals sought assistance from an external professional development provider.

In some schools, however, principals developed their own professional learning sessions. This was more common when principals had prior knowledge of LGBTQ topics or identified as a member of the LGBTQ community. For example, the Evergreen Elementary principal, who identified as lesbian, explained how she combined her own secondary research with legal information provided by the district attorney to design training for her teachers:

> I trained my own staff about the terms, the definitions, what their roles and responsibilities are. I provided them with some handouts. We talked about some of the laws, the ones I felt they needed to know about in terms of bathroom issues, parental rights, and student rights. We used two faculty meetings to address how we were supporting Eric and then just educating them in the laws and our responsibilities as educators.

Because this principal was knowledgeable about LGBTQ topics and comfortable discussing gender with her faculty, she was able to design and lead her own transgender education learning session. At least three other supportive principals, all with links to the LGBTQ community, acted as a resource to their school community, while simultaneously inviting expert organizations and consultants to provide professional learning to their staff.

Despite having little prior knowledge about transgender and gender-expansive children, numerous principals and teachers described working collaboratively with colleagues to build their knowledge base, often reading books together. For example, at Talbot Elementary School, the principal, counselor, and school psychologist read and discussed *Becoming Nicole* as a way to deepen their understandings.[6] Teachers also reported initiating their own learning, seeking information online or sharing reading materials.

One Mercer Elementary teacher remarked, "We are big readers, so we read a lot of books." A parent backed up this statement saying, "[The fifth-grade teachers] have read more books on transgender families or young adult novels with transgender characters than most of the immediate members of our family." In this way, many educators worked independently to develop their knowledge in addition to the learning opportunities provided by their school or district.

In some instances, the transgender student's family paid for professional learning. The principal at Mercer Elementary explained that in addition to the state department's LGBTQ liaison, who presented at a faculty meeting, the transgender child's family paid for five key staff members to receive additional training: "It was one day at the children's hospital. At that point, Meredith was going into third grade, and they wanted to make sure that we all collectively knew. It was just school staff, and [the family] arranged for us to go." Given the lack of resources in schools, financial support from the family increased the likelihood that school personnel would receive adequate professional learning. While this scenario may be less common, there were numerous instances of families providing professional learning resources in the form of books, training, and speakers. These examples demonstrate how a lack of financial resources can constrain professional learning and raise the question of whether teachers in lower-income schools and children from less financially stable families receive adequate supports.

While most of the supportive principals described providing school-level professional learning, in some instances, professional learning took place at the district level, especially when district administrators were aware of having multiple transgender or gender-expansive students enrolled across the district. The principals from Dixon Primary and Iroquois Valley Elementary, which are located in the same small district, explained that their superintendent offered professional learning to district administrators first, before providing whole-school training. The primary school principal explained:

> An outside organization that specializes in supporting transgender students came in and talked to us about best practices and things we could

do. That definitely helped guide us. It was a half-day with the entire district leadership team. From there, we made plans to have that trainer come back and speak to each of the faculties in a faculty meeting in the fall.

In this example, a supportive superintendent helped ensure that everyone in the district received similar access to professional learning, increasing the consistency and accuracy of information across the district.

The most effective learning opportunities are ongoing rather than one-shot workshops.[7] In each of the five case study schools—Mercer, Jefferson, Northstar, Pacificus, and PS 25—educators had multiple opportunities to engage in transgender-related learning. Providing multiple opportunities for transgender education enabled teachers to deepen their knowledge over time. Danny Carver, a PS 25 kindergarten teacher and dedicated LGBT activist, described the learning that occurred when Leo, an openly transgender boy, enrolled in kindergarten:

> For the initial training, they sent one representative from every grade as sort of like a crash course on LGBT and transgender issues in the classroom and in the school, what children's rights are and what is mandated, and how to provide support. Then we had [an external organization] that works on classroom issues around oppression, and they did a training with the staff. Then at the end of the year, we did a whole morning workshop with me and Leo's mother facilitating. It was for the whole teaching staff. I basically gave a little introduction to general LGBT history. . . . Mom basically told her story about Leo and the dramatic emotional shift and confidence level when they began accepting him as a boy. It was very touching . . . I thought it was very powerful and impacted a lot of teachers who may have been skeptical.

When teachers have extended opportunities to learn about a new topic, they are more likely to make changes to their classroom practice. Chapter 5 examines some of the strategies that teachers in the case study schools used to create more gender-inclusive classroom practices.

Learning for Noncertified Staff[8]

Beyond teachers, schools employ a wide range of noninstructional support staff. Some of these support staff, such as the school psychologist, counselor, social worker, or nurse, hold professional certifications and work directly with students. These school staff were commonly included in professional learning related to transgender students. Their inclusion may be due, in part, to the perception that gender-expansive and transgender children could experience emotional distress in school, need access to counseling, or request to use the nurse's gender-neutral bathroom. Thus, it was common for these certified, noninstructional staff members to participate in professional learning related to gender, sometimes even receiving more training opportunities than the teaching staff.

By comparison, noncertified school staff seldom had opportunities to learn about gender or transgender students. Generally speaking, positions such as lunch monitor, hall monitor, cafeteria cook, recess aide, crossing guard, security guard, custodian, bus driver, and bus aide involve limited training. Cafeteria cooks and bus drivers need appropriate licensure for employment, but other noncertified positions have minimal requirements for job entry. Moreover, employment contracts for noncertified employees may not require learning beyond initial job training. These hiring practices contrast sharply with those of certified teachers, who are required to complete a minimum number of hours of yearly professional development to maintain certification.

Although noncertified support staff lack training related to gender-expansive and transgender students, they often supervise spaces where these children may be most at risk. Primary and secondary students report that some of the most dangerous school spaces—places where they are most likely to be bullied or harassed—include the bathroom, locker room, playground, school corridors, and cafeteria.[9] Research further suggests that the noncertified staff who supervise these spaces may be less likely to identify and intervene in instances of bullying.[10] Thus, school spaces that are under the supervision of noncertified staff, who are unlikely to receive adequate professional learning, could present real risks to gender-expansive and transgender children. An uninformed adult in a position of authority could exacerbate a bullying situation or inadvertently disclose a student as transgender, violating the Family Educational Rights and Privacy Act (FERPA) and placing the student at risk.[11] Unfortunately, many noncertified staff are exempt from having to participate in learning sessions that fall outside of their contracted job training specifications.

The topic of noncertified staff and their lack of access to training and information came up repeatedly, often in response to observed problems. Danny Carver, the kindergarten teacher at PS 25, raised his concern with the principal, after observing practices that exacerbated, rather than decreased attention to gender differences. He explained:

> There are lunch staff who are basically hired from outside that don't have any training on this. When it's line-up time outside, they still do it boys and girls. I've talked to the person I work with and was like "Don't do that and this is why," but they haven't actually been trained. I think that would be useful because at lunchtime they're with all of the students. So, I feel like they should have training too.

In this instance, the teacher observed the lunch staff lining up children into binary girl-boy lines. This procedure contradicted practices Danny had implemented in his classroom, where gender was not used to sort children or structure classroom activities. Danny had worked especially hard to eliminate such practices because one of the children in his class had socially transitioned that year. Even though Danny spoke directly to the staff member working with his students, lack of systematic training for all the support staff gives children mixed messages and can create the context for gender-based bullying.

The teachers at Jefferson Elementary intervened in one such instance of bullying on the school bus. Multiple factors converged to create a high-risk situation for Jacob, who transitioned over the summer between kindergarten and first grade. Although the teachers had spoken at length with Jacob's mother and had received training related to transgender children, support staff in the school had not been informed. To complicate matters, Jacob's birth name (sometimes called a deadname) and original gender marker were still part of his school record. The second-grade teacher reflected on what happened when Jacob started first grade as his true self:

> Mom wrote a letter, and then the guidance counselor read the letter to the school, to the whole faculty, including the PE teacher and the librarian—they all knew. But as far as the cafeteria and the recess aides and people like that, it was just word of mouth for them; they didn't hear the letter. I don't believe it was communicated to the bus drivers because there was an incident later. Somebody was bothering Jacob on the bus, saying "You're really a girl." He was like "No, I'm not. I'm a boy." The bus driver said, "No, my list says you're a girl, so you're a girl." It was not a shining moment for our district.

Even though the certified staff had been informed about Jacob's gender identity, formal school records had not yet changed, and in this instance, the bus driver's lack of knowledge created a dangerous situation for Jacob. Although teasing from peers and learning to navigate social relationships are common aspects of childhood, malicious teasing about one's gender can threaten children's safety, leading to acts of harassment, violence, and even self-harm.

In this instance, the bus driver exacerbated the situation. By rejecting Jacob's gender identity and using written records as proof, he invalidated Jacob's authority over his own identity and gave others power over him. The kindergarten teacher, Sarah Molino, who had taught Jacob prior to his transition, offered an extended description of the steps she took to support and protect Jacob:

> **SARAH:** I was worried about the bus because I thought these kids all know Jacob as [deadname] and now all of the sudden he is Jacob and they're just little kids. They could say something that's offensive just out of curiosity. So, I remember that was a big issue for me. I get emotional. Could you imagine what could have happened? So, I met with the bus driver that Jacob had, and another bus driver came with him that knew the situation. We watched that Ryland Whittington video

together. I was like, "You need to watch this [video] because this [situation] could really be disastrous."[12]

MELINDA: You contacted the bus driver and invited the bus driver to watch a video?

SARAH: Yes, I called the bus driver. I also called this other bus driver [who runs] a bus safety program, and he ended up coming with the bus driver. I think he knew this was not going to go over very well. I remember the one bus driver was like, "What are you talking about?" and looking at me like I made this thing up.

So, we watched the video, and then we talked about it. At first [Jacob's bus driver] was just very abrasive and "What are you talking about?" and said something not so nice. I was really like, "You have to get on board with this." I said, "You're going to have to wrap your head around this. You're a key person. Because, in the nucleus of the school we've got support systems here and if something happens, there's someone that will be able to scoop up the pieces and make it okay, but on the bus you're alone. It's you and all of these kids."

The bus driver, I don't think got it. So, they left. Then later in the day, the other guy who got it, not the actual bus driver [the one who runs the safety program], he came back and said, "I want you to know there's going to be an aide on the bus." So, they had an aide and nothing really came up for a while, and so it ended up being okay. I was just fearful. When the transition happened, I just didn't want things to be horrible for him.

In this description Sarah identifies the bus driver as a "key person" and points out that he is alone on the bus, making it difficult to assist Jacob, if needed. Because the bus driver struggled to "get on board," there was increased potential for further incidents on the bus that could jeopardize Jacob's safety. While Sarah's efforts to educate the bus driver may seem out of the ordinary, Jacob's experience on the bus was not unusual. Educators and parents regularly shared stories of transgender and gender-expansive children being harassed and having to defend themselves in these less-supervised school spaces.

In addition to their regularly employed, noncertified staff, schools also host a wide array of temporary staff and visitors. This could include guest speakers, after-school caregivers, and substitute teachers. Interactions with these visitors can place children at increased risk of being misgendered, being directed to the wrong bathroom, or having their transgender identity disclosed. The principal at Belmont Elementary shared: "We had a lunch teacher who was a substitute, and she didn't understand why Bailey was going in the different gender bathroom." In this instance, six-year-old Bailey reported the substitute's behavior, prompting the principal to respond reactively after Bailey had been misgendered and singled out. A more proactive approach to professional learning—one that includes noncertified staff and school visitors—could contribute to a more knowledgeable school community and decrease the risks that transgender children face in schools.

LEARNING FOR THE SCHOOL COMMUNITY: "SHOULD WE? SHOULDN'T WE?"

While supportive principals unequivocally reported that teachers benefit from transgender-related professional learning, they were less certain about creating learning opportunities for other adults in the school community. Principals and parents alike wondered about the benefits and risks of engaging the larger school community in dialogue about gender and transgender identities. The primary concerns centered on student privacy and the relevance of gender-focused professional learning for a wider audience. Ultimately, decisions about whether to extend learning opportunities to the larger school community were made with input from the known transgender child and their family and reflected individual needs and circumstances.

Learning for Parents and Guardians

Decisions about what and how to communicate with parents and guardians differed by school and family. In line with their child-centered approach, supportive principals described working closely with the parents of the known transgender child to identify and develop appropriate learning opportunities for other parents or guardians with children enrolled in the school. A key consideration was whether to send a letter home and, if yes, for what purpose? Families with children who transitioned at school were more likely, but not guaranteed, to send a letter to other parents and guardians. Such letters were sent with two primary purposes: to educate and to express pride in their transgender child. Parents who decided not to send letters described wanting to protect their child's privacy.

Across the eighteen children who served as introductory entry points for this study, six families opted to send letters home to parents and guardians. Each of the six children had transitioned subsequent to enrolling at their school, and the families anticipated receiving questions from adults and students alike. Sending letters home was one way to provide parents and guardians with the vocabulary and knowledge they would need to respond to their children's questions. For example, at Lincoln School, a class-specific letter was sent to parents and guardians explaining that one child in the class was socially transitioning. The principal explained:

> Mom wrote a letter to all fifth-grade parents explaining "We have a daughter who continually said I'm not a girl, I'm a boy." So, the letter recounted the experience from the parents' perspective and ended with "We just want our child to be happy and healthy, and we ask that you embrace this as much as you can. Here are some questions your child may ask and here are some answers you can give them." It was very useful because parents want to say the right thing, and a lot of times they didn't know the answers. It was truly an education because, as much as you want to do the right thing, you don't want to use the wrong terminology.

Class-specific letters were one way to educate and support parents' and guardians' ability to respond to questions their children might ask at home.

When thinking through "Who needs to know what?" families often concluded that varying levels of proximity necessitated varying levels of information. At Quail Road Elementary, Quinn's family was new to town when Quinn, a third grader, announced he was ready to transition. Mom explained how they decided to communicate their son's transition using

two different letters, one to the entire school community and a more personal letter to a smaller group of parent-friends:

> We worked with the principal and school psychologist to come up with
> a communication plan. The principal sent a generic letter out to the
> whole school community about what it means to be transgender, how
> the community would support him, what the school valued, and how
> it was an accepting school. It listed a lot of resources, websites, and
> books. It didn't include names, but it said the parents were available to
> talk to anyone that had questions. Our letter was a lot more personal
> and really told our story. We hoped that the friends we had made in
> the town in that short year would help us disseminate that information. It
> included our phone numbers, and we got a lot of phone calls.

In this instance, the principal distributed a general letter to the school community aimed at building knowledge and awareness in the larger parent/
guardian population. At the same time, the family's letter, which they distributed to a smaller friend circle, provided more personal information and
solicited questions. This way, they hoped to cultivate a supportive network
of goodwill ambassadors who could spread positive information about
Quinn and his family.

Deciding how much information to share with other parents was sometimes difficult. Families wanted to share enough information to educate
and build support without oversharing or jeopardizing the child's privacy.
One mom tailored her communication approach to target first-grade families who were most likely to remember that her son, Jacob, had presented
as female in kindergarten:

> I decided to ask for the list of kids who were going to be in his first-grade
> class who had known him before. It was five kids that had been with him
> in kindergarten. I emailed their parents individually. I told the school I
> was going to do that. I emailed [the parents] and I said, "I have some
> information that I don't think will surprise your child but it might surprise
> you." I said, "so and so," his old name, "will be entering school as Ja-

cob, the boy that he's always been." I gave some basic education, and I said, "If you have questions, please call me and I really appreciate your support" or something like that.

This parent's decision to limit communication about her child to a select number of families reflects a general desire to foster opportunities for the community to learn about being transgender without making a broad-scale announcement that would make the transgender child the focus of unwanted attention.

Sending letters home to parents and guardians was not just about sharing factual information; it was also a way to express transgender pride. For some families, being open about having a transgender family member helped to preempt and counteract the stigma and shame that deficit perspectives confer upon transgender and gender-expansive people. Jacob's mother explained that being open about her son's transgender identity was a way to exhibit pride in her son:

> I just remember early on saying, "I'm never going to do anything to make my child feel ashamed." To me, shame would have been not talking about it, not being open about it, not having conversations about it with people. I felt [sending the letter] was the best thing to do so that there weren't people whispering in the hallways.

By being open and communicating directly with other parents and guardians, Jacob's mom hoped to circumvent gossip and shame and, instead, nurture her son's self-esteem and confidence. This desire to be open and "out" mirrors the gay pride movement of the 1980s and 1990s, which associated the "closet" and nondisclosure with secrecy and shame.[13] Sending letters to other parents and guardians in the school was one way for the parents to assert their transgender pride, a message they wanted their transgender children to internalize.

Parents' also described tension between their desire to express and develop transgender pride and the need to protect their child's privacy. For many parents, pride and privacy seemed to be at odds. Openly identifying as transgender can promote pride; however, disclosing one's transgender identity can also jeopardize privacy and safety. Meredith's mom shared:

> That is something we, as parents, are always thinking about because I don't want it [her transgender identity] to be a secret. I don't want it to be something that we have to be ashamed of, but I want her to be safe. So, how do you talk about it in a way that doesn't induce shame?

Parents worried that their efforts to maintain privacy would be mistaken for secrecy and shame. This balancing act between pride and privacy led parents to make different decisions about sending letters home to other parents and guardians.

Ultimately, most families preferred not to send out formal communication that would call attention to their transgender child. Across the eighteen families, twelve opted not to send formal communication to parents and guardians, expressing a desire to maintain privacy. The principal at Iroquois Valley explained:

> We really followed their lead, and they are pretty private. So, we did not do any formal notification of people. I know there were conversations with the other parents and students, privately, outside of school, but we did not do any sort of big notification.

Similarly, the principal at Dixon Primary said, "We had a lot of discussion about it. Should we? Shouldn't we? What does it mean? We decided no . . . partly because we just didn't want to draw attention to it." For these families, the desire to protect their child's privacy and avoid unwanted attention was a central factor in their decision not to send letters to other families within the school community.

In some cases, even families whose children transitioned during the school year decided not to send informational letters home. One mother, whose transgender child transitioned while attending Aberdeen Academy, explained:

> I just felt "Let's see how it rides out," you know. I wanted to draw less attention to it and make it just a normal, smooth transition, so yeah, I didn't

want any of that [letters home]. And it's such a small school. It doesn't exceed fifteen children in a classroom, so I felt I was able to speak with families on my own, if they came forward.

Even though her child socially transitioned mid-year, this mom preferred to communicate individually with parents who asked. At Mercer Elementary, where Meredith presented as gender expansive before socially transitioning to live fully as a girl, the principal explained:

> I try not to over-inform. I try to be communicative with parents, and I think we are very communicative, but there are some things where [I think], "What would the benefit of that be?" So, it probably fell in that category. Everyone and all of her friends in fifth grade, everybody knows, I'm pretty sure. They've been with her at some point throughout the grades. So, it just didn't seem to warrant a larger kind of announcement.

For this principal, a larger-scale announcement felt unnecessary because Meredith's transition had been gradual, and she believed most were aware of the situation. For many families and schools, opting not to send an informational letter was a way to minimize unwanted attention, safeguard the child's privacy and, potentially, protect their safety.

Learning for the Larger School Community

Some schools and districts took a broader view of learning about gender and transgender identities, recognizing its relevance to a larger group of stakeholders beyond the circle of people in direct contact with the known transgender child. These leaders understood the likelihood that multiple transgender and gender-expansive students attended their schools, even if they were not out or visible. Principal Tavoli remarked, "There are probably other Jamies in our school whose parents aren't as proactive. Maybe [children] who are older or maybe even younger who haven't fully realized or can't articulate as clearly as Jamie had." This understanding—that learning about transgender identities is not a single-student issue—enabled educational leaders to see the topic as broadly relevant to the entire school community. As a result, they sought to create learning opportunities that would extend beyond targeted groups of parents and guardians to the larger school community. While these kinds of learning opportunities were uncommon, they merit discussion because they demonstrate the full range of possible learning opportunities and provide examples for other schools and districts seeking to broaden the scope of learning to extend outside their school walls.

One way that learning extended to the larger school community was through districtwide events. Although this study did not explicitly examine district-level practices, through conversations with principals it became apparent that having a supportive district context made it more likely that learning about transgender identities would extend to the larger community. Although all of the principals described their district-level leadership team as generally encouraging of their efforts, most indicated that district-level leaders were relatively uninvolved in the details of working with transgender students and their families. In contrast, principals in three public school districts described having district-level leaders who exhibited a more proactive stance. In each of these districts, the central office conveyed a clear message about the value of learning about transgender identities and took steps to extend learning opportunities to the larger school community.

The superintendent in the school district with Mercer and Griffin Elementary Schools made a point of clarifying the district's stance in response to the Trump administration's 2017 decision to rescind the Title IX guidelines established under the Obama administration. Meredith's mom summarized the superintendent's letter:

> After Trump announced the trans education changes that he was making, our superintendent released a letter that went home to every family that [said] "In light of this change, just to let people know, we live in Massachusetts. These are our laws. These are our rules. We'll continue to support the gender identity and expression of everyone."

In this example, the state context provided a supportive environment for the superintendent's public stance on transgender students. In addition to state laws that protect the rights of transgender and gender-expansive people, the district is located in a politically progressive community. Superintendents are typically appointed by elected school boards and may avoid topics that don't align with voters. This district's supportive context raises questions about whether superintendents in states without legal protections or supportive constituents would take a positive stance on transgender students and the need to learn about transgender identities.

Further evidence that supportive superintendents play a role in creating learning opportunities for the larger school community surfaced in the small New York district where Dixon Primary and Iroquois Valley are located. This city suburb enrolled at least two openly transgender elementary-level students. The Dixon Primary school principal described the superintendent's positive leadership role with regard to transgender students:

> Our superintendent is kind of at the forefront of the issue and has definite stances and feelings about it. I think our middle school and high school principals have struggled more with it . . . so we are always sitting and talking about it, talking about trainings that we've been to, and if there are any guest speakers, just making sure that our network is connected.

By facilitating communication among school administrators, superintendents can promote coherence across schools and facilitate administrators' support for one another. This superintendent also conveyed his support for transgender students by providing learning opportunities for the larger school community. The Iroquois Valley Elementary principal described a district-sponsored event that was open to the public:

> We had a panel that the Family Support Center put together. It included three transgender people who were willing to talk about their experience and take questions from a public forum. It was mainly parents from our district, but there were definitely parents and community members from other districts as well. . . . It was very respectful. Everybody who came walked out of there appreciating that we put that together and feeling better informed and able to be more supportive.

This community-oriented educational event extended learning outside the school walls, involving others in a conversation about how to support transgender people and create gender-inclusive schools. The availability of such learning opportunities depended on supportive district-level administrators.

The next example of a district that developed learning opportunities for the larger school community comes from Greater Prospect School District, home to Jefferson Elementary. The district-level administrators in Greater Prospect formed a districtwide committee dedicated to developing inclusive practices for transgender and gender-expansive students. This Pennsylvania school district did not benefit from progressive state legislation, but its proximity to a cosmopolitan city and its wealthier demographics may have facilitated the district's willingness to initiate discussions about gender. The district-level committee, formally known as the Gender and Sexuality Advisory Committee (G-SAC), was facilitated by an external consultant. Initially, the committee focused on developing a district policy related to transgender students. Once the district policy was complete, the committee shifted to examining educational practices, facilities, and school-related activities. An announcement for one of their meetings read:

> G-SAC functions as an advisory group within Greater Prospect to support and address the unique needs of students who are gender expansive and transgender. This meeting is open to adult family members who would like to share concerns and perspectives around students' issues related to gender identity, thereby, informing the process of making our school community a safe environment where all students thrive and reach their potential. The structure and goals of the meeting will be to share updates on the following topics: Athletics, Student GSA Groups, Curriculum, Restrooms, Technology, and Library Holdings. Parents/Guardians will be invited to share updates regarding community activities relevant to the group.

As this announcement suggests, G-SAC engaged in numerous tasks that collectively conveyed the importance of learning about and supporting transgender students. In turn, the district sponsored educational events aimed at increasing awareness and understanding. For example, Jefferson Elementary hosted an early morning information session and an evening book discussion for parents and guardians. Unlike most opportunities to learn about transgender identities, these events did not target people in direct contact with the known transgender child but were intended to raise overall awareness in the larger school community.

In the absence of proactive district contexts, another way that schools provided learning opportunities for the larger school community was to tap into and promote public events sponsored by other organizations. For example, educators at Pacificus Learning Collaboratory promoted a talk, "Transforming My Family," sponsored by Equality Delaware and presented by TV writer Joan Rater, who shared her experience having a transgender son. Similarly, PS 25 promoted a free community event, Genderful!, which was hosted at the local library for children ages six to twelve and focused on "exploring gender through curiosity, creativity, and community." Another example comes from the Kirby Learning Center, a progressive independent school, which received a generous donation to host Lori Duron, author of the blog and book *Raising My Rainbow*.[14] The event was held at a local liberal arts college and open to the public. By promoting community events, the educators at Kirby, Pacificus, and PS 25 provided opportunities for their school community members to learn about gender and simultaneously conveyed their support for transgender students.

Although these examples were not typical, they provide evidence of the kinds of proactive practices that are possible. Perhaps the biggest obstacle to delivering learning opportunities to the larger school community is the failure to see transgender identities as broadly relevant and the lack of understanding that gender-inclusive school environments are beneficial to all students. When educational leaders understood the broad relevance of gender and transgender identities, they were more likely to create and promote learning opportunities that extended beyond the classroom and school building.

MISSED LEARNING OPPORTUNITIES: "HOW MUCH, OR HOW LITTLE, DO YOU INFORM THE PARENTS?"

While supportive principals were proactive about providing learning opportunities to teachers who were in direct contact with transgender students, they also missed opportunities to teach others about transgender and gender-expansive identities. When asked about possible regrets or missteps, principals reflected on their practice and shared what they might have done differently with the benefit of hindsight. While few had overt regrets, many wished they had created more learning opportunities for everyone. The Northstar principal reflected:

> It makes me question whether we should have sent that letter to the families because I think maybe it was a lost learning opportunity or educational opportunity for the families. Just because no one complained, they still might have had some uninformed conversations in their homes that we could have interjected some information into.

Although this principal had honored the student's request not to send letters home to parents and guardians, she imagined that a letter may have offered insights and information that could have been useful to families. It is also possible that a more generic informational letter could have been sent, rather than a letter that named and exposed the specific child who had initiated the school's attention to gender. The principal at Griffin Elementary wished she had provided more learning opportunities to teachers and staff. She shared:

> We did not do enough professional development for our staff, so I would really recommend getting the best resources that you can for your whole staff. . . . [Start by] preparing the school staff first, and then even if necessary, the full school community.

Educators know that deep learning comes from sustained engagement and opportunities to discuss and collaborate. This is certainly true for learning about gender and transgender identities, topics that may be unfamiliar and steeped in misinformation.

In some instances, learning opportunities were limited due to a common belief that learning about transgender identities is relevant only to educators who are in direct contact with a known transgender student. This belief is problematic in two regards. First, not all transgender people are disclosed. Children are increasingly enrolling in school as their affirmed gender and without sharing their gender history with school officials. Second, the topic of gender is relevant to all people, whether cisgender or transgender. Knowing about gender and the negative effects of gender stereotypes can lead to more gender-inclusive educational practices. Nevertheless, some principals struggled to see the broader relevance, commenting that "it hasn't been necessary" or "it wasn't really an issue."

In one telling example, the principal at Silas Country School lamented that the known transgender student at her school wasn't disclosed to anyone beyond the principal, school adjustment counselor, and classroom teacher. From the principal's perspective, this lack of disclosure constrained her ability to provide learning opportunities to teachers, students, parents, and guardians. She remarked:

> What communication did we have with staff? Basically, we have never had communication with our school population. . . . We brought up talking to the class and the parents in the class. The [transgender student's] parents did not want to do that, and they still do not want to do that. . . . I want the parents to drive this, yet, we're sort of a school that throws everything on the table. We really talk a lot about inclusiveness and feelings and disabilities or differences and how we treat one another, so my concern is that secrets aren't really good. . . . I want to protect her; of course, I want to protect her. And like I said, the family drives everything that we do for her, [but] I can't implement a lot of [communication] here because of that constraint of not wanting to out her in any way.

As this example demonstrates, the principal's child-centered approach combined with her respect for the family's decisions made her reluctant to create learning opportunities beyond those for the few educators who were aware of the student's transgender identity. Of course, this principal could have provided learning opportunities without revealing the identity of any particular student. However, principals may feel ill equipped to justify transgender-related learning if they cannot point to the kind of immediate and pressing need that a specific child represents.

CONCLUSION

This chapter describes the kinds of learning opportunities that were available to adults including learning for teachers, staff, and the larger school community. Generally speaking, having an identified transgender or gender-expansive student prompted principals to create learning opportunities as a way to build knowledge and support for transgender students. Supportive principals also missed opportunities to provide transgender-related learning to a broader set of educators and the larger school community, not understanding its broader relevance.

Keeping in mind the burden of responsibility that children face when they are the poster child for transgender identities, proactive schools should develop learning opportunities for all educational professionals even when no visible transgender students are enrolled. Statistically, it is certain that nearly all schools will have at least one or, probably, many transgender and gender-expansive students. Equally important, opportunities to learn about gender need to extend beyond basic introductory information. In contrast to a "pedagogy of exposure," Elizabeth J. Meyer and Bethy Leonardi advocate for a culture of conversation that includes critical self-reflection.[15] Limiting educators' learning to simplistic exposure or an overview of terms can actually have a negative effect, situating transgender people as "other" and perpetuating simplistic and hurtful stereotypes.[16]

Educators need opportunities to learn how gender norms constrain everyone, including cisgender children and adults. Educators need to interrogate their own beliefs about gender and critically consider how they, as individuals, contribute to the reproduction of gender norms. Moreover, high-quality learning requires ongoing opportunities for educators to build their collective capacity to deconstruct gender stereotypes and develop shared beliefs that shift the cisnormative status quo to create school and classroom cultures where all gender identities are affirmed.

CHAPTER 5

Gender-Inclusive Classroom Practices

Like other New York City schools, Rosa Parks Public School (PS 25) sits in a dense, mixed-use neighborhood that includes homes, businesses, bodegas, and cafés. PS 25 serves just over eight hundred children in grades preK through fifth. Students are drawn from a small school zone that encompasses a ten-block radius. While the PS 25 community celebrates their diverse student population, the school leaders describe gentrification as a pressing problem that has pushed them to have difficult conversations about race, class, and privilege. Today, warm spring weather makes it possible for the PS 25 students to play outside while they wait for the first morning bell to ring. The children are running and shouting on the playground, their backpacks lined up along the chain-link fence. Inside, Danny Carver, a kindergarten teacher in his second year at PS 25, is getting ready for a special visitor, Afsaneh Moradian, author of the children's picture book *Jamie Is Jamie*.[1] The story introduces children to the idea that toys are for everyone, regardless of gender. Teachers from seven classrooms signed up to participate—four kindergarten and three first grades.

Danny invited Moradian to PS 25 because of his commitment to equity and his desire to create an affirming environment for Leo, a transgender boy in Danny's kindergarten classroom. Danny explained that Leo had been placed in his class intentionally:

> I identify as gay, and I have a lot of friends in the LGBT community, including some trans friends. I'm thirty-four now, and since my twenties,

I've been an activist fighting for marriage equality and LGBT rights. So, I think that makes me more confident to take on some of these issues.

While Danny may not seem like the stereotypical kindergarten teacher, the administrators at PS 25 didn't hesitate to hire him or to place Leo in Danny's classroom. The assistant principal described Danny's "knowledge of equity and creating democratic practices inside classrooms" as key qualities that made him an excellent teacher and a leader among his colleagues, who are learning how to navigate the topic of gender with young children.

The first stop for Afsaneh Moradian's PS 25 book tour is Ms. Fiore's kindergarten classroom where twenty wriggly children sit criss-cross applesauce on a multicolored carpet. Moradian sits in the teacher's chair at the front of the carpet, smiling and making eye contact as she introduces herself. When she begins to read, Moradian holds the book high, rotating it so everyone can see the colorful pictures, which depict a classroom similar to their own. Ms. Fiore's students crane their chins forward, examining the pictures and listening to the story of Jamie, a young child who is new to town. On the first day of school, Jamie engages in many different activities: fixing a toy car, performing a perfect pirouette, feeding a baby doll, and playing with superhero action figures. At the end of the day, Jamie's classmates wonder whether Jamie is a boy or girl. One of Jamie's classmates concludes, "I don't know, but I can't wait to play with Jamie tomorrow. That was a lot of fun!"

When the story ends, Moradian, Ms. Fiore, and the assistant teacher, Ms. Maria, help the PS 25 students explore their thinking about gender through whole-group discussion:

MORADIAN: What is the problem in the story?

STUDENT 1: They don't know whether Jamie is a girl or a boy.

STUDENT 2: Another problem is they didn't think Jamie could put together the car.

STUDENT 3: Jamie doesn't want to be a girl or a boy.

STUDENT 4: Boys can do what they want, and girls can do what they want.

STUDENT 1: Is she is a boy or a girl?

MORADIAN: We don't know. Jamie didn't say, "I'm a boy or I'm a girl." Jamie said, "I'm Jamie." I hope when you hear this book it makes you think, "People are just people." It doesn't matter what they look like or whether they are a girl or a boy. It just matters that you have fun with them, right? What would you want to play with Jamie?

STUDENTS: [One-by-one] Voltron. Ballet. Tag. Cars. Hide-n-seek. Freeze-tag. Creepy clown.

MORADIAN: Can I tell you why I wrote this book? I have a daughter who is six years old. Jamie is not my daughter, but I think that Jamie and my daughter would be friends. When my daughter was three, we were at a restaurant, and there was a boy with some action figures. He had Iron Man and Hulk, and she loves the Avengers. So, she asked him, "Can I play with you?" and he said, "No, action figures are only for boys." What do you think about that?

STUDENT 2: Action figures aren't just for boys. They're for girls and for everybody.

STUDENT 5: Girls can like Hulk. My sister is a girl, and she likes Iron Man.

STUDENT 6: My sister likes Batman. She also likes Darth Vader.

MORADIAN: I felt bad for my daughter, but you know what? I felt really sad for that boy because he didn't get to play with my daughter. She's a really fun kid. She loves to climb. She loves to jump. She loves to play with action figures and spies and tag. That little boy missed out on playing with her because somebody had taught him that he wasn't supposed to play with girls. I thought, "You know what? There really needs to be a book about kids just being themselves and playing what they want to play."

STUDENT 7: One time I was with my cousin and my cousin was a girl and I wanted to wear her dress and she was like, "You can't wear a dress. Only girls can wear dresses." But that's not true. Boys can wear dresses.

STUDENT 8: One time I saw a boy named Oliver, and he was wearing a skirt.

MORADIAN: Do you like wearing skirts?

STUDENT 8: Yes.

MORADIAN: It's fun sometimes, right? Twirly dresses are fun. So, you could understand why he would want to wear it, right? It's kind of fun.

MS. MARIA: I want to tell you a story that happened here at PS 25. I had an afterschool class called Spa where children polished their nails and we had facials and we put cucumbers on our eyes. A boy in my class started polishing his nails, and one of the girls stopped him and said, "Boys aren't supposed to be polishing their nails." And I said, "If he wants to use the nail polish, that's totally fine. He can choose whatever color he likes, and he can polish his nails." And, you know what? He did. When he finished, everyone said, "Your nails look so nice."

STUDENT 1: I have a friend named Gabe that used to be in my old school, and he put on nail polish.

STUDENT 8: Sebastian always wears nail polish.

MS. MARIA: Your brother showed me. He showed me his nails. He said, "Look, Ms. Maria." I've even seen adult men wearing nail polish.

The story depicted in Afsaneh Moradian's picture book is deceptively simple: a child plays with new friends at school. But the author also challenges the reader to consider how the enforcement of narrow gender categories can limit our experiences. This chapter presents three principles that teachers employed to help children think more expansively about gender and make their classrooms more inclusive and affirming.

GENDER-INCLUSIVE CLASSROOM PRACTICES

While principals have an indirect effect on students, teachers directly influence children's school experience through their classroom practices and interactions. A great deal of effort has been put into determining what kinds of teacher behaviors yield the best student outcomes and under what conditions. Much of this research focuses on the importance of teachers' pedagogical content knowledge for students' academic achievement.[2] However, research also shows a link between children's social, emotional, and ethical competencies and their academic success.[3] Effective teachers attend to children's social-emotional well-being as part of students' overall development.

A key component of social-emotional well-being is having a sense of belonging to a larger community. In an extensive review of research, Karen F. Osterman found that students who feel a sense of belonging in school demonstrate multiple positive effects:

> They have more positive attitudes toward school, classwork, teachers, and their peers. They are more likely to like school, and they are also more engaged. They participate more in school activities, and they invest more of themselves in the learning process. They have a stronger sense of their own social competence, and they are more likely to interact with peers and adults in prosocial ways.[4]

Conversely, students who experience rejection or exclusion exhibit

> behavioral problems in the classroom (either aggression or withdrawal), lower interest in school, lower achievement, and dropout. More important are the findings that link rejection to various forms of emotional distress including loneliness, violence, and suicide.[5]

These research findings remind us that children are not inherently at risk, but rather unsupportive school environments can create the conditions that put children at risk for failure. A sense of belonging in school can help counteract other negative environmental influences that could otherwise decrease children's well-being.

Belonging in schools is often addressed using the language of *inclusion* and *diversity*. The idea that schools should "include diverse students" has become a common refrain that is often accepted at face value. Yet, how we act on this idea matters, especially for students from historically oppressed populations.[6] Frequently, *diversity* is a euphemism for Black and Brown students, students for whom English is not their first language, or students whose country of origin is not the United States. Having a so-called diverse classroom does not ensure that everyone feels a sense of belonging. *Inclusion* commonly refers to the assimilation of differently abled students into so-called general education classrooms. Typically, inclusion is conditional—dependent on the student's capacity and willingness to conform to the existing educational system. So, even when we "include diverse students," we can fail to disrupt power structures and, instead, normalize inequity. In a truly inclusive classroom, belonging is not contingent upon conformity.[7] Inclusive classrooms recognize and affirm students' varied ways of being, their complex histories, and their multiple identities.

Knowing that students' social-emotional well-being is vital for their academic and life success, how can teachers create a classroom environment where transgender and gender-expansive students experience affirmation and belonging? Thirty-one teachers shared their stories, depicting three main principles for gender-inclusive classroom instruction:

- Decrease gendered practices.
- Increase discussions about gender.
- Affirm children's gender identity and expression.

Collectively, these classroom practices have potential to benefit all students. Not only do they contribute to transgender children's sense of belonging, but these practices also help cisgender students learn about and accept experiences that differ from their own.

DECREASE GENDERED PRACTICES: "'BOYS AND GIRLS' DOESN'T INVOLVE EVERYBODY."

Gendered activities in elementary classrooms are so pervasive that the casual observer may not notice how extensively schools plan and categorize around the binary notion of "boy" and "girl." Teachers often use gender as an easy organizing principle—a simple way to sort students quickly. Some gendered activities are intended to increase equitable participation in classroom activities like alternating between calling on boys and girls during discussion. Typically, when teachers critically reflect on gender in the classroom, they usually do so with an eye toward gender biases, such as the overrepresentation of boys in disciplinary infractions or the underrepresentation of girls in mathematics. These kinds of gender-based differences point to real biases that need to be actively addressed.[8] At the same time, examining inequities between binary genders doesn't provide a mechanism for critiquing the larger social system of gender or the problematic nature of binary gender representations.

As a binary category, gender limits us to dualistic thinking even though the range of gender variation found in society is wildly diverse. Gendered classroom practices emphasize the categories of "boy" and "girl" as opposites and defined in contrast to one another. This binary, constructed to be mutually exclusive, reinforces gender stereotypes and limits forms of expression that cut across gender categories. The first-grade teacher at Northstar Charter School explained that students constantly receive messages about gender. "Even just coloring a picture. At indoor recess there's a coloring station and there's a Transformers pile and there's a princess pile. It's always like that. People don't even realize the students are taking that in." The unconscious and ubiquitous nature of gendered teaching practice means many educators are unaware of its role in their classroom. Even teachers who understand the limitations inherent in binary gender may be uncertain about how to decrease gendered practices in the classroom.

Many teachers in this study wanted to reduce gendered classroom practices because of the possible negative impact on gender expansive and transgender children. These teachers aimed to incorporate more inclusive language, gender-neutral classroom management strategies, and gender-expansive play into their classrooms.

Inclusive Language

Teachers' language may be the most explicitly gendered practice in elementary schools. Teachers commonly refer to students as "boys" and "girls" to get their attention and give instructions. In contrast, the teachers in this study had begun to question this terminology, recognizing that binary gender terms may cause feelings of distress or exclusion for some students. Students who identify outside the gender binary, somewhere on a gender continuum, are explicitly excluded when binary gender categories are used to describe students. Even for children who generally fit into binary categories of "boy" and "girl," these demarcations create pressure to be the "right" kind of boy or girl and to be an easily identifiable boy or girl. Reducing gendered language can decrease the pressure children feel to conform to binary gender norms.

Many teachers worked to replace "boys and girls" with alternate language such as "friends," "scholars," or "children." A fourth-grade teacher at Northstar Charter School explained:

> [The use of] "boys and girls" doesn't involve everybody. I teach a whole social studies unit on gender identity, and we discuss that many people believe there are two genders, but there are actually many ways that people identify their gender. People create their own words. People choose words that match the way they feel. We talk about the difference between gender and sex, but I don't say "boys and girls" because those aren't words that everybody identifies with. That would be like saying "blondes and brunettes" when there were redheads in the classroom, right? It doesn't include everybody.

This teacher ingeniously conveys the limiting nature of binary gender in her comparison to hair color. As she explains, when we rely on dualistic terms to describe a diverse continuum of genders, we risk excluding and unintentionally marginalizing students. Dualistic terms limit our ability to see and validate people who challenge binary gender norms. Helping children learn about and build understanding around a wide range of life experiences is an important component of children's social and emotional development.

Children who defy gender norms underscore the importance of using inclusive language, and teachers were particularly sensitive to gendered language when they had gender-expansive children in their class. At Mercer Elementary, the teachers described being "hypersensitive" about gender as a result of meeting Max, a gender-expansive child who had been assigned male at birth. While others commonly read Max as female, based on clothing and hairstyle, Max used the boys' bathroom and male pronouns.[9] Max's third-grade teacher explained, "That year I used no pronouns all year long, for anybody. 'She' and 'he' were not part of my vocabulary because it was just too uncomfortable for me." This teacher's discomfort with male and female pronouns in the context of a gender-expansive student led her to avoid pronouns altogether and, instead, refer to children exclusively by their names. Given the teacher's discomfort with pronouns, one would imagine that a gender-expansive student would feel even greater distress having to conform to binary gender categories when neither accurately conveys their gender experience. Teachers who want to use more inclusive language can refrain from using pronouns even if there is no known transgender or gender-expansive student in the classroom. These kinds of gender-inclusive practices can benefit children along the entire gender spectrum.

Gender-Neutral Classroom Management

In addition to language, classroom management is another highly gendered practice in schools. Teachers use gender to categorize and organize children, particularly when lining up, making seat assignments, creating groups, selecting partners, and the like. Binary gender is perceived as a quick and easy sorting mechanism that allows teachers to effectively manage classroom activities. However, it can cause distress for nonbinary children. At Mercer Elementary, the fourth-grade teacher shared a story from when Meredith was presenting as a gender-expansive boy:

> Meredith's parents told us a story about music class. All the girls were instructed to play one note, and all the boys were told to play another note, and Meredith froze because she didn't know what note to play. I thought, "We've got to get rid of girl/boy stuff." I used to have separate boy and girl lists [to sign out for the bathroom], and so I changed to one list. Now the students just sign out. When you go to the bathroom, you just go to the bathroom.

Meredith's negative experience in music class helped this teacher realize that gendered classroom management strategies are problematic for some students. In response, she changed the procedures in her classroom so that students could visit the bathroom without the use of gendered bathroom passes or gendered sign-out sheets. Many classroom teachers shared that they had eliminated "boy" and "girl" bathroom passes in favor of generic passes that any child could use, regardless of gender. For a child who is gender-expansive, transgender, or questioning, repeatedly having to choose between two gender options mirrors the kinds of microaggressions that contribute to children's decreased sense of belonging and jeopardize their emotional well-being.

Seemingly simple changes to classroom management were not without controversy. Some teachers worried that the lack of gendered bathroom passes would allow same-gender classmates to visit the bathroom simultaneously, leading to socialization, and maybe even misbehavior. At PS 25 the principal mandated that all teachers eliminate boy/girl bathroom passes and line-up procedures, prompting teachers to rethink their management strategies. One of the first-grade teachers shared:

> Now we have two or three passes, same color, that say "bathroom pass." That's it. We had to change our rules though because it was concerning to some teachers how many kids you're sending to each bathroom. If we have two passes, that means two kids can go to either bathroom. It used to be one girl was out and one boy was out, and all of a sudden, we often have two boys are messing around in the bathroom and climbing windows.

As this teacher explained, changing bathroom passes required some additional procedural changes as well so that only one child at a time could use the bathroom pass. Another PS 25 teacher explained how the change to nongendered lines affected her kindergarten classroom procedures:

> We had to change our lines from girls' line and boys' line to mixed lines. Now we just have line A, line B. It's funny because people complain about stuff and then it happens and you're like it's easy. [Except for] the recess aides, because they don't really know, so that was a big thing for them. My recess aide, that was really mind-blowing for her, it was really hard.

The shift to gender-neutral line-up procedures was easier than expected for most classroom teachers; however, it was a significant challenge for non-teaching staff. Noncertified staff were less likely to receive training related to gender and transgender identities; however, their need for training is equally important. As these examples demonstrate, even small changes to traditional management procedures required effort, so a lack of opportunities to learn about gender and how to implement gender-inclusive practices is likely to make change more difficult.

Gender-Expansive Play

Beyond language and classroom management, teachers also worked to facilitate gender-expansive play in their classrooms. Much of the gender policing that occurs in schools comes from children themselves as they try to make sense of their relationship to gendered roles in society.[10] For example, during independent play, children may make "boys only" or "girls only" rules that delineate membership in gendered groups and what kind of play is permissible based on gender. Education scholar Harper B. Keenan explains that we need to unlearn these gender scripts. Keenan advocates for critical pedagogy, a constant process of "unscripting" gender that is marked by free play and experiential inquiry.[11] When children have permission to engage in gender-expansive play, they can try on complex identities and create their own understandings rather than being relegated to prescriptive, mutually exclusive, boy/girl categories and forms of expression.

Teachers described trying to reduce gendered play and encourage mixed-gender groupings. One first-grade teacher with a transgender boy in her classroom explained, "With the games they play or the centers they choose, I try to mix it up. It's not like, 'Legos is a boy center, blocks is a boy center.' It's not like that. They can all go everywhere." An important aspect of creating opportunities for gender-expansive play is adults debunking the gender stereotypes associated with certain kinds of play and explicitly framing activities as gender neutral. Too often, adults make assumptions about the kinds of activities children will prefer based on traditional gender norms. To make space for more expansive play, adults must refrain from making gender-based presumptions and be explicit that all toys and activities are for all children.

One space in elementary schools that has potential to be highly gendered is the dramatic play center, where children engage in imaginative,

play-based learning. Typically, this play includes experimenting with gender roles and gendered occupations. At Pacificus Learning Collaboratory, a
small independent school, the lead teacher in the K–1-combined classroom
described her approach to dress up in the dramatic play center:

> There have been several boys who are interested in what some might
> consider feminine things like wearing dresses. So, in dramatic play we
> have all kinds of dresses, and anybody can dress up in a dress. Some
> of the kids haven't seen that before. If it becomes something contentious,
> a misunderstanding between two people, we have that discussion. We
> talk about how, if it makes you happy to wear a dress, then you wear
> a dress. That's just how it goes. We don't want anybody to be unhappy
> because of what they're wearing.

In this example, the dramatic play center is framed as a space where children can express themselves in whatever way makes them feel good about
themselves. Rather than reproducing gender norms, the space becomes a
place where norms can be disrupted. Having opportunities to engage in
gender-expansive play can help children develop a sense of self that is free
from gender restrictions. As such, the benefits of gender-expansive play
are not confined to transgender or gender-expansive students but include
gender identity development for cisgender children as well.

Across school contexts, decreasing gendered educational practices is
highly dependent on the ways in which educators frame and introduce
those practices to children. When adults use gender-inclusive language,
engage in gender-neutral classroom management, and set expectations for
gender-expansive play, children are less likely to self-censor or engage in
gender policing. A third-grade teacher at Jefferson Elementary School explained how she set expectations regarding gender:

> From the very beginning I teach that I don't identify my students in that
> way, by gender. When I do seating arrangements and I have four kids
> at a table, it does not have to be two boys and two girls. Oftentimes
> I've had tables where there might be three girls and a boy or three boys
> and a girl. And I say this from the beginning of the year. "I see you

all as students. The end." Your gender is just one thing to know about you, but I do not use those rules when doing bathroom passes or when doing seating arrangements. And I find that if you set that expectation at the beginning, you sort of lower their awareness of *gender*, which is so strong from such an early age, and you kind of work with them on seeing each other as *people*. They actually start to see each other as classmates and as whole people and see that your gender is just one little thing about you. So, I don't actually see the boys only passing to the boys and the girls only passing to the girls, but that's because there is an expectation set that they don't need to just see each other in that way.

When educators decrease gendered practices, it liberates students from the confines of binary gender norms and contributes to gender equity.

INCREASE DISCUSSIONS ABOUT GENDER: "SOME BOYS WEAR SKIRTS."

Adults often question whether gender is an appropriate topic in elementary classrooms. Parents worry that elementary-age children are too young to discuss gender, that it could introduce mature concepts, unnecessarily complicate children's understandings, or create gender confusion. The idea that children are too young to learn about gender stems, in part, from the misconception that gender is somehow linked to sexuality. It also fails to recognize that gender is already a pervasive component of schooling, albeit, from a cisnormative perspective. In fact, talking about gender in ways that encourage students to think critically about gender norms may *reduce* children's confusion, particularly, the confusion children may have about whether it's okay to challenge gender norms. As the opening vignette demonstrates, even kindergarteners have insights and opinions about gender.

Discussing gender with children offers multiple benefits. Learning gender-related terms provides children with language to better express themselves. Talking about gender can build awareness of gender diversity and help refute negative gender stereotypes. In classrooms, discussing gender creates space for self-expression, reduces gender-policing, and increases children's acceptance of creative gender expression. Conversations about gender do not cause children to become gender expansive or transgender. However, talking about gender-expansive behavior as a normal part of gender expression may help children feel accepted.[12] Teaching children about gender contributes to children's healthy identity development and increases their sense of belonging.

The teachers in this study increased gender-related discussions, even while they decreased gendered classroom practices. Foremost, teachers increased children's exposure to literature with gender-diverse characters. In addition, teachers implemented lessons or curriculum related to gender.

Literature with Gender-Diverse Characters

Nearly all the teachers added gender-diverse books to their classroom libraries. Books are a doorway to conversations about new topics. Stories with transgender or gender-expansive characters present an opportunity for children to find points of commonality across divergent gender experiences, which can foster understanding and empathy. For transgender children, gender-inclusive literature offers the possibility of seeing oneself represented in text, which can foster a sense of pride and validation.

Critiques of gender representation in children's literature have focused primarily on the underrepresentation of girls and negative gender stereotypes for girls and boys. Children's books published in the United States consistently represent boys and male animals at higher rates than girls and female characters.[13] A large-scale study of nearly six thousand books found that, on average, boys are central characters in 57 percent of children's books in comparison to girls who appear as central characters in 31 percent of books.[14] Thus, boys are nearly twice as likely to play a central role in children's literature. Moreover, girls are frequently portrayed as passive, dependent on others, and without paid occupations, which perpetuates negative stereotypes about girls.[15] Not surprisingly, unequal gender representation in published works is mirrored in the kinds of books available to children in schools and classrooms.[16]

While valuable, studies that limit their gender critique to unequal representation of males and females fall short with regard to gender diversity.

Most studies fail even to conceptualize questions about gender identities other than cisgender males and females. One study that did examine instances of transgender representation in early childhood classroom libraries found that none of the 691 books depicted transmen, transwomen, or other transgender identities.[17] While this is grim news for transgender and gender-expansive children, the fact that researchers are beginning to ask about transgender representation in children's literature is a positive indicator that societal norms are shifting to create space for diverse gender identities.

For elementary teachers who want to diversify their classroom libraries, numerous books with explicitly transgender and gender-expansive characters are available. Danny Carver, the openly gay kindergarten teacher at PS 25, described his efforts to create an inclusive classroom library:

> I already was conscious of trying to have some books in my classroom that supported gender diversity. Most of the books I had, though, were very much boys into feminine things or boys feeling like princesses, but there wasn't anything like female-to-male or gender nonconforming. So, Leo's mom actually brought me a book, *About Chris*, that is basically a preK boy, a little trans boy, coming out to his teacher. That was a book that Leo and his mom used to read a lot together. One of the days when Leo decided to talk about himself we read *About Chris* and then he talked about it.[18]

Danny understood the importance of exposing his students to diverse texts. Adding *About Chris* to the classroom library provided Leo with a representative text where he could see himself. It also became a teaching tool that helped Leo tell his story and helped Danny navigate the topic of transgender children with other students. Ideally, classroom and school libraries would have multiple books that legitimize and validate transgender identities.

Many teachers took a facilitative approach to gender-diverse literature. That is, they made texts available as a way to facilitate conversation but waited for children to initiate discussion. This approach helped ease teachers' discomfort about introducing potentially controversial books to young children. In contrast, some teachers used a more instructive approach to gender-diverse texts. Teachers commonly used read-alouds—when teachers read out loud to the class—to introduce and create opportunities to discuss gender-diverse characters. Read-alouds capitalize on children's capacity to comprehend oral text that is more advanced than their reading level. The fifth-grade teachers at Mercer Elementary used a read-aloud format for a story about a transgender girl. "We read *George*, by Alex Gino, as a read-aloud to all our students, all forty of them. It was awesome." In this example, a fictional transgender character, rather than a real-life classmate, created a point of entry to talk about transgender identities. This use of literature helps protect the privacy of transgender and gender-expansive students. In addition, the read-aloud format provides the teacher with an opportunity to present new information and guide students in whole-group discussion about gender.

Lessons About Gender

In addition to using literature to teach children about gender diversity, teachers can also develop specific lessons, or even curricula, related to gender. LGBTQ-centric lessons have become increasingly common in secondary schools, particularly in English classes where teenagers may be exposed to LGBTQ characters through literature and the media.[19] As of 2019, four states—California, Colorado, Illinois, and New Jersey—had implemented laws that require schools to include curriculum that discusses the positive contributions LGBTQ people have made to society. New texts and materials for all age levels are being developed to help teachers incorporate information about gender, sexual orientation, queer families, and anti-bullying into classrooms.

While gender-focused lessons were less common than literature with gender-diverse characters, several teachers found ways to explicitly address gender as part of their instruction. In one example, a kindergarten teacher at PS 25 incorporated a discussion of gender into her regular routine. Each day, during morning meeting, this teacher would have students vote on ordinary matters—for example, "Do you prefer pizza or hamburgers?" Then she would use the results to build children's numeracy skills through activities like counting, making pie charts, and drawing comparisons. Here she explains how a student's comment about make-up led her to construct a morning meeting activity that would challenge children's conception of gender:

> One of the girls in my class was talking about "Mommies wear makeup," and I was like "Actually, I'm not a mommy, but I am a woman but I don't wear makeup. But also, some boys do." Then [during morning meeting] I showed them two different looks of James Charles. He is a CoverGirl model. I had two different makeup looks of his. We have a vote every day. Every day, we just vote on two different things. So, we looked at and we voted on them, and then we had a whole discussion. I was like "Some boys wear makeup." And there is boy in another classroom that wears skirts and tutus. That hasn't happened in my room. But we have spoken a lot about, "Yeah, some boys wear skirts."

This kindergarten teacher used her daily routine to engage a conversation about gender norms and demonstrate variation in gender expression.[20] Even though this teacher did not have a transgender student in her room (to the best of her knowledge), she created an opportunity for the children to critically reflect on gender and the way that binary gender norms constrain and limit self-expression.

Two teachers, both from Northstar Charter School, described creating curriculum related to gender even though neither teacher had a known transgender student enrolled in their classroom. In this extended passage, the first-grade teacher describes the gender unit she created:

> I've tried to create sort of a unit, and essentially what I focus on is this idea of "girl things" and "boy things." Colors, toys, clothing, activities. We read some books, like *Not Every Princess* and *Jacob's New Dress*. What I find at this age, most of them get the idea that girls can do anything that boys can do, but the idea that boys could express themselves in any way has been a huge unlearning. That's something many of my students had never seen, so we talk about that. It took a lot of processing to really change what they had seen and heard and just be open to a new idea. So, that's really been the focus.

> Then we created a toy store. I worked with an art teacher a couple of years ago, and then I kept going myself. We created toys that we thought didn't fit the stereotypes. We sort of talked back to that idea. They really take it on. Sometimes some of my students would ask, "Does that mean I have to start wearing dresses?" "No, but if someone chooses to, what's your response to that? It's that you are accepting of the choices others make." The unit ends with we make these belief posters where we put them up and we tell the world what we believe. One example is "We believe that all toys should be for all kids." It's been really fun to see.[21]

In describing this gender unit, the teacher further explained that she waited until the second half of the school year to raise the topic of gender with her first graders. At that point, "the community is established, their language is more developed, and their stamina for this kind of thinking is there." The unit starts with extensive conversation: having book talks and read-alouds, sharing stories at morning meetings, and addressing gender conflict during the community meetings after lunch. The unit unfolds over several months, allowing the children time to think and process new understandings.

Importantly, each of the lessons described in this section was developed and delivered in classrooms where there was no known transgender child; rather, the teachers understood that learning about gender is an important component of all children's learning. Increased discussions and explicit lessons about gender have potential to challenge, rather than reinforce, the binary gender norms that constrain gender identity development.

AFFIRM CHILDREN'S GENDER IDENTITY: "IF YOU LIKE THAT, WE LIKE THAT."

The fields of medicine and psychology have a long history of pathologizing children who do not conform to gender norms.[22] Traditionally, children who expressed interest in the attire and activities associated with the "opposite" gender were subjected to harsh treatment intended to correct supposed deviant behaviors. These so-called treatments, described as "conversion" or "reparative" therapy, commonly included restricting children's toys, play, and friendships. For children who continued to demonstrate nonconforming behavior, treatment could include punishment, isolation, medication, and even institutionalization. Doctors speculated that gender-nonconforming children were confused, perhaps as a result of inconsistent gender messaging from parents. This idea that transgender children are confused has been debunked by research demonstrating that transgender and cisgender children are similarly certain about their gender identity, with transgender children expressing no greater gender confusion than their cisgender peers.[23]

Currently, the fields of medicine and psychology agree: conversion therapy is ineffective and harmful. Adults who experienced transgender conversion therapy as children describe experiencing emotional trauma and negative effects on their health and well-being as a result. Some states have banned transgender conversion therapy, including New Jersey, Rhode Island, Delaware, and New York. Moreover, new research conducted by Kristina Olson as part of the Trans Youth Project found positive outcomes associated with social transition.[24] Thus, current best practice is to support transgender children whose identity is consistent, persistent, and insistent.[25] In fact, transgender experts in the fields of medicine and psychology contend that failure to support social transition is tantamount to abuse and may be as harmful to children as conversion therapy.[26]

Given that social transition is considered best practice for promoting transgender children's well-being, it is increasingly clear that truly supportive schools must demonstrate an affirmative, not merely inclusive, approach to gender-expansive and transgender children. Gender affirmation is the process of recognizing, validating, and supporting another person's gender identity regardless of whether that identity conforms to social norms. Gender affirmation involves seeing someone as they are and "honoring their humanity," as one supportive principal explained. Affirming a child's gender identity promotes children's sense of belonging in schools and positively affects their sense of self and overall mental health.[27]

Educators affirmed children's gender identity in multiple ways. These included using children's chosen names and pronouns without requiring "proof" or legal documentation. Educators also affirmed children's gender expression including students' choice of clothing, toys, and activities. A teacher from Pacificus Learning Collaboratory explained that they affirmed gender-nonconforming play and dress, and as a result, it was not unusual for children to wear clothing that might be considered atypical. She shared:

> One of our students comes in a lot of the time wearing a button-up shirt and a necktie, sometimes a little bowler hat, not what you would normally wear, but she likes to experiment. When she comes in that way, we make a point to say, "You look wonderful" and let her know "We see how you chose to dress today and we love it." It's kind of modeling for the rest of the kids before anybody even has a chance to make a comment. It sets the tone for anybody who would want to dress differently—just congratulating them on their bravery and their experimentation, and letting them know we notice and we love it and keep going. If you like that, we like that.

One way to affirm gender-expansive identities and expression is to recognize and validate students' clothing choices.

Another important way that educators affirmed gender-expansive and transgender children was to create a supported space for the children to tell their gender story when, and if, they chose to do so. Teachers and principals offered sometimes emotional accounts of children sharing their gender identity with their classmates. The head of school at Kirby Learning Center described a coming out story that demonstrates sincere affirmation, as opposed to mere acceptance:

> The family and child worked out a process with the teachers. They read a book aloud, and the child told the class that she was transgender and explained what that meant with help from her teacher. The parents wrote a letter the same day to the parent community. Then—we're a constructivist school, so a lot of the work is child led—the children wanted to make Katie a book. So, the kids all sat down and drew pages in the book. One said, "Katie, you're a beautiful butterfly and I'm so proud of you." It's just this beautiful book that she got to take home.

Like Katie, transgender children commonly used books with transgender or gender-expansive characters to help tell their gender story. Having such books in the classroom library enabled students to make connections between a familiar storybook character's experience and a friend's experience and, thus, facilitated children's sense making. Through such activities, transgender and cisgender children co-construct their classroom culture and learning experience, and thus, they collaboratively create a space where all gender identities can truly belong.

One school psychologist with more than thirty years of experience explained that students' sense of belonging is facilitated when educators affirm and validate their identities. Failing to see children for who they are can cause feelings of inadequacy, exclusion, school avoidance, and worse. She explained:

> It's really about understanding the whole student and supporting them and their identities, because if you're not supporting their identities, there's no bloody way they're learning. . . . The foundation is belonging. How do you help a student feel like they belong? And all students, not just certain ones. We can include people, but sometimes when you're included, it doesn't mean you belong. I can include you, I can invite you to a party, and you're included, but you don't feel like you belong. You need that belonging connection.

When schools honor and affirm children's gender identities, students are more likely to feel a sense of belonging, which is necessary for engagement and learning.

CHALLENGES TO GENDER-INCLUSIVE CLASSROOM PRACTICES

In general, the teachers strove to create classroom environments where transgender and gender-expansive students would experience affirmation and belonging. Supportive principals intentionally placed transgender students with these teachers because they were perceived as accepting and willing to learn. These qualities were evident in teachers' self-descriptions, classroom observations, and in the parents' depictions. At the same time, it would be overly simplistic to present these teachers as uniformly and easily changing their classroom practices. In reality, some teachers struggled, and despite good intentions, their classroom practices remained gendered.

Sometimes, teachers explained their inability to change classroom practices as an unintended outcome of deeply entrenched practices. A first-grade teacher from PS 25 shared: "We've been trying for the past couple of years to call them our students or friends. I try so hard, and I feel like half the time I do it successfully and half the time it's 'ladies and gentlemen' because it's so ingrained in me." This admission speaks to the difficulty of changing practice even when educators work in a supportive context with opportunities to learn. Changing gendered classroom practices requires constant self-monitoring, effort, and reflection. Moreover, meaningful change requires simultaneously dismantling the larger system of gendered norms that privileges cisnormativity. This means thinking beyond the actions of individual teachers to intentionally and systematically interrogate the ways in which gender is reproduced in schools.

Other times, teachers simply did not see the need to change their classroom practices. This point of view was especially true when the transgender or gender-expansive child had moved on to the next grade level. Without an identifiable transgender student, some teachers perceived that gender-inclusive practices were no longer relevant.[28] For example, one teacher removed books with gender-diverse characters and placed them in storage after her transgender student moved to the next grade. The idea that gender-inclusive practices are exclusively for the benefit of transgender students fails to recognize that cisgender children also benefit from learning about gender diversity. Moreover, it presumes that teachers know their students' gender identities. In reality, it is increasingly common for young transgender children to enter school as their affirmed gender, and some of these students choose not to disclose their sex assigned at birth. Not to mention, children may be questioning their gender or exploring their gender identity, unbeknownst to the teacher. Thus, these teachers are misguided in their belief that gender-inclusive classroom practices are relevant only when a known transgender child is in the classroom.

Some teachers did not view gender-inclusive classroom practices as necessary when their transgender student conformed to binary gender norms. A fourth-grade teacher at Jefferson Elementary explained that she didn't want to draw any additional attention to her openly transgender student by talking about gender. Therefore, she did not add books with gender-diverse characters to her classroom library, maintained gendered classroom practices, and refrained from initiating conversations about gender. This approach may help to guard the child's privacy. It may also validate transgender children who conform to binary gender norms. However, the absence of gender-inclusive practices also reduces students' opportunities to learn about diverse genders and to challenge harmful gender stereotypes.

Even when the known transgender student conforms to binary gender norms, teachers can still create gender-inclusive classrooms. A teacher at PS 25 explained that the transgender boy in her classroom conformed to traditional gender norms, "He generally plays with the boys. He likes 'boy' things. He wants to be a baseball player. So even though we're going against these gender stereotypes [in the classroom], it's interesting how he's fixated on that." In this instance, the teacher recognized and made space for her transgender student's stereotypical "boy" identity, but that did not prevent the teacher from developing more gender-inclusive practices in her classroom. This perspective was shared by the majority of teachers, who understood that gender-inclusive practices provide an opportunity for cisgender and gender-conforming transgender children to learn about the range of gender identities and expressions.

Classroom practices may also remain gendered due to teachers' fear of complaints from the families of cisgender students. While such complaints were rare, and handled by school administrators, the mere specter of backlash may have an indirect negative effect on teachers' willingness to create gender-inclusive classrooms. Teachers may prefer to maintain their existing gendered practices rather than risk potential complaints and conflict. In fact, across the twenty schools, concerns about gender-inclusive practices seldom escalated beyond the kinds of clarifying questions that would be expected. That said, in the rare instances when concerns did escalate, educators had to put significant effort into responding. One such example comes from the principal at Harborside Cooperative School:

> Our first-grade curriculum has a unit on community activists, and so they do case studies of various people who have been agents of change in the world. Some of the people are Malala [Yousafzai], and César Chávez, and they do Jazz Jennings. There was a parent who didn't

object specifically to our bathroom policy or to the way that Hope's situation was being handled, but when his kid was in first grade and she came home talking about transgender people, he was like, "Wait, what?" He felt like it was developmentally inappropriate to be teaching about that stuff in first grade, and he also interpreted that it was not about gender, but about sexuality, and accused us of trying to indoctrinate his daughter into becoming a lesbian. He actually wrote an email to the Chancellor of Schools in New York City and got a response from senior counsel in the Chancellor's office. I had to spend weeks providing all this evidence to support what we do and why we do it and how it is research-based. It was a big waste of my time, honestly, but they needed to make sure all their i's were dotted and so on. In the end I was blind-copied on the final response back to this parent from the senior counsel's office saying, "What this school is doing is 100 percent appropriate and in line with our policies on transgender students and we support the principal's decisions. Thanks for raising your concern, but it's not substantiated." It was a very supportive letter of what we did. I felt kind of validated in that.

While escalated complaints were rare, they required significant energy that distracted educators from the work of teaching and learning. Absent a supportive principal, teachers' concerns about the potential risks may be warranted. Teachers who preserve binary gendered practices may avoid possible backlash; however, maintaining the status quo will not create the conditions needed to facilitate all students' sense of belonging.

Overall, relatively few teachers reported challenges to their efforts to create more gender-inclusive classrooms. Having a supportive principal and opportunities to learn about gender identities helped smooth the way for teachers to develop inclusive and affirming classroom practices.

CONCLUSION

In the schools examined here, teachers have taken proactive steps to make their classrooms more inclusive for transgender and gender-expansive students. They have made efforts to decrease gendered classroom management strategies, increase discussions about gender, and affirm children's gender identities. Collectively, these efforts may help increase transgender students' sense of belonging and their overall well-being.

Having a transgender or gender-expansive student does not automatically make a classroom gender-inclusive. Educators need to intentionally create spaces where all gender identities can be expressed safely, without ridicule or shame. At the heart of genuine inclusion is unconditional affirmation, including affirmation of gender identities that do not conform to gender norms. Inclusive practices disrupt gender stereotypes and facilitate gender-expansive play and self-discovery. Too often, gender-expansive children feel pressure to conform to either norms for boys or girls. When affirmation and inclusion are contingent on cisnormative expression, gender norms are reinforced in ways that hurt transgender children's sense of belonging and their social-emotional well-being. Elementary classrooms should not be spaces where transgender and gender-expansive children learn to hate themselves.[29]

To reduce the burden that children feel to conform, efforts to include children with diverse gender identities must also entail meaningful changes to classroom practice. Adding new practices that affirm all gender identities is part of the solution. Equally important, we must continually engage in conversations that deconstruct gender norms and challenge systems of power that privilege some people and oppress others.[30]

CHAPTER 6

What to Do About Gendered School Spaces?

Greater Prospect prides itself on being a forward-thinking school district. Located in an exurb of a large metropolitan community, the majority of students come from wealthy and moderate-income families and approximately 20 percent are students of color. Despite its reputation as a liberal-minded district, in 2006 Greater Prospect captured unwanted attention when they declined to accept a donated children's book, *And Tango Makes Three*, which describes a same-sex penguin family in the Central Park Zoo.[1] The negative publicity that Greater Prospect received in response to this incident may have influenced their 2015 decision to form a committee dedicated to writing a district-level policy protecting the rights of transgender and gender-expansive youth.

To facilitate policy development, Greater Prospect hired a consultant who had worked with the district for more than ten years providing professional learning on a wide range of sociocultural issues including class, race, and sexual orientation. The consultant described the vision for the committee and how it was formed:

> The deal was to make the best school district policy in the country and to do it as a team. We put out a call [to district employees] to see who wanted to do it. School counselors, teachers from all three grade levels, administrators, bus drivers, anyone could be on this team, and we called it the "Gender Identity Policy" (GIP) team at that point. There were

like thirty people that showed up the first time. I said, "It's going to be a lot of work because here's how we're going to do it. Here are the six best policies in the country that I know of right now. We're going to look at them and then break into teams. One is going to look at Phys Ed and sports. One is going to look at restrooms, and so on. Then, we're going to meet once a month and the groups are going to present, and we're going to talk as teams about what parts we should keep and to figure out what's missing." The next time, about eighteen people came back and about fifteen were there in the end.

As explained, the committee broke into teams, each focused on a different subtopic. Over the course of the 2015–16 school year, they wrote the policy, building on what they learned from other districts. According to the consultant, "some were calling the school districts and talking to the directors who wrote the policies. They were really engaged." Toward the end of the school year, the committee presented their work to the school board in two separate public sessions. The consultant prepared for a contentious set of meetings:

I went to the team and said, "Go to that parent who's an advocate who's going to bring half of her friends and get advocates there." It was standing room only, packed. People signed up to talk, maybe thirty people presented. The second or third person said something slightly negative, but then everybody else negative dropped out. There was so much positive three-minute support from people in the community, from rabbis, from ministers. I was thinking we're going to get beat up, but it became like, this love fest. We answered some of the tougher, scarier questions that the board had, you can imagine—"What about bathrooms? What about this?" We took time to parse it out, and they felt much more secure. Then we had the second meeting, and I thought, "Oh my gosh, it's been in the news now." But, again, another love fest. It was a unanimous vote.

Following the passage of the Gender Identity Policy, the committee restyled itself and became the Gender and Sexuality Advisory Committee (G-SAC). The purpose of the G-SAC was to guide and support the policy implementation process. First on their list of things to do was figuring out what to prioritize. The consultant explained, "I went to the GSAs, the Gender and Sexuality Alliances, and asked the students 'Where do you think we need to start?' The big ones were restrooms, restrooms, restrooms, restrooms, and bullying, and gym." In addition to asking students, the G-SAC also sought input from the families and guardians of gender-expansive and transgender students, inviting them to an evening meeting in the fall of 2016. One member of the G-SAC, who worked at Jefferson Elementary School, described the meeting, the families' impatience, and the challenges they faced:

> We invited parents to a meeting this fall. It was less than twenty parents and equally as many people from the school district. It was a terrible meeting. But it was the coolest thing ever that curriculum supervisors, principals, counselors, and teachers were there. You had the movers and the shakers—the people that could make the decisions. Operations was there too because our bathrooms are still the binary system. When the parents came, they wanted more action, more now. They wanted to be heard. So, it was a really hard meeting because we felt like we were doing an awful lot already, and they were saying you're not doing enough. They wanted the bathrooms taken care of now. They wanted the school district to do more training than we already have done. They just wanted more.
>
> Again, it didn't go well, but everybody was able to speak their truth and figure out what's needed, why parents are worried. Again, parents were talking about bathrooms. That seems to be the biggest thing for parents is the bathroom. Since the meeting in the fall, we went into every bathroom in the school district to see, what do we have? How can we retrofit? What do we need? What's missing? The thing is a bathroom is an expense. You don't just put in a bathroom because we want one. In a building that recently had a renovation, that's a huge expense. It's an expense that parents just wanted taken care of now. It's not going to be now. It's going to take time to first figure out what needs to be done, then budget the right amount, and then figure out the steps to get us to a better place. At the high school level, you can't just put in single bathrooms because those are then spaces where kids can do drugs or have sex. I mean it seems so simple to parents—"Just do it. My kid needs it."

It's not that simple. But we're an advisory group, so we're going to try and figure it out.

Greater Prospect is an example of a school district that is willing to put their resources into figuring out how to protect the rights of transgender and gender-expansive students. At the same time, it is a difficult process. Even when there is clarity about what should be done, there are practical and financial obstacles. In this chapter, we examine three ways that schools attend to gendered spaces, focusing primarily on bathrooms, which may be the most controversial gendered space in schools.

GENDERED SCHOOL SPACES

Schools are inherently gendered spaces, physically and conceptually.[2] As socializing institutions, schools reflect and perpetuate our societal norms, including norms related to gender. Consequently, in the United States, school cultures preserve cisnormative and heteronormative beliefs. From the beginning, children are enrolled in school as boys or girls, and gender continues to be a part of their social, academic, and extracurricular activities. Gender is infused into school routines and traditions in a way that reinforces gender norms. For example, a school event such as "Muffins with Mommy" or "Doughnuts with Dad" is meant to build school-family connections, but it also preserves a narrow definition of family as heterosexual and cisgender. Children with two mommies, two daddies, blended families, donor parents, nonbinary parents, polyamorous parents, or nonparental custodians do not fit into this simplistic family depiction. In addition to excluding some children, gendered spaces also reinforce gender roles. Having a "daddy-daughter dance," for example, perpetuates cisnormative ideals that would not be reinforced if schools opted to host a "parent-child dance" or a more inclusive "all-families" dance party.

Cisgender people are often unaware of the ubiquitous role that gender plays in schools. Adults may even assert that children are too young to learn about gender, when, in fact, children are immersed in gendered spaces daily. The pervasive nature of gender in schools is often invisible to cisgender people because gendered school spaces are inherently cisnormative. As such, cisgender people experience few, if any, discomforts while navigating gendered spaces. The ease that cisgender people experience reflects their cisgender privilege and generally makes them unaware of the ways that binary, cisnormative spaces exclude and stigmatize transgender people. Tasks that cisgender people take for granted can present daunting obstacles for people whose gender identity or expression differs from their sex assigned at birth. Constantly having to navigate binary, cisnormative school spaces can exacerbate dysphoria, increase the risk of harassment and bullying, and may result in school avoidance.

As educators become aware of how cisnormative spaces are harmful, some schools have altered their practices to become more gender inclusive; however, gender continues to be a common way to categorize, sort, and define children. For example, it is not unusual for schools to formally sanction gendered attire in the form of graduation gowns, school uniforms, or clothing required for school performances and events. As one parent noted, "When you're inducted into the Honor Society, the girls wear dresses and boys wear suits." Activities may also be gendered such as Junior Olympics or Colonial Days.[3] A teacher explained, "There's a gender marker for every kid, either male or female, so it comes up on your standardized testing, it comes up on your Google account, it comes up in all sorts of different places." Perhaps the most visible cisnormative school space is the bathroom.[4] "Use of bathrooms, I get asked about that a lot," remarked one principal. Bathrooms are emblematic of our most entrenched societal beliefs about binary sex/gender, wherein male/boy and female/girl are perceived as stable, immutable, and mutually exclusive categories. As such, when educators discuss how they might make schools less cisnormative, bathrooms are the perennial lightning rod. Subsequently, bathrooms take center stage in this discussion of cisnormative school spaces.

Knowing that we have transgender and gender-expansive children in our schools, how should schools attend to gendered spaces? This chapter examines three broad approaches:

- Accommodate students.
- Assimilate students.
- Modify spaces for universal accessibility.

The first two approaches were common across the schools, and the third, modifying spaces for universal accessibility, was seldom observed. While each approach can provide support to gender-expansive and transgender students, these approaches diverge dramatically in the extent to which they deconstruct binary gender categories. Therefore, they also differ in the kinds of experiences they facilitate for transgender and gender-expansive children in school and their capacity to produce cultural change.

ACCOMMODATE STUDENTS: "I NEEDED TO FIND A COMFORTABLE AND SAFE PLACE FOR HIM."

When considering how to help transgender and gender-expansive children navigate gendered school spaces, a common approach is to provide students with accommodations. *Accommodations* is a term borrowed from the field of special education and refers to supports and services that remove barriers and help a student access the general education curriculum so that they can learn alongside their peers. In the realm of special education, accommodations allow a student to learn the same material as their peers. For example, a student with a visual impairment or reading disability might listen to, rather than read, a text. A student with difficulty concentrating may be seated next to the teacher or wear noise-cancelling headphones. In these examples, accommodations alter how the child learns without changing what the student learns.

In contrast to students who are diagnosed and classified with special education needs, being transgender or gender expansive is not a disability; however, in a cisnormative school culture, these children may face barriers that decrease their access to education.[5] For example, in a traditional school setting with bathrooms designated for either boys or girls, a gender-expansive student would lack access to appropriate facilities. Lack of access to school bathrooms can result in toileting accidents, urinary tract infections, and school avoidance. Thus, so-called single-sex bathrooms become a barrier, making it difficult for gender-expansive children to learn alongside their cisgender peers. A possible accommodation would be to identify an alternate bathroom for the student to use, perhaps the bathroom in the nurse's office or a bathroom previously reserved for adults. As such, accommodations are an attempt to ameliorate the negative effects of gendered spaces on gender-expansive and transgender students. Accommodations facilitate access to education that might otherwise be compromised.

In some schools, accommodations for transgender or gender-expansive students are formalized in a written "504 plan," named for Section 504 of the Rehabilitation Act of 1973. This federal statute prohibits discrimination based on disability, including physical impairments or health conditions that may not be obvious to others. In such cases, a school may document the child as having gender dysphoria, depression, anxiety, or being at risk for self-harm or school avoidance. Accordingly, a 504 plan might include any number of accommodations. A student might be assigned to a designated bathroom and given access to counseling services. Teachers might be required to use the student's chosen name and appropriate pronouns and to implement nongendered classroom activities. A student could be exempt from some requirements, such as participating in sex-segregated puberty education or changing clothes for physical education. Accommodations that are formally documented in a 504 plan are legally binding and, thus, enforceable. Families who make use of a 504 plan to identify accommodations are often concerned that, without a legal document, the educators in their school may not comply with requested accommodations.

None of the schools or families in this study took a formal approach to accommodations. Rather, the school faculty—administrators, teachers, and counselors—worked with families to informally determine what kinds of accommodations might be needed, without formally documenting any kind of "disability" or "impairment" as required for a 504 plan. For some families, this informal approach to accommodations is more fitting because gender identity alone is not a disability, health condition, or impairment. Rather, transgender people face barriers in the context of rigid enforcement of binary, cisnormative school spaces. Many transgender and gender-expansive people reject and actively resist definitions that construct transgender identities as "disability" or "pathology" out of concern that such representations perpetuate dangerous deficit perspectives that construe transgender people as deficient and diseased. At the same time, the medical professions and insurance companies often require transgender people to meet diagnostic criteria to receive needed services, such as hormone replacement therapy.

In the realm of education, being able to access accommodations informally, without the deficit framing entailed in a 504 plan, may reinforce that transgender identities are part of the gender spectrum and may better position transgender children to develop a positive sense of self.

Accommodations for transgender and gender-expansive students can help address health and safety concerns that arise in the context of cisnormative school spaces. While anti-trans rhetoric falsely posits transgender people as predatory, in reality transgender people are at higher risk of discrimination, harassment, and assault than cisgender people.[6] This risk is highest in cisnormative spaces, especially those spaces where dichotomous girl-boy gender identities are reinforced, such as bathrooms. Of the various kinds of possible accommodations, those related to bathroom usage received the most attention, likely owing to the real dangers presented in these unmonitored and highly gendered spaces. One parent feared that her gender-expansive son would face increased animosity upon moving to the school's upper-elementary wing and sharing the bathroom with older boys. "I'm worried about next year because it's one thing to have a kindergarten boy wonder about a sparkle barrette in the boy's bathroom, but some of those fifth-grade boys are like men. They're huge. I'm worried about [my child] being in the bathroom with those people." For this parent and many others, the potential physical threat that unmonitored bathrooms pose for transgender and gender-expansive children raised serious concerns about how their children would navigate these spaces.

In addition to the potential safety risks that so-called single-sex bathrooms pose, they can also cause transgender children significant distress and anxiety. Gender-expansive children may struggle to determine which bathroom to use when neither aligns with their gender identity. Gender-conforming transgender children may worry about being outed or having their legitimacy challenged. Faced with girl-boy bathrooms, these children worry: Will someone question me? Will the other boys ask why I always use the stall? Will they look under the door or through the crack? Will they say I'm not a real girl? Will I be bullied? The cumulative stress of these daily pressures can be severe. One mother explained, "I needed to find a comfortable and safe place for him to use the bathroom because that wasn't happening. The toileting is a big deal because Quinn had some health issues from avoiding going to the bathroom." It is not uncommon for transgender and gender-expansive children to avoid the bathroom completely and, as a result, suffer toileting accidents or urinary tract infections. The Lincoln School principal commented:

> He was not comfortable using the boy's bathroom, but the nurse's office was there for him. This child just didn't go to the bathroom though. He has the strongest bladder in the world because he just wouldn't go to the bathroom. Mom was, of course, monitoring that and making sure there were no other issues.

When faced with imperfect options, transgender children may even limit their food intake and avoid drinking to minimize the likelihood of needing to use the bathroom. Too often, cisgender people underestimate the negative effects of this chronic distress. In fact, the dysphoria that transgender people feel is not exclusively a result of their body but is directly affected by their environment and having to navigate cisnormative spaces.[7]

Educators described collaborating with the transgender child's family and using a child-centered approach to determine the kinds of accommodations that could prove useful, including bathroom access. Therefore, accommodations differed by child and situation and changed as the children's identities developed and needs shifted. The Evergreen Elementary principal explained, "Initially, he felt comfortable using the nurse's bathroom. That was something we worked out with his parents. This year, he may be using the boys' room." Because gender is not a fixed identity but evolves and develops over time, supportive principals were careful to communicate with families to continually monitor and revise accommodations as needed.

In most cases, the school's physical structure limited the kinds of bathroom accommodations available to children. Conventional school buildings in the United States are characterized by pink tile bathrooms for girls, blue tile bathrooms for boys, and single-occupancy bathrooms for teachers, usually located in the teachers-only workroom. That said, most schools have a gender-neutral bathroom in the nurse's office, and in many cases, this becomes the default bathroom for gender-expansive and transgender students. The principal at Forrest School shared a common scenario:

> The bathroom became an issue, very soon. By third grade, fourth grade, we had had the conversation. Bek no longer felt comfortable being referred to as "she" at all and wasn't comfortable using the girls' bathroom. Nobody knew what to do, so that is where the relationship with the parents came along, and Bek. We have three bathrooms that are gender nonspecific in the school. So Bek went to the nurse's bathroom, where many students go, or one of the two adult bathrooms, and those are single-person bathrooms.

In this example, the student had several options to choose from, including access to the "adult" bathrooms that would typically be reserved for teachers or school visitors. This kind of arrangement is not always possible due to structural limitations. Often, the gender-neutral adult bathroom is located in teacher-only work rooms, and educators may be reluctant to give up the adult-only spaces that allow them to recharge and face the demands of classroom instruction. Given the limitations of conventional school-building design, principals and families worked to provide the best accommodations possible.

Whether formal or informal, accommodations are intended to remove barriers and increase access to education; however, accommodations do not solve the problem of cisnormative school spaces, which remain intact. In fact, accommodations may merely substitute one set of problems for another. Access to the nurse's bathroom or a gender-neutral bathroom may allow the child to avoid stresses associated with so-called single-sex bathrooms; however, accommodations often come with other challenges. When gender-expansive and transgender children are using bathroom facilities that are different from their peers, they may worry: Why am I using the nurse's bathroom if I'm not sick? What do I tell my friends about using a different bathroom? What if the gender-neutral bathroom is occupied— should I wait or return to class? What if the wait is long and I have to return to class without using the bathroom and the teacher won't let me use the bathroom again? What if an adult tells me I'm not allowed in the adult bathroom? Given this set of worries, it becomes clear that accommodations may merely shift rather than alleviate children's distress. For example, Quinn's mom explained the challenges he experienced in association with the nurse's bathroom saying, "If the nurse would leave, just to go to a meeting, she'd have to lock it because of whatever she has in there, medicine and stuff. It was not good. . . . The nurse's bathroom didn't really work." Subsequently, the accommodations intended to provide Quinn with a healthy and safe bathroom were an imperfect solution, at best.

Providing accommodations to students is one way for schools to address the challenge of gendered school spaces; however, accommodations come with multiple drawbacks. Foremost, accommodations do not change the cisnormative school spaces that cause barriers, distress, and anxiety; rather, an accommodations approach asks children to change. It would be most accurate to say that the children make accommodations so that schools can maintain gendered spaces. In the process, transgender children are separated from their peers and marked as "different" or "other." Instead of being freed from distress, the children merely trade one set of worries for another. Even when accommodations prove helpful to a particular child, the cisnormative spaces remain intact and continue to reinforce rigid, dichotomous gender norms that underlie and perpetuate harmful stereotypes.

ASSIMILATE STUDENTS: "SHE WAS ABLE TO PASS."

A second approach that schools use is to assimilate transgender and gender-expansive children into gendered school spaces. The term *assimilate* is used in a variety of contexts and generally refers to the process of becoming similar to, being integrated into, or absorbed by another entity. The term may be most closely associated with the idea of cultural assimilation, which refers to the process by which a minority culture, over time, conforms to the norms of a majority culture. For example, cultural assimilation is the process by which immigrants become integrated into a new society, perhaps adopting the language and traditions of their new homeland. Assimilation can be viewed positively, as a desirable goal that provides new members of a society with greater access to cultural capital. Assimilation can also be interpreted negatively, as a loss of one's culture of origin.

In the context of schools, assimilating transgender and gender-expansive students refers to the idea of integrating them into traditionally cisnormative spaces. Rather than diverting the students to other spaces, as with accommodations, an assimilation approach provides them with access to cisnormative spaces and affirms their right to occupy such spaces based on their gender identity. For example, transfeminine children would have access to the girls' bathroom, be grouped with other girls for gendered activities, and conform to girl-specific dress codes. Similarly, transmasculine children would have access to facilities and activities designated for boys.

Many of the schools used an assimilation approach, particularly when the known transgender child conformed to binary cisgender norms. Educators were quick to point out that these children looked and behaved like their affirmed gender, making it easy to assimilate them into cisnormative spaces. The Iroquois Valley Elementary school principal explained, "It has been almost zero effort, in terms of needing to do anything special, because the student presents as a boy and uses the boys' bathroom and hangs out with the boys." When transgender children socially transition in a way that preserves dichotomous, boy-girl gender representations, schools had fewer concerns about assimilating transgender students into cisnormative spaces or how others might react. In some cases, members of the school community may not even realize that a transgender child is using restrooms designed as cisnormative spaces.

Transgender people who are perceived, or "read," by others as cisgender are commonly described as "passing." For prepubescent children, who have not developed secondary sex characteristics, such as facial hair or breasts, passing is relatively easy. Typically, children merely need to wear the clothing and hairstyles associated with their affirmed gender to pass as cisgender. The head of school at Kirby Learning Center explained, "The students' understanding was that the child was in fact a girl, which aligned perfectly with what the child felt, so there was no need for that child to come out. She was able to pass." As in this example, transgender children who "pass" as cisgender may remain "nondisclosed" to their peers or other members of the school community.[8] Transgender children often express a desire to be "just a boy" or "just a girl," even when parents intentionally cultivate pride in their children's transgender identity.

Passing is a complex and controversial topic. Being able to pass as cisgender confers privilege in the form of legitimacy, status, and access to spaces that might otherwise be inaccessible or even dangerous. As a result, transgender people who are able to pass as cisgender may benefit from the preservation of dichotomous cisnormative spaces. At the same time, passing is not feasible or desirable for all transgender people. The broad transgender umbrella includes many people whose gender identities do not conform or overtly reject conventional gender expression. Cisgender people often mistakenly presume that passing as cisgender is a goal for transgender people. The reality is that transgender people vary in their views on passing, and those who benefit from passing in a cisnormative society do so at the same time that nonpassing or gender-expansive transgender people suffer from the same system. Of course, the primary beneficiaries of cisnormative social systems are cisgender people who generally fail to question the inequities inherent in a social order that recognizes only two genders and historically privileges one gender, men, over all others.

Whether or not they pass as cisgender, transgender students in the United States have the legal right to use the bathroom of their choosing. To date, ten legal rulings across eight states have upheld existing protections for transgender students including equal access to bathrooms for transgender students.[9] In one high-profile legal case, high school student Gavin Grimm fought for equal access to gendered school facilities. Grimm and his legal team successfully argued that separate facilities for transgender people, as might be provided through accommodations, do not constitute equal treatment. Thus reasoned, all transgender people, regardless of whether they conform to gender norms, are legally entitled to access whichever programs and facilities they feel most comfortable using. In this way, schools that decide to use an assimilation approach are supporting their students' constitutional and educational rights.

Educators reported very few negative reactions from their school communities in response to transgender students' assimilation into cisnormative spaces. In those instances where other parents did complain, principals drew upon their child-centered approach to address the situation. One parent described her son's principal as saying, "If they have a problem with it, their kids can use a different bathroom." The Griffin principal, who previously worked at Mercer Elementary, took a similar approach when a parent called with concerns that Meredith, who had been assigned male at birth, was using the girls' bathroom:[10]

> A parent called me and was out of her mind saying, "What are we sup-
> posed to do? That's a boy [sic] using a girl's bathroom. He [sic] shouldn't
> be allowed to do that. My daughter doesn't feel comfortable." . . . I said
> to her, "Your child is welcome to use the nurse's bathroom."

In this example, the quick-thinking principal offered to accommodate the cisgender child. This principal not only demonstrated a child-centered approach but also upheld the law, which permits students to use whichever bathroom they feel most comfortable using.

While many schools successfully used an assimilation approach, families also reported drawbacks. Foremost, when transgender children are assimilated into cisnormative spaces, they may feel their acceptance in those spaces is contingent on their ability to conform to rigid cisgender norms. As a result, assimilation can be stressful for transgender children who may become anxious about having to keep their gender identity a secret. Even in the context of strong parental and school support, assimilation can be a heavy burden for children. At Mercer Elementary, Meredith's decision to use the girls' bathroom brought anxiety. Her mother explained:

> She had been using the girls' bathroom those first few weeks of school,
> and we had been checking in to see how it was going. She was always
> like, 'It's fine.' Then, a few weeks into the school year, Meredith asked
> if she could address the class. She stood up and said, "I just want ev-
> eryone to know that I'm allowed to use whichever bathroom I feel com-
> fortable using and the principal knows and all the teachers know. My
> parents know and everyone says it's okay." So, when we found out, I
> said, "I'm really proud of you, but I'm also curious. Why did you want to
> make that announcement?" She said, "It felt like I was carrying a secret,
> and I didn't want to do that anymore."

In this example, Meredith experienced assimilation as a secret that was difficult to bear. Even though Meredith was able to "pass," being open about gender identity helped to relieve the burden of secrecy. Meredith's capacity to identify the source of stress and self-advocate demonstrates a high level of self-awareness. Meredith continued to use the girls' bathroom without incident and with the added confidence that comes with not having to hide her gender identity.

Whether or not transgender students disclose their transgender identity, being assimilated into cisnormative spaces often caused anxiety about being "outed." Children frequently devised elaborate strategies to avoid being identified as transgender while in the bathroom. These approaches included using the bathroom only at certain times of day, selecting particular stalls, and sitting or standing in a specific way. These considerations demonstrate the level of chronic stress transgender children face while navigating cisnormative spaces. Leo's mom shared her son's experience using the boys' bathroom as a transgender first-grader:

> Leo is using the boys' room. Just last week he told me he has to wait until all of the other kids are out of the bathroom. I asked, "What exactly is happening?" He said, "I'm afraid." He's very anxious that somebody is looking in the crack of the stall. I said, "That's scary. I'd be nervous if somebody was doing that to me, so I completely get where you're coming from." I said, "Let's practice. What could you say to somebody?" I gave my own example. I said, "Maybe you could say 'leave me alone.' You don't have to scream, but you can stand up for yourself." With that, he just fell apart. He just started to cry.

Even in supportive contexts, children feared being outed in the bathroom, where they may interact with older or unfamiliar students. Fear of being exposed or confronted in this highly gendered and unmonitored space was stressful even for those children who preferred assimilation in cisnormative bathrooms over accommodations in other facilities.

Perhaps the biggest drawback to the assimilation approach is that not all transgender children can comfortably assimilate or want to assimilate into cisnormative spaces. Bathrooms designated for boys or girls may feel ill suited or unsafe for gender-expansive children, children who are questioning their gender, or children going through a social transition. The educators at Harborside Cooperative School had to address this challenge when Henry, a second grader, began to socially transition. The principal explained:

> Very early on we were saying, "If Henry wants to use the boys' bathroom, that's okay; go ahead and use the boys' bathrooms." We were okay with that, but it wasn't that simple. There was about a year where he didn't want to use any bathroom at all in our school. It wasn't like he really wanted to use the boys' bathroom; he didn't want to use either. The nurse's office does not have a bathroom. He kind of wanted to use a single-person bathroom, which we don't have in our school, except in the preK classrooms and the adult bathrooms. And so we offered up some of those options. He did use the preK bathroom for a while. He would walk down the stairs to the preK classroom, but I don't think he really liked that very much.

Even though the school was willing to assimilate Henry into cisnormative bathroom spaces, neither the boys' nor girls' bathroom felt right. Henry's desire to use a single-stall bathroom meant that he had to remove himself from his peers and either use a bathroom for younger children or adults. As this example demonstrates, both the accommodation and assimilation approaches ask children to adapt in ways that can cause stress and anxiety.

MODIFY SPACES FOR UNIVERSAL ACCESSIBILITY: "BATHROOMS JUST AREN'T PRIVATE ENOUGH FOR ANYONE."

The third approach to dealing with gendered spaces is to modify physical spaces for universal accessibility. Unlike accommodations and assimilation, a modification approach does not ask people to adapt to gendered spaces; rather, it changes those spaces so that all people can access them regardless of their gender identity. The idea of universal accessibility comes from the field of design and the notion of "universal design."[11] Products, services, and facilities that are designed for universal accessibility are easier for everyone to use. For example, curb cuts and doors that open automatically facilitate universal accessibility for a wide range of people including those with packages, wheelchairs, crutches, strollers, decreased mobility, visual impairments, etc. As such, universal design facilitates accessibility for the widest range of people possible, beyond those people who might be considered average users.

Recently, architects, engineers, and designers have taken up the challenge of designing bathrooms for universal accessibility including "gender-neutral" or "all-gender" bathrooms.[12] These new designs include separate spaces for grooming, washing, and eliminating. While grooming and washing areas are open, elimination stalls are designed for a single user with floor-to-ceiling walls and doors for both visual and olfactory privacy. Previously, these innovative designs were difficult to operationalize due to widespread, state-level construction codes that mandate sex-segregated bathrooms in addition to all-gender multi-user bathrooms. For many facilities, having both all-gender and sex-segregated bathrooms is cost prohibitive. Gradually, these codes are being revised, as evidenced by so-called family restrooms that allow multiple, mixed-gender users to access a single-user bathroom for the purposes of caregiving and toileting assistance. Even bigger changes are on the horizon. Two new amendments to the International Plumbing Code, which establishes industry standards, further relax gender restrictions and take effect in 2021. They state

- Single-user restrooms require signage to indicate that they're open to any user regardless of gender.
- Multi-user restrooms can now be offered to all users. They need shared sinks and each toilet must have a private compartment.[13]

These changes to international plumbing codes will make it easier for states to rewrite existing ordinances so that facilities can offer multigender facilities exclusively, instead of as an addition to sex-segregated bathrooms.

Generally speaking, bathroom design and access are influenced by a confusing compilation of state-level legislation, state building and plumbing codes, and municipal codes and ordinances. This labyrinth of regulations may be enough to dissuade schools from attempting to change their bathrooms, despite the clear need to make these gendered spaces more comfortable for a wider range of users. While the majority of schools added all-gender signage to their single-user restrooms, only three schools took steps to modify their multi-user bathrooms to create greater accessibility for transgender and gender-expansive students. This small number is not surprising. Families were relatively satisfied with assimilation and accommodations and did not press for bathroom modifications. Moreover, schools likely lack the knowledge and resources needed to significantly modify bathrooms in ways that are cost effective and code compliant. Most school administrators were resigned to the structural constraints of their buildings. As the Lincoln School principal remarked, "The bathroom is a big thing, but we can't change that. I wish I could, but I also need another floor and I'm not getting that either. It's more a structural issue than anything." Structural limitations were often seen as insurmountable obstacles.

In the three schools that did modify their multi-user bathrooms, the changes were improvised alterations rather than permanent structural solutions. On one hand, improvised changes were immediate and inexpensive; they did not require significant funds or new construction. On the other hand, they were imperfect fixes. For example, at Pacificus Learning Collaboratory, a small independent school, signs for the multi-user "boys" and "girls" bathrooms were replaced with all-gender signs. However, the rest of the bathroom fixtures remained unchanged, which meant that one bathroom still had a urinal, making it appear to be a "boys" bathroom despite the all-gender signage. Accordingly, students continued to use the bathrooms as they had prior to the new signs. In this case, the signage appeared largely symbolic. It is difficult to know whether the children could comfortably use either bathroom, if they desired to do so, or whether gender-expansive children felt affirmed and included by the new signage.

Another school that took steps to modify both their single-user and multi-user bathrooms was the Kirby Learning Center, also a small independent school serving students preK through eighth grade. Kirby's social justice mission seemed to attract LGBTQ families, and they had a handful of students who were transgender or gender expansive. In fact, the head of school, Principal Jackie Kendall, openly identified as part of the

LGBTQ community, and her spouse identified as agender. Principal Kendall conveyed deep understanding of anti-transgender discrimination, and she actively engaged the school community in conversations about gender. Principal Kendall shared one incident that catalyzed their desire to take action with regard to bathroom modifications:

> A set of parents and a child came to visit. One parent hadn't come out and said whether they used "he" or "she" pronouns, and it was not obvious what this parent's identity was. So, that parent asked the admissions director to help find a bathroom and it was this moment of like, 'Oh my God." [The admissions director] just pointed in the general direction of the hallway because she didn't want to make an assumption. That was a moment where we were just thinking, "We're not there. We're not where we need to be to make everybody feel safe and comfortable."

This incident with a prospective parent, combined with the increasing visibility of transgender and gender-expansive children at Kirby, helped galvanize Principal Kendall and her teaching staff to take action.

The actual work of modifying bathrooms to make them all-gender is not as straightforward as one might assume. Principal Kendall described bringing the matter to the teachers in her school, who agreed that sex-segregated bathrooms were problematic, especially in the context of their social justice mission and their gender-diverse school community. The teachers suggested that all bathrooms should be single stall and lockable, a solution that would be costly and slow to implement. In search of a more expedient solution, Principal Kendall turned to the seventh-grade students for advice:

> The solution our students came up with was to take the stalls we already have and simply put weather stripping on the doors and in the cracks so, if someone's in a stall, no one is able to peek in. This wasn't an issue of people being in bathrooms with the opposite gender. This was an issue of them saying, "These bathrooms just aren't private enough for anyone." So, we put weather stripping on the doors. We also built a stall around the urinal in what was the boys' bathroom so that became a private space. And in any of the bathrooms that were multi-stall, they

came up with the ingenious idea of putting a lock on the main front door, so if you found yourself alone in the bathroom and wanted to create a private space, you could lock the main door. So, we've now transitioned our bathrooms to being all-gender bathrooms with private stalls that also convert into single-occupancy bathrooms.

The Kirby students recognized that bathrooms were problematic for two reasons: they were sex/gender-segregated, and they also lacked privacy. The students' approach to problem solving mirrors the components of universal design, wherein the solution benefits everyone. Principal Kendall reported that the new bathroom design was announced and implemented without any complaints from the school community. Being an independent school and serving a niche group of parents may have facilitated Kirby's nimble response and creative problem solving.

The third school that modified their sex-segregated, multi-user bathrooms was Jefferson Elementary, located in Greater Prospect, the district featured in the opening vignette to this chapter. Over the years, Greater Prospect had enrolled several transgender students, who were supported using an accommodations approach. At Jefferson, however, the family of a transgender second-grader, Jacob, requested assimilation and full access to the boys' bathroom. The school counselor recalled the conversation:

> One of the solutions was to use the nurse's bathroom, and I knew that wasn't fair or appropriate; they're not sick. The principal at the time said, "Jacob can use whatever bathroom he wants. Everybody can use whatever bathroom they want. I want him to be comfortable."

For the family and administrators at Jefferson, assimilation represented an improvement over accommodations, a way for Jacob to be integrated with his peers. However, the presumed benefits of assimilation were short-lived. As the year progressed, Jacob reported that the boys' bathroom was not comfortable. It lacked privacy. His mother explained:

> Jacob told me that the boys were looking under or in the cracks in the boys' bathroom. I told the counselor. I wanted them to know that Jacob is

doing okay in the bathroom, but he's afraid sometimes. The next thing I knew, like a couple of weeks later, she came back to me and said we've retrofitted the second-grade boy's bathroom. They added rubber strips and lowered the stall doors, which I was thrilled with. I hadn't asked for it, but they did it. So, there's this genuine attempt to solve the problem at a kid-specific level, which I've really appreciated. The unfortunate thing is when I checked back in with Jacob, he said, "Oh, now they just stand on the toilets and look over." So, while they considered it a success, it's an inexpensive solution that seems good, but it's not.

Jefferson Elementary had been proactive, quickly agreeing to Jacob's request to use the boys' bathroom and then, unprompted, modified one stall to offer more privacy. Unfortunately, the improvised modifications were insufficient in the context of active, curious children. One might imagine that a single altered stall could attract even more attention than the standard stalls. As such, both assimilation and the improvised modifications proved inadequate for meeting Jacob's needs and, presumably, the needs of other children who might need privacy or more gender-inclusive facilities.

This example from Jefferson Elementary highlights the potential tension between families and schools as they figure out how to address gendered spaces. On one hand, the school and district are actively seeking solutions that will meet the needs of their transgender and gender-expansive student population. As such, these supportive educators may expect families to be grateful or ask students to be patient as they figure out a path forward. But, as Jacob's mom alluded, even the most understanding families can feel frustrated if their children's basic needs and civil rights are not being met. Parents of transgender children have been known to say, "I'm not a hero for loving my transgender child." In a similar fashion, schools are not heroic for providing transgender children with access to educational facilities and programs to which they are legally entitled. So, while Jacob's mom is appreciative of the school's efforts, she is justifiably frustrated with the shortcomings inherent in improvised bathroom modifications. Lack of adequate bathroom facilities jeopardizes the health, safety, and learning for transgender and gender-expansive children, particularly those who remain undisclosed or lack familial supports, resources, or cultural capital.

BEYOND BATHROOMS

Bathrooms are not the only gendered spaces in schools. Schools reinforce and reproduce cisnormative views of gender through school-sponsored programs, events, and activities. The three approaches highlighted here—accommodation, assimilation, and modified spaces—can be employed broadly across the many gendered spaces we find in schools. For example, schools commonly used an accommodations approach with regard to health education, allowing students to engage in an alternate activity instead of participating in either of the "boys'" or "girls'" puberty talk. One school used an assimilation approach for their annual Colonial Day event, permitting the known transgender student to wear the clothing that felt most comfortable, either knickers and a white shirt with suspenders or a long skirt and bonnet.

A modification approach to gendered spaces can also be applied beyond bathrooms as a way to create greater accessibility for everyone. For example, at Lincoln School the principal modified the dance residency program so that it was no longer structured around gender-based dance roles. She explained:

> Fifth grade does a dance residency, and it was ballroom dancing. How will I deal with this? I wasn't aware of how many boy-girl things I was doing until this experience. So, when Luke was in fourth grade, I changed it. I said we're going to do group dancing. It's not going to be boy-girl. I'm not sure if Luke noticed, but then, when Luke was a fifth grader, we did group dancing again and it worked out beautifully. It was just as wonderful without the male-female roles.

In this example, Luke was not excused from the dance residency as he might be if an accommodations approach were employed. Nor did Luke assimilate into a boy's role in ballroom dancing, which some transgender boys might want to do if given the opportunity. Rather, the principal modified the dance residency altogether, using gender-neutral group dance, such as square dance and contra dance, to make all aspects of the activity fully accessible. This approach enables all children to participate in the dance equally regardless of their gender expression or identity. Modifications like this might even be characterized as liberatory because they completely remove gender constraints.

In most cases, schools and educators fail to interrogate the utility of gendered school spaces, accepting them at face value and as inevitable. Increased awareness of diverse gender identities can prompt educators to reflect on and be more intentional about the role of gender in school-sponsored programs, events, and activities. Jackie Kendall, the principal at Kirby Learning Center, described her school's efforts to be attentive to gender and gender identity development for both cisgender and transgender students and the challenges it presented. She explained:

> We had a Frisbee clinic, and we wanted the girls to have a chance to really play because the boys were always diving in front of them and stealing the Frisbee. So, we said, "We're going to divide you by gender today." Then this child—who started to come out as gender nonconforming or genderqueer and then maybe as trans but that was unclear—is in the bathroom sobbing. So, we were really kicking ourselves for not remembering what that might have brought up. It's these traps you fall into. We still have not resolved this issue. Some teachers really still feel that the girls need space, and how are we going to have that space when we can't necessarily say who's a girl? I don't know.

This example illustrates the formidable challenge that gender presents in schools. The reflective educators at Kirby Learning Center wanted to create space for girls to develop strong identities, and simultaneously, they wanted to deconstruct those spaces that delegitimize transgender and gender-expansive students. These competing needs emerge from a shared social context that constructs gender as binary and hierarchical.

CONCLUSION

Among the schools in this study, elementary school educators worked with families to help transgender children navigate gendered spaces, particularly bathrooms, using three approaches: accommodating students, assimilating students, and modifying school spaces. Across the schools, the first two approaches predominated. In contrast, efforts to modify spaces to create universal access were limited or nonexistent.

Just as these three approaches can be applied broadly to an array of gendered spaces, the depth of their application is also important to consider. Frequently, educators explained that the accommodation, assimilation, and modification strategies they implemented were in place only for a limited time, usually while the known transgender or gender-expansive child was enrolled and directly impacted by prior practices, programs, activities, and facilities. Once the child moved on to another classroom or school, educators often reverted back to gendered practices. For example, gender-neutral bathroom passes might once again be labeled "boy" and "girl." One parent expressed disappointment that her younger cisgender child brought home forms with boy-girl identifiers, even though those labels had been removed previously when the older gender-expansive sibling had been in that teacher's classroom. Even the gender-neutral dance at Lincoln School reverted back to ballroom dancing after Luke had moved on to sixth grade.

The brevity of these changes meant that schools remained cisnormative, continuing to reproduce traditional gender norms that situate transgender and gender-expansive students as different or "other." This reality reflects what we already know. Deep, sustained change is difficult, particularly when those changes demand shifts in our understanding and a redistribution of power. While it may be disappointing to know that these supportive schools did not maintain the practices that transgender students found helpful, we can build on this knowledge to imagine how we might promote gender-affirming practices that are implemented broadly and deeply and are sustained over time.

CHAPTER 7

Reculturing Schools for Gender Equity

Deodorant, of course, is gendered and Mickie Cullen [the fifth-grade health educator] used to put out boy deodorant and girl deodorant. So, one thing that she changed after we talked was, she just held up the deodorant and said, "This is Axe. This is for those of you who like to feel more sporty. This is Secret Powder. This is if you like to smell like you just had a bath and put powder on like a baby. This is Tom's. This is if you care about chemicals in your body." She didn't present it as gendered but more about the scent or the lifestyle. She said that for the first time ever she saw girls coming over and picking up the Axe and boys coming over and picking up the powder or picking up the Tom's and that she saw this real kind of open change in the kids, like they were open to whatever, based on how she had pitched the different deodorants. I thought that was great. Even though it says "women's deodorant" or whatever, they didn't care. They were listening to what she said, and when she framed it that way, the kids really responded and took what felt appropriate.

—MEREDITH'S MOM

In the preceding vignette, we learn how Mickie Cullen, the health educator, redesigned her hygiene lesson to remove gendered associations from deodorant, relying instead on descriptors such as scent to characterize the various types of deodorant. This shift in language, although simple, is not trivial. For one thing, it takes critical self-reflection and concerted intentionality to change long-standing educational practices. In addition, although gendered deodorant may appear insignificant, it is emblematic of deeply entrenched binary gender norms that pervade our education systems. In this sense, a seemingly simple change related to deodorant marks a bold challenge to entrenched beliefs. It would not be an overstatement to say that, in changing how she talked about deodorant, Mickie helped shift the status quo, which relies on binary gender norms to maintain power imbalances and perpetuate inequity.

To lift the constraints imposed by binary gender norms, we need to reculture our schools for gender equity. This formidable task depends, in part, on individual educators' willingness to deliberately shift the status quo in small but significant ways. It also requires systemwide change aimed at cultivating new gender norms. This means conceptualizing gender equity as more than equality between girls and boys, to include all gender identities. It requires developing cultures of critical self-reflection, dismantling our cisnormative beliefs, actively deconstructing gender norms, and unconditionally affirming transgender and gender-expansive identities. To create truly equitable educational spaces where all children are encouraged to develop their gender identities, free from binary constraints, we need to aim beyond temporary fixes directed at individual children. We need to reculture schools so that a new conceptualization of gender—as expansive and complex—permeates our structures, practices, and relationships. We need to reculture schools so that the gender norms include deeply held beliefs that transgender and gender-expansive children bring value to our schools—that they belong.

This final chapter reviews the lessons learned from more than seventy-five educators in twenty schools across six states. In each of the schools, individual transgender and gender-expansive children prompted educators to think differently about gender and consider how they might develop more supportive and affirming educational spaces. The changes that educators made to their practice resulted in real benefits to transgender and gender-expansive students. The educators' stories and insights can help other educators more confidently take up the challenge of creating more gender-equitable schools and classrooms. At the same time, it is instructive to turn a critical eye toward the practices described in this volume and ask, "What are the shortcomings? And, how might we do even better?"

The discussion that follows is not meant to diminish the many positive ways that educators supported transgender and gender-expansive students; rather, it challenges us to dream bigger. Critically reflecting on the limits of educators' efforts to support transgender children points us toward new goals and can inspire even more meaningful change.

LESSONS LEARNED

In each of the twenty schools, individual children served as the impetus for educators' efforts to learn about transgender identities and change gendered school practices. Using a child-centered approach, the educators worked to create a supportive environment for the individual transgender or gender-expansive student. The educators' responsiveness to transgender students is impressive given the numerous factors that deter educators from addressing gender in schools. These factors include a lack of formal training, the belief that gender is irrelevant to children's school experience, misconceptions about gender being synonymous with sexuality, and fear of reprisals. In contrast, these educators were eager to learn how to support their transgender students. They provide positive examples for other educators who want to implement more gender-affirming educational practices in their classrooms and schools.

Each of the chapters provides important lessons for educators. Foremost, leadership matters. Principals' efforts to support transgender and gender-expansive students set the stage for other educators to develop supportive practices. Principals served as lead learners and created learning opportunities for other educators and the larger school community. Equally important, individual educators can positively affect transgender students' school experiences. Teachers decreased gendered classroom management strategies, increased critical discussions about gender, and affirmed children's gender identities. The stories in this book also teach us that educational spaces are adaptable. In addition to assimilating and accommodating students, schools can modify spaces for greater accessibility for everyone. Perhaps most importantly, the educators' stories resoundingly demonstrate that having a transgender or gender-expansive student is an opportunity. Educators expressed gratitude for having known the transgender student and their family, describing unexpected personal and professional growth. As a result of their work with transgender and gender-expansive students, educators became more empathetic and affirming of identities and experiences they might have previously dismissed.

Across these stories we see how educators leveraged their knowledge to create supportive and affirming environments for individual transgender children, employing a child-centered approach to guide their practice. The educators' successes, however, are tempered when we reflect on the limitations inherent in a child-centered approach. First, a focus on individual students privileges children with supportive parents who can leverage their cultural and economic capital to advocate for a gender-inclusive educational environment for their child. Second, the supportive practices that the educators developed for individual transgender children were often temporary, implemented only while the known transgender student was enrolled or only in classrooms where the child was present. Thus, supportive practices that resulted from a child-centered approach lacked depth, breadth, and sustainability. A narrow focus on individual children fails to tackle the larger problem: binary gender norms that perpetuate gender inequity and constrain gender identity development for all children.

RECULTURING SCHOOLS FOR GENDER EQUITY

To facilitate gender equity in schools, we need a two-pronged approach that includes changing school cultures in addition to meeting individual children's needs. School cultures continue to reproduce the gender norms that contribute to the dehumanization of transgender identities, even when individual children are affirmed and supported. Cultural change is hard to achieve because it requires critical self-reflection, ongoing conversation, and collective action. Dean Spade, a legal scholar and transgender activist, warns about the dangers of "pinkwashing," which gives the illusion of support without substantially shifting the beliefs and norms that underlie and perpetuate inequity.[1] Actions meant to signal change such as "safe school" stickers, rainbow flags, and anti-bullying posters remain largely symbolic in the absence of deeper cultural change. Changing educational practice is difficult under the best circumstances, that is, when educators are eager to try out new ideas. When change threatens to destabilize existing power dichotomies and deeply entrenched societal beliefs, such as binary gender norms, resistance is likely.

In the context of schools, meaningful change is inhibited by a lack of time and competing priorities. Educators in the United States are over-worked and underappreciated. Constant pressure to improve, without adequate support, commonly results in shallow, short-lived change. Most school reform is characterized by changes in degree, doing more or less of the same, rather than changes in kind—engaging in different practices needed to yield different results.[2] Educators may be uncertain about how to begin the process of reculturing schools for gender equity. They may also be skeptical that individual educators can alter deeply entrenched binary gen-der norms. While it can be helpful to have school and district administra-tors out front and leading the change effort, norms do not shift in response to heavy-handed mandates. Change *can* begin with individual educators, just as the individual transgender children featured in this book motivated educators to develop more gender-inclusive practices.

Even though children can inspire action, educators should not wait for individual transgender children to disclose their gender identity before en-gaging in the work necessary to shift gender norms. Transgender children and their families should not have to sacrifice their privacy and bear the burden of facilitating change. Instead, educators must be proactive about reculturing schools for gender equity. The need and rationale are unequiv-ocal. First, gender-expansive and transgender children and those who are questioning their gender are already enrolled in our schools, even if they are not disclosed. Second, binary gender norms constrain everyone, including cisgender children. Simply stated, our failure to challenge binary gender norms in schools perpetuates inequity and limits learning and development for all children.

To reculture schools for gender equity, educators need to be proactive along three dimensions:

- Make space for transgender and gender-expansive identities.
- Invite difficult conversations about gender.
- Develop formal policies and written curriculum.

We can make schools more equitable. Those of us who are cisgender can use our privilege to challenge binary gender norms, shift the status quo, and reculture schools. Our proactive efforts can facilitate gender equity and liberate, rather than limit, children's gender identity development.

Make Space for Transgender and Gender-Expansive Identities

One proactive way to shift gender norms is to make space for transgender and gender-expansive identities. Here, the idea of making space is not about physical space that a person might occupy, such as a chair or desk; instead, this is about creating conceptual space. Making space for transgender and gender-expansive identities is distinct from and stands in contrast to the idea of making space for individual transgender children. That is, a known transgender person should not have to be present to recognize and affirm transgender identities. A focus on identities, rather than individuals, presumes that transgender identities are real, valid, and inherently worthy. It presumes that transgender people are present even when they are not disclosed, and thus, transgender identities are always relevant. A focus on identities recognizes that transgender people should not have to ask for space to exist; rather, transgender and gender-expansive identities, like cisgender identities, should be expected.

Presently, transgender identities are not inherent within the social constructs of schooling. Adrienne Rich, poet and essayist, aptly describes the feeling of erasure that results from systemic exclusion:

> When those who have power to name and to socially construct reality choose not to see you or hear you, whether you are dark-skinned, old, disabled, female, or speak with a different accent or dialect than theirs, when someone with the authority of a teacher, say, describes the world and you are not in it, there is a moment of psychic disequilibrium, as if you looked into a mirror and saw nothing.[3]

So long as gender remains salient in our educational institutions, we need to make space for transgender and gender-expansive identities so much that excluding them from school frameworks and narratives would conflict with how we make sense of the world. If equity is truly an educational ideal, then those of us who are privileged, who possess the "authority of a teacher," must describe the world in ways that include transgender identities as an intrinsic part of society, as inherently belonging.

How, then, can we make space for transgender and gender-expansive identities in schools and classrooms? Generally speaking, educators must widen their lens and attend to gender more broadly instead of focusing narrowly on the needs of individual transgender children. Educators also must explicitly create space for identities other than boy or girl. Not everyone feels like a boy or a girl, and making this point clear, repeatedly, legitimizes transgender and gender-expansive identities. Some of the ways we can make space for transgender identities were discussed earlier in this book and include reducing an emphasis on binary gender categories and increasing conversations about gender. Educators described actions such as eliminating boy/girl bathroom passes and adding books with gender-diverse characters to the school and classroom libraries. Mickie Cullen provides an additional example in the introductory vignette to this chapter when she presents deodorant as being gender-neutral. These actions create space for us to think differently about gender and develop new understandings about gender-expansive identities. Importantly, these practices need to be implemented broadly and sustained over time, beyond classrooms with known transgender children, if we want to shift our gender norms. As the educators in this book have demonstrated, these practices can, and should, begin in the earliest grades with all students.

Another way to make conceptual space for transgender identities is to include pronouns as part of a self-introduction. This can be done by simply stating, for example, "Melinda, she/her/hers." For people who are never misgendered, adding pronouns to an introduction may feel unnecessary, but claiming pronouns isn't just a way to keep from being misgendered. On the contrary, it is also a way to remind others that gender should never be assumed based on external appearance or based on names. Even though we think of Melinda as a so-called girl's name, we can't know Melinda's pronouns without being told. Claiming pronouns creates conceptual space for transgender and gender-expansive identities to be imagined and articulated. It reminds us that gender identity may not fit neatly into binary categories of boy/man, girl/woman. At the same time, claiming pronouns should not be a way to force others to disclose their gender. Some people aren't comfortable with any of the pronoun options currently in use, or they may not want to share personal information. It is usually unnecessary to know someone's gender or pronouns to interact with them.

When someone's pronouns are unknown and we need to refer to <u>them</u> in the third person, it is appropriate to use <u>their</u> name or use *they/them/ their/theirs* as a singular, gender-neutral pronoun. We commonly use *they/ them/their/theirs* to refer to individuals, as demonstrated in the underlined text of the previous sentence, although this usage often goes unnoticed.[4] Because singular *they* challenges binary gender norms, it is a useful way to make space for transgender and gender-expansive identities. In addition to singular *they* used as a gender-neutral pronoun, it can also be used to convey gender-expansive identity. Some gender-expansive people use other pronouns, such as *ze/hir/hirs* or *ze/zir/zirs*.[5] Admittedly, learning new pronouns or using singular *they* can feel clumsy, but, as with any new language, practice brings greater ease. When individuals make an effort to learn and use new pronouns, they make space for increased awareness and affirmation of transgender and gender-expansive identities. As such, individual actions can contribute to the larger task of cultural change and, specifically, reculturing schools for gender equity.

Making conceptual space for transgender and gender-expansive identities to exist takes pressure off transgender children to be the poster child or sacrificial lamb.[6] At the same time, conceptualizing gender in more expansive ways affirms individual transgender and gender-expansive students. Making space for transgender and gender identities also legitimizes children who may be questioning or exploring their gender identity. Widening the scope of gender-affirming practices facilitates more effective support for the entire population of transgender students, known and unknown, present and future.

Invite Difficult Conversations About Gender

Binary gender norms will not change unless we engage in difficult conversations that make gender inequity visible, especially to those people who benefit from inequity. Difficult conversations demand that we analyze our participation in systems of inequity and take responsibility for changing the attitudes, beliefs, and behaviors that contribute to power imbalances. Difficult conversations about gender are distinct from learning about gender and transgender identities. Learning opportunities, absent critical self-reflection, do not facilitate a sense of ownership or obligation to make change. The end goal of difficult conversations extends beyond mere acquisition of information. Rather, the aim is to apply new knowledge in ways that disrupt binary gender norms, challenge power inequities, and, most importantly, benefit transgender and gender-expansive people. If we truly want to make schools more equitable spaces, then opportunities to learn about transgender and gender-expansive identities must include difficult conversations.

Shallow learning fails to inspire meaningful change, and, more specifically, shallow learning about gender can cause harm to transgender and gender-expansive people. The idea that learning has potential to harm may appear illogical, particularly to educators who are dedicated to children's learning. Consider, however, that shallow learning can reinforce stereotypes and situate transgender people as "different" or "other," which reinforces and justifies exclusion and perpetuates inequity and discrimination. Julia Serano, author and transgender activist, explains how questions directed at transgender people, under the guise of learning, undermine and delegitimize transgender identities:

> [W]henever people ask me lots of questions about my previous male life and the medical procedures that helped facilitate my transition to female, I realize that they are making a desperate and concerted effort to preserve their own assumptions and stereotypes about gender, rather than opening their minds up to the possibility that women and men do not represent mutually exclusive categories. When they request to see my "before" photos or ask me what my former name was, it is because they are trying to visualize me as male in order to anchor my existence in my assigned sex.[7]

Opportunities to learn about complex transgender identities commonly reduce identity into a single story that is told in the context of a one-shot workshop, a solitary guest speaker, or a single resource.[8] These kinds of isolated, depoliticized learning opportunities objectify rather than empower transgender people.

To shift binary gender norms and reculture schools, educators need to invite one another to engage in deep learning characterized by difficult conversations about gender. This work is especially important for cisgender educators, who may be unaware of how their actions and inactions contribute to the oppression of transgender and gender-expansive people. Moreover, transgender people are not responsible for educating cisgender people. Cisgender educators need to challenge one another to do the work required to reculture schools. This means raising the topic of gender again and again, as long as the gender binary continues to constrain gender identity development and marginalize transgender identities.

One way to initiate difficult conversations about gender is to conduct a gender audit aimed at identifying all the ways binary gender is implicitly and explicitly reflected in schools. Making this a collaborative endeavor, shared by a team of educators, can spark conversation about school norms and the ways that gender influences children's school experiences. A gender audit examines the role of gender in the design of facilities, oral and written language, procedures and practices, and in programs and curriculum. Consider, for example, whether gender influences how students are seated in classrooms, for performances, on field trips, or during lunch? Are school forms gendered? Do library books, textbooks, and assignments feature gender-expansive children and include gender-neutral pronouns? Are classroom pets or the school mascot gendered? A gender audit creates an opportunity to discuss promising and troubling practices. Difficult conversations can help uncover and challenge deeply held beliefs that contribute to gender inequity. Setting and monitoring specific goals aimed at developing new practices that disrupt binary gender norms can contribute to a more gender-inclusive school culture.

Educators can also form gender study groups that utilize multiple resources and intentionally foster difficult conversations aimed at interrogating cisgender privilege. In our cisnormative culture, being cisgender means never having to articulate and justify one's identity to gatekeepers with the power to confer legitimacy and determine access to human and civil rights. Interrogating cisgender privilege entails critically reflecting on personal narratives of gender and identity and how they contribute to the reproduction of cisnormative school cultures. Questions that can facilitate critical self-reflection include

- How did you figure out your sex and your gender identity? Was there any conscious process? What internal and external clues have helped you figure them out?
- How have your interactions with others affected your own gender identity or expression either in general or at particular times?
- How do you make visible or camouflage this gender identity?
- Have you had opportunities or obstacles in expressing your gender identity? That is, does your gender expression match your gender identity as much as you would like?
- To what extent do you see your gender identity reflected in organizational spaces, such as schools?[9]

These kinds of questions make cisgender identity an object of study and expose the privileges afforded to people with cisgender identity.

Inviting difficult conversations about gender can facilitate the kind of deep learning needed to make gender inequity visible. Moreover, deep learning characterized by critical self-reflection can reveal our complicity and compel us to act. Intentional actions are needed to challenge the binary gender norms that privilege cisgender identities at the expense of transgender children's sense of belonging.

Develop Formal Policies and Written Curriculum

To increase the likelihood of reculturing schools for gender equity, we must also develop educational policies and written curriculum that facilitate meaningful changes to school practice. Formal policies that support transgender rights can decrease educators' fear of reprisals and increase willingness to change existing practices that reproduce binary gender norms. It is true that mandates alone are insufficient for changing school culture, but supportive policies and curriculum can both guide and reinforce the efforts of educators who want to create more gender-affirming schools.[10] When policy is thoughtfully implemented, monitored, and enforced, it can be a useful tool for changing educators' practice and beliefs.

Some schools, districts, and state departments of education already have policies that explicitly support transgender students and educators.[11] At minimum, all schools must have policies that comply with Title IX of the Education Amendments of 1972, which states, "No person in the United States shall, on the basis of sex, be excluded from participation in, be denied the benefits of, or be subjected to discrimination under any education program or activity receiving Federal financial assistance."[12] Although the language here refers to sex, courts have repeatedly ruled that gender, which is assigned on the basis of medico-legal sex, is similarly protected under Title IX.[13] A first step, then, is to investigate the policies that exist. Knowing the extent of protections for transgender students and educators, as articulated in formal education policies, establishes the starting point for change efforts. Where formal gender policies exist, educators need to be proactive about updating policies so that they remain consistent with new laws and reflect the educational practices recommended by transgender rights advocates.

In the absence of supportive gender policies, policy development can be a formidable task. Importantly, development efforts should include a broad set of stakeholders, opportunities to learn, and extensive communication. Involving stakeholders in the policy-making process can increase stakeholders' sense of ownership and commitment. One example of this is the policy-making efforts of Greater Prospect School District. The district sought assistance from an experienced education consultant who acted as the facilitator and involved a wide range of stakeholders in the policy-making process. Various resources are available to assist school districts with policy making. In addition to local consultants and advocacy groups, numerous national organizations have regional offices and staff dedicated to assisting educators and schools. Some organizations that advocate for the educational rights of transgender students include GLSEN, Gender Spectrum, PFLAG, the Southern Poverty Law Center, and the Human Rights Campaign.

The limits of policy for changing practice should not be underestimated. Written guidelines do not guarantee implementation, monitoring, or enforcement. Higher education scholar Z Nicolazzo describes the limits of policy for protecting transgender students:

> It's important that we have nondiscrimination policies that include gender identity and gender expression, but that's insufficient to create environments where trans students can have more livable lives. . . . I can't carry around a nondiscrimination policy and say, "You shouldn't look at me weird because look here, gender identity and expression are listed under the nondiscrimination policy." While that policy is necessary, it's insufficient at actually changing the way we think about gender and how gender structures college environments.[14]

Policy is similarly limited in the context of K–12 schools, which may lack consequences for failing to implement policy guidelines. The limits of policy underscore the vital role of deep learning and difficult conversations for shifting cultural norms in addition to formal structures.

Although policy alone is insufficient for reculturing schools, policy can be influential in changing educators' beliefs and practices. Change theorists explain that, paradoxically, changes in beliefs often follow changes to practice, not the inverse. Consider, for example, a teacher who believes elementary-age children are too young to discuss gender. A policy that requires instruction on gender as part of the curriculum could compel the teacher to change their practice and, subsequently, develop new beliefs about young students' capacity to engage in discussions about gender. As such, changes in practice can precede and facilitate changes in beliefs. At the same time, changes to practice may not be possible unless policy implementation also includes high-quality learning opportunities. Even willing educators may be uncertain about *how* to translate policy demands into practice. Therefore, policy mandates that lack opportunities for learning are unlikely to produce meaningful changes to practice or beliefs.

Like policy, written curriculum plays an important role in reculturing schools. Just as policy establishes guidelines for practice, curriculum also guides the instructional practices that take place in schools. When teachers have access to curricular materials that facilitate gender-affirming lessons, they are more likely to engage students in conversations about gender. In the context of instructional norms that include collegial collaboration and constructive critique, gender-affirming curriculum may also prompt teachers to engage difficult conversations about gender. Several organizations, including Gender Spectrum, the Southern Poverty Law Center, and the Human Rights Campaign Foundation, have developed teaching materials related to gender that are publicly available online. Alternately, teachers can write their own gender-affirming curriculum. Done collaboratively, curriculum writing presents an additional opportunity for teachers to develop shared norms about gender-affirming classroom practices.

Teachers can also adapt existing curriculum to be more gender inclusive. In the current educational context of accountability and standardization, teachers are under great pressure to cover the required curriculum. Writing new curriculum may not be feasible; however, existing lessons can offer opportunities to engage students in conversations about gender. In *Reading the Rainbow: LGBTQ-Inclusive Literacy Instruction in the Elementary Classroom*, authors Caitlin Ryan and Jill Hermann-Wilmarth, present classroom scenarios that demonstrate how to incorporate LGBTQ topics in English language arts using existing curriculum and reading materials.[15] Their suggestions include strategies for expanding the representation of LGBTQ people and applying a queer lens to straight books. Adapting curriculum to be gender-inclusive does not have to be onerous. As we saw in the opening vignette, Mickie Cullen significantly altered the hygiene lesson simply by reframing the content using gender-neutral language.

Developing formal policies and written curriculum intended to support transgender students signals that gender equity is a priority and legitimizes individual educators' efforts to shift gender norms to be more inclusive and affirming. At the same time, new policies and curriculum require dedicated resources for successful implementation. Not only do educators need opportunities to engage in the kind of deep learning that can help change practice, but those practices also need to be monitored and accountability systems need to be in place as a way to provide both pressure and support. In that context, new curriculum, in tandem with policy guidelines that support gender-affirming educational practices, can positively influence our capacity to reculture schools for gender equity.

CONCLUSION

The educators featured in this book embraced opportunities to learn about transgender identities, and as a result of their new understandings, they actively supported the transgender and gender-expansive students in their schools. Supportive principals set the stage, and as a result, educators honored transgender students' names and pronouns; they developed new, gender-affirming practices; they defended their students' interests and needs. Collectively, these educators demonstrate what is possible and provide an exemplar to other educators who want all students to feel a sense of belonging in schools. At the same time, educators' efforts to support individual students were insufficient to disrupt binary gender norms and sustain meaningful change. The larger problem of gender inequity remained.

For schools to become spaces of belonging and affirmation for transgender and gender-expansive students, we need to reculture schools for gender equity. This is not a simple task. Reculturing schools for gender equity is a process that depends on individual educators' willingness to challenge binary gender norms and engage collaboratively with colleagues to co-construct new shared norms that recognize and affirm the diversity of gender identities. New norms do not develop from a checklist. Reculturing for gender equity is a formidable task that requires sustained commitment to deep, meaningful change. Individually and collectively, educators will need to make space for transgender identities, engage in difficult conversations about gender, and develop policies and curriculum needed to make schools gender-affirming spaces of belonging for transgender and gender-expansive children.

Methodology

The stories and information presented in this book are drawn from a qualitative research project that was supported by the Spencer Foundation. The study design conformed to Institutional Review Board (IRB) approved procedures for use with human subjects including informed consent and confidentiality safeguards. Data collection was executed in two phases over eighteen months, January 2017 through June 2018.

PHASE ONE

The first phase focused on supportive elementary school leaders, primarily principals. Drawing on my network of support organizations for parents of transgender children, including but not limited to PFLAG and GLSEN, I asked parents for recommendations of supportive principals. I sampled for variation, including participants from different states to represent a range of legal, political, and educational contexts. All participants met three criteria for participation. First, they were educational leaders working in an elementary school setting. Second, they had experience working with transgender youth in their school setting. And, third, the leaders were perceived as supportive by the parents recommending them for participation in the study. For the purpose of this study, the notion of "supportive" was entirely subjective and defined by the parents. As such, there is no common understanding across parents about what constitutes support. Moreover, I accepted the parents' perception at face value and with no effort to measure or categorize different types of support. This decision recognizes that children's needs differ, and the kinds of support they require from educators may similarly differ.

Some additional sampling considerations from phase one focused on the following criteria. When principals worked in schools with both elementary and middle school populations, they were included if the transgender student was enrolled prior to grade 6. All of the schools had at least one transgender or gender-expansive child, whose parent recommended the principal as a possible participant. The child did not have to be a current student. Some schools had more than one identifiable (known to the principal) gender-expansive or transgender student.

The final purposeful sample of supportive elementary school leaders was drawn from twenty schools in the Northeast region of the United States. Of these leaders, nineteen were principals. One school, Pacificus Learning Collaboratory, used a collaborative teacher-run model of leadership; therefore, I interviewed the teacher who led efforts to support the transgender student. When the term *principal* is used in this volume, the lead teacher from Pacificus Learning Collaboratory is included. The final sample of schools was drawn from six states: New Jersey (n = 2), New York (n = 6), Delaware (n = 1), Rhode Island (n = 1), Massachusetts (n = 8), and Pennsylvania (n = 2). The schools included fifteen public, one public-charter, three private-independent, and one private-religious school. The community populations ranged from four thousand people to 2.6 million. Median family income within the communities ranged from $26,000 to $160,000 annually and skewed more heavily toward middle and upper incomes. Thirteen communities were predominantly White, with populations ranging from 60 to 92 percent White. In the seven communities that were majority People of Color, there was a mix of racial and ethnic identities. For example, one community was 64 percent Latinx and another was 42 percent Black (see table 1).

Data for phase one were collected using semistructured interviews with the school leader and lasted approximately forty-five minutes. Two interviews were conducted by phone, and all others were conducted face to face at the principals' schools.

TABLE 1

School Community Demographics

	SCHOOL NAME	SCHOOL TYPE	COMMUNITY POPULATION	COMMUNITY RACIAL/ETHNIC MAKE-UP	COMMUNITY MEDIAN FAMILY INCOME
A	Aberdeen Academy School	Private-independent	150,000	45% Latinx (any race) 33% White (non-Latinx) 19% Black 2% Asian	$37,000
B	Belmont Elementary	Public	40,000	44% White (non-Latinx) 27% Black 19% Latinx (any race) 8% Asian	$108,000
C	Crescent Elementary	Public	75,000	60% White (non-Latinx) 28% Latinx (any race) 7% Black 3% Asian	$45,000
D	Dixon Primary	Public	210,000	42% Black 37% White (non-Latinx) 16% Latinx (any race) 3% Asian	$31,000
E	Evergreen Elementary	Public	5,000	92% White (non-Latinx) 4% Latinx (any race) 2% Black	$84,000
F	Forrest School	Public	23,000	70% White (non-Latinx) 25% Asian	$156,000
G	Griffin Elementary	Public	68,000	65% White (non-Latinx) 13% Latinx (any race) 6% Black 6% Asian	$100,000
H	Harborside Cooperative School	Public	1,600,000	46% White (non-Latinx) 26% Latinx (any race) 17% Black 12% Asian	$72,000
I	Iroquois Valley Elementary	Public	210,000	42% Black 37% White (non-Latinx) 16% Latinx (any race) 3% Asian	$31,000
J	Jefferson Elementary	Public	58,000	81% White (non-Latinx) 7% Asian 5% Black 3% Latinx (any race)	$115,000
K	Kirby Learning Center	Private-independent	17,000	87% White (non-Latinx) 7% Latinx (any race) 2% Black	$46,000

(continues)

	SCHOOL NAME	SCHOOL TYPE	COMMUNITY POPULATION	COMMUNITY RACIAL/ETHNIC MAKE-UP	COMMUNITY MEDIAN FAMILY INCOME
L	Lincoln School	Public	12,000	78% White (non-Latinx) 11% Asian 7% Latinx (any race)	$160,000
M	Mercer Elementary	Public	68,000	65% White (non-Latinx) 13% Latinx (any race) 6% Black 6% Asian	$100,000
N	Northstar Charter	Public-charter	19,000	64% Latinx (any race) 20% White (non-Latinx) 14% Black	$26,000
O	Ovid Preparatory	Private Religious	2,600,000	36% White (non-Latinx) 35% Black 20% Latinx (any race) 12% Asian	$45,000
P	Pacificus Learning Collaboratory	Private-independent	33,000	72% White (non-Latinx) 10% Black 9% Asian 7% Latinx (any race)	$75,000
Q	Quail Road Elementary	Public	4,000	91% White (non-Latinx) 4% Asian 3% Latinx (any race)	$150,000
R	Rosa Parks Public School PS 25	Public	2,600,000	35% White (non-Latinx) 35% Black 19% Latinx (any race) 11% Asian	$45,000
S	Silas Country School	Public	1,500	90% White (non-Latinx) 6% Latinx (any race)	$72,000
T	Talbot Elementary	Public	15,000	75% White (non-Latinx) 13% Latinx (any race) 8% Asian 2% Black	$122,000

Source: www.census.gov

Note: Percentages for community racial/ethnic make-up do not always equal 100 percent. In some instances, rounding to whole numbers produces a total greater than 100 percent. In other instances, groups with populations under 1 percent do not appear in the table and, therefore, some totals are less than 100 percent.

PHASE TWO

The second phase of the research involved case studies of a subset of schools drawn from the sample of schools with supportive elementary school principals. All schools with an identifiable (known to the principal) transgender or gender-expansive student currently enrolled were invited to participate in the case study phase. Principals were informed that the case studies would include voluntary interviews with approximately ten educators and, possibly, voluntary observations of typical school activities and interviews with parents of the transgender or gender-expansive student. Five principals from five different states expressed interest in participating, and all were included in phase two of this study.

To recruit educators for participation in the case studies, principals either notified their colleagues or provided me with contact information so that I could directly invite educators to participate. The only criterion for participation was that educators have some knowledge of or experience interacting with the transgender or gender-expansive student. The case study participants included educators from the child's school as well as other persons knowledgeable about school- and district-level policies or practices. All except four of the semistructured interviews were conducted in person and typically lasted forty-five minutes although parent interviews lasted two to three hours. In addition to interviews, I conducted observations and collected artifacts such as written policies, letters, and emails, plus curricular and training materials (see table 2).

In addition to the phase one principal interviews and phase two cases study interviews, I conducted nine additional interviews with participants associated with non-case study schools. These were parents or educators who either asked to be interviewed and/or were recommended by the participating principal even though their school was not participating in phase two of the study. Specifically, two parents requested to be interviewed, along with four teachers and two school psychologists. I also interviewed one state-level Department of Education LGBTQ program provider. The total number of formal interviews conducted as part of this study was seventy-five.

For both phases of the study, data trustworthiness was facilitated through in-depth interview techniques, including strict confidentiality for participants and sequencing of questions from recall and descriptive queries to more interpretive and feelings-based inquiries.[1] All interviews were audiorecorded and transcribed verbatim. Data analysis procedures were ongoing and inductive, building on insights from the study participants.[2] The names of all study participants, students, and schools in this book

TABLE 2

Case Study Data Sources

SCHOOL/STATE/ STUDENT	FORMAL INTERVIEWS	OTHER DATA SOURCES
Mercer Elementary, Massachusetts, Meredith	1. Principal, Mercer Elementary 2. Principal, Griffin Elementary (former Mercer Principal when Meredith was in grades K–3) 3. Fifth-Grade Teacher 4. Fifth-Grade Teacher 5. Fourth-Grade Teacher 6. Third-Grade Teacher 7. High School Educator (engaged in district-level policy development) 8. Social Worker 9. Health Educator 10. Meredith's Parent	Observation/participation in regional transgender conference. Observation of professional learning session. *Review of* • school handbook from Mercer elementary school • emails between parents, teachers, counselor, principals, superintendent (n = 26) over four years • resource list provided by parent to schools • online posts to gender forum by Meredith's parent • State Department of Education transgender policy • related local news articles
Jefferson Elementary, Pennsylvania, Jacob	1. Principal, Jefferson Elementary, K–5 2. Fourth-Grade Teacher 3. Third-Grade Teacher 4. Second-Grade Teacher 5. First-Grade Teacher 6. Kindergarten Teacher 7. School Counselor 8. Middle School Educator (engaged in district-level policy development) 9. Learning Consultant 10. Jacob's Parent 11. Principal at Jackson Elementary, K–5 (another school in this district; this principal was not part of phase one) 12. Jackson Parent with transgender child	Observation/participation in regional transgender conference. Inspection of Jefferson bathroom facilities. *Review of* • district policies and guidelines • Gender and Sexuality Advisory Committee (G-SAC) agendas • related local news articles • district website materials, including name change forms • online posts to gender forum by Jacob's parent • letters to other parents introducing Jacob's new name and pronouns; letter to Jefferson teachers; letter to the health and sexuality teacher

SCHOOL/STATE/ STUDENT	FORMAL INTERVIEWS	OTHER DATA SOURCES
Northstar Charter, Rhode Island, Natalia	1. Principal 2. Sixth-Grade Teacher 3. Fourth-Grade Teacher 4. First-Grade Teacher 5. Preservice Teacher 6. Middle School Teacher 7. Middle School Teacher 8. Special Education Teacher 9. Behavioral Specialist 10. School Psychologist 11. Director of Social-Emotional Support	Observation/participation in day-long professional learning session. Observations of school and classroom practices over two days. *Review of* • State Department of Education transgender policy • school website and policies • related local news articles • curricular materials related to gender • student work related to gender including video
Pacificus Learning Collaboratory, Delaware, Sophie	1. Lead teacher 2. School founder 3. Grades 5/6 Teacher 4. Grades 5/6 Teacher 5. Grades 3/4 Teacher 6. Grades K/1/2 Teacher 7. Spanish Teacher 8. Sophie's Parent 9. Parent of a gender-questioning child	Observations of school and classroom practices over two days. Observation/participation in community learning event sponsored by Equality Delaware. *Review of* • school website and policies • related local news articles • curricular materials related to gender • student work related to gender
Rosa Parks Public School (PS 25), New York, Leo	1. Principal 2. Assistant Principal 3. Fifth-Grade Teacher 4. First-Grade Teacher 5. First-Grade Teacher 6. First-Grade Teacher 7. Kindergarten Teacher 8. Long-term Substitute Teacher 9. Afsaneh Moradian, author 10. Leo's Parent	Observation of professional learning session. Day-long observation of school/classroom practice. *Review of* • State Department of Education transgender policy • school website and policies • related local news articles • curricular materials related to gender • student work related to gender • online posts to gender forum by Leo's parent

are pseudonyms, with the exception of Afsaneh Moradian. All cities and districts are also pseudonyms, with the exception of New York City. State names are not pseudonyms.

Despite a robust study design, two methodological limitations merit mention. First, the findings were drawn from participants' self-reports, which may be partial representations or not reflect the experiences of other school community members. Second, as part of the sampling criteria, the study participants were characterized as supportive of transgender and gender-expansive students. Likewise, the students' parents were also supportive of their children's gender identities. As a result, findings from this study may not generalize to other school populations where either educators or parents may not support transgender and gender-expansive children.

Resources for Educators

RESOURCES: WEBSITES

The following list of resources is not comprehensive. Descriptions are drawn from each resource's website, and additional information can be found online.

Organizations with K–12 Lesson Plans Related to Gender Identity

Welcoming Schools, a project of the Human Rights Campaign Foundation

www.welcomingschools.org/

Welcoming Schools is a professional development program that provides training and resources to elementary school educators to embrace all families, create LGBTQ and gender-inclusive schools, prevent bias-based bullying, and support transgender and nonbinary students.

Teaching Tolerance, a project of the Southern Poverty Law Center

www.tolerance.org/

Teaching Tolerance provides free resources to K–12 educators that can be used to create civil and inclusive school communities where children are respected, valued, and welcome participants. The program emphasizes social justice and anti-bias.

Gender Spectrum

www.genderspectrum.org/

Gender Spectrum's mission is to create a gender-inclusive world for all children and youth. The website includes a broad range of downloadable school-specific resource materials including sample training materials, how-to guides, and policy guidelines.

GLSEN

www.glsen.org/

GLSEN is an education organization working to end discrimination, harassment, and bullying based on sexual orientation, gender identity, and gender expression and to prompt LGBT cultural inclusion and awareness in K–12 schools. The website includes lessons, research, activities, and downloadable infographs and posters.

LGBTQ+ Organizations That Provide Services and Informational Resources

National Center for Transgender Equality

https://transequality.org/

The National Center for Transgender Equality advocates to change policies and society to increase understanding and acceptance of transgender people. The website includes information related to legal rights including health care, employment, housing, legal documents, and schools.

PFLAG

https://pflag.org/

PFLAG extends support to LGBTQ families, friends, and allies through a vast network of local chapters that include support groups and educational activities.

Transgender Training Institute

www.transgendertraininginstitute.com/

The Transgender Training Institute provides national training and consulting services that are informed and provided by transgender and nonbinary people, for the benefit of transgender and nonbinary communities. The organization provides services including expert facilitation of transgender-related professional development trainings, training of trainers/facilitators, and ally skill building.

Trans Youth Equality Foundation

www.transyouthequality.org/

The Trans Youth Equality Foundation is a nonprofit organization that provides education, advocacy, and support for transgender and gender-nonconforming children and youth and their families. The website includes, among other materials, a list of books with gender-diverse characters that are appropriate for elementary-age children.

Trevor Project

www.thetrevorproject.org/

The Trevor Project provides crisis intervention and suicide prevention services to lesbian, gay, bisexual, transgender, queer and/or questioning (LGBTQ) young people under age twenty-five.

Other Online Resources

The Trans Language Primer

www.translanguageprimer.org/

The Trans Language Primer is an extensive guide to the language of gender, sexuality, accessibility, and acceptance. Terms are listed with their definition(s), part(s) of speech, examples, and links for extended context.

US Department of Education, Office for Civil Rights (OCR)

www2.ed.gov/about/offices/list/ocr/docs/howto.html?src=rt

Historically, the Office for Civil Rights' mission has been to ensure equal access to education and to promote educational excellence through vigorous enforcement of civil rights in our nation's schools. Any person or organization may file a complaint, including on behalf of another person, if they believe someone has experienced discrimination or their civil rights have been violated. Complaints can be filed electronically, and anonymously, via the OCR website.

RESOURCES: BOOKS

Introductory Resources for K–12 Educators

About Gender Identity Justice in Schools and Communities by sj Miller (Teachers College Press, 2019)

> "This book carefully walks readers through both theory and practice to equip them with the skills needed to bring gender identity justice into classrooms, schools, and ultimately society. The text looks into the root causes and ways to change the conditions that have created gender identity injustice."

Everything You Ever Wanted to Know About Trans by Brynn Tannehill (Jessica Kingsley Publishers, 2018)

> "This book aims to break down deeply held misconceptions about trans people across all aspects of life, from politics, law and culture, through to science, religion and mental health, to provide readers with a deeper understanding of what it means to be trans. The book walks the reader through transgender issues, starting with "What does transgender mean?" before moving on to more complex topics including growing up trans, dating and sex, medical and mental health, and debates around gender and feminism."

Gender: Your Guide: A Gender-Friendly Primer on What to Know, What to Say, and What to Do in the New Gender Culture by Lee Airton (Simon and Schuster, 2018)

> "Professor and gender diversity advocate Lee Airton, PhD, explains how gender works in everyday life; how to use accurate terminology to refer to transgender, non-binary, and/or gender non-conforming individuals; and how to ask when you aren't sure what to do or say. It provides the information you need to talk confidently and compassionately about gender diversity, whether simply having a conversation or going to bat as an advocate."

Safe Is Not Enough: Better Schools for LGBTQ Students by Michael
Sadowski (Harvard Education Press, 2016)

> "*Safe Is Not Enough* illustrates how educators can support the posi-
> tive development of LGBTQ students in a comprehensive way so as
> to create truly inclusive school communities. Using examples from
> classrooms, schools, and districts across the country, Michael Sadowski
> identifies emerging practices such as creating an LGBTQ-inclusive cur-
> riculum; fostering a whole-school climate that is supportive of LGBTQ
> students; providing adults who can act as mentors and role models;
> and initiating effective family and community outreach programs."

Transgender 101: A Simple Guide to a Complex Issue by Nicholas Teich
(Columbia University Press, 2012)

> Written by a social worker, popular educator, and member of the
> transgender community, this well-rounded resource provides an acces-
> sible portrait of transgender life and its unique experiences of discrim-
> ination. Chapters describe the coming-out process and its effect on
> family and friends, and the relationship between sexual orientation
> and gender. This book is written for students, professionals, friends,
> and family members.

Picture Books for Children

Annie's Plaid Shirt by Stacy B. Davids (Upswing Press, 2015)

> "Annie loves her plaid shirt and wears it everywhere. But one day her
> mom tells Annie that she must wear a dress to her uncle's wedding.
> Annie protests, but her mom insists and buys her a fancy new dress
> anyway. Annie is miserable. She feels weird in dresses. Why can't her
> mom understand? Then Annie has an idea. But will her mom agree?"

I Am Jazz by Jessica Herthel and Jazz Jennings (Dial Books, 2014)

> "From the time she was two years old, Jazz knew that she had a
> girl's brain in a boy's body. She loved pink and dressing up as a
> mermaid and didn't feel like herself in boys' clothing. This con-
> fused her family, until they took her to a doctor who said that

Jazz was transgender and that she was born that way. Jazz's story is based on her real-life experience and she tells it in a simple, clear way that will be appreciated by picture book readers, their parents, and teachers."

Introducing Teddy: A Gentle Story About Gender and Friendship by Jessica Walton (Bloomsbury USA Children's Books, 2016)

"Errol and his teddy, Thomas, are best friends who do everything together. Whether it's riding a bike, playing in the tree house, having a tea party, or all of the above, every day holds something fun to do. One sunny day, Errol finds that Thomas is sad, even when they are playing in their favorite ways. Errol can't figure out why, until Thomas finally tells Errol what the teddy has been afraid to say: 'In my heart, I've always known that I'm a girl teddy, not a boy teddy. I wish my name was Tilly, not Thomas.' And Errol says, 'I don't care if you're a girl teddy or a boy teddy! What matters is that you are my friend.'"

Jack (Not Jackie) by Erica Silverman (little bee books, 2018)

"Susan thinks her little sister Jackie has the best giggle! She can't wait for Jackie to get older so they can do all sorts of things like play forest fairies and be explorers together. But as Jackie grows, she doesn't want to play those games. She wants to play with mud and be a super bug! Jackie also doesn't like dresses or her long hair, and she would rather be called Jack."

Jacob's New Dress by Sarah Hoffman and Ian Hoffman (Albert Whitman & Company, 2014)

"Jacob loves playing dress-up, when he can be anything he wants to be. Some kids at school say he can't wear 'girl' clothes, but Jacob wants to wear a dress to school. Can he convince his parents to let him wear what he wants? This heartwarming story speaks to the unique challenges faced by boys who don't identify with traditional gender roles."

Jacob's Room to Choose by Sarah Hoffman and Ian Hoffman (Magination Press, 2019)

"When Jacob goes to the boys' bathroom he is chased out because the boys think he looks like a girl because of the way he is dressed. His classmate, Sophie, has a similar experience when she tries to go to the girls' bathroom. When their teacher finds out what happened, Jacob and Sophie, with the support of administration, lead change at their school as everyone discovers the many forms of gender expression and how to treat each other with respect."

Jamie and Bubbie: A Book About People's Pronouns by Afsaneh Moradian (Free Spirit Publishing, 2020)

"Jamie is excited to spend the day walking around the neighborhood with great-grandma Bubbie. They meet so many friends and neighbors along the way . . . but Jamie has to correct Bubbie when she assumes Ms. Wallace is a he and their server is a she. Jamie helps Bubbie understand that it's important not to assume a person's pronouns based on appearance, and to always use the name and pronouns they go by: he, she, they, or something else. The story stays lighthearted and sweet, while diving into an often misunderstood, evolving topic, so children can build empathy and begin to explore their own feelings about gender identity. A section at the back of the book includes tips for teachers, parents, and caregivers for expanding on the concepts in the book and for talking with children about gender."

Jamie Is Jamie: A Book About Being Yourself and Playing Your Way by Afsaneh Moradian (Free Spirit Publishing, 2018)

"There are so many fun things to play with at Jamie's new preschool—baby dolls to care for, toy cars to drive—and Jamie wants to play with them all! But the other children are confused . . . is Jamie a boy or a girl? Some toys are just for girls and others are just for boys, aren't they? Not according to Jamie! This book challenges gender stereotypes, shows readers that playing is fundamental to learning, and reinforces the idea that all children need the freedom to play unencumbered. A special section for teachers, parents, and caregivers provides tips on how to make children's playtime learning time."

Julián Is a Mermaid by Jessica Love (Candlewick, 2018)

"While riding the subway home from the pool with his abuela one day, Julián notices three women spectacularly dressed up. Their hair billows in brilliant hues, their dresses end in fishtails, and their joy fills the train car. When Julián gets home, daydreaming of the magic he's seen, all he can think about is dressing up just like the ladies in his own fabulous mermaid costume: a butter-yellow curtain for his tail, the fronds of a potted fern for his headdress. But what will Abuela think about the mess he makes—and even more importantly, what will she think about how Julián sees himself?"

Morris Micklewhite and the Tangerine Dress by Christine Baldacchino (Groundwood Books, 2014)

"Morris is a little boy who loves using his imagination. But most of all, Morris loves wearing the tangerine dress in his classroom's dress-up center. The children in Morris's class don't understand. Dresses, they say, are for girls. And Morris certainly isn't welcome in the spaceship some of his classmates are building. Astronauts, they say, don't wear dresses. One day when Morris feels all alone and sick from their taunts, his mother lets him stay home from school. Morris dreams of a fantastic space adventure with his cat, Moo. Inspired by his dream, Morris paints the incredible scene he saw and brings it with him to school. He builds his own spaceship, hangs his painting on the front of it and takes two of his classmates on an outer space adventure."

One of A Kind, Like Me / Único Como Yo by Laurin Mayeno and Robert Liu-Trujillo (Blood Orange Press, 2016)

"Tomorrow is the school parade, and Danny knows exactly what he will be: a princess. Mommy supports him 100% and they race to the thrift store to find his costume. It's almost closing time—will Danny find the costume of his dreams in time? *One of A Kind, Like Me / Único Como Yo* is a sweet story about unconditional love and the beauty of individuality. It's a unique book that lifts up children who don't fit gender stereotypes and reflects the power of a loving and supportive community."

Phoenix Goes to School: A Story to Support Transgender and Gender Diverse Children by Michelle Finch and Phoenix Finch (Jessica Kingsley Publishers, 2018)

"Phoenix is preparing for her first day of school. She is excited but scared of being bullied because of her gender identity and expression. Yet when she arrives at school she finds help and support from teachers and friends, *and* finds she is brave enough to talk to other kids about her gender! This is an empowering and brightly-illustrated children's book for children aged 3+ to help children engage with gender identity in a fun, uplifting way."

Pink Is for Boys by Robb Pearlman (Running Press Kids, 2018)

"Pink is for boys . . . and girls . . . and everyone! This timely and beautiful picture book rethinks and reframes the stereotypical blue/pink gender binary and empowers kids—and their grown-ups—to express themselves in every color of the rainbow. Featuring a diverse group of relatable characters, *Pink Is for Boys* invites and encourages girls and boys to enjoy what they love to do, whether it's racing cars and playing baseball, or loving unicorns and dressing up. Vibrant illustrations help children learn and identify the myriad colors that surround them every day, from the orange of a popsicle, to the green of a grassy field, all the way up to the wonder of a multicolored rainbow."

Red: A Crayon's Story by Michael Hall (Greenwillow Books, 2015)

"Red has a bright red label, but he is, in fact, blue. His teacher tries to help him be red (let's draw strawberries!), his mother tries to help him be red by sending him out on a playdate with a yellow classmate (go draw a nice orange!), and the scissors try to help him be red by snipping his label so that he has room to breathe. But Red is miserable. He just can't be red, no matter how hard he tries! Finally, a brand-new friend offers a brand-new perspective, and Red discovers what readers have known all along. He's blue! This funny, heartwarming, colorful picture book about finding the courage to be true to your inner self can be read on multiple levels, and it offers something for everyone."

Sparkle Boy by Leslea Newman (Lee & Low Books, 2017)

"Casey loves to play with his blocks, puzzles, and dump truck, but he also loves things that sparkle, shimmer, and glitter. When his older sister, Jessie, shows off her new shimmery skirt, Casey wants to wear a shimmery skirt too. When Jessie comes home from a party with glittery nails, Casey wants glittery nails too. And when Abuelita visits wearing an armful of sparkly bracelets, Casey gets one to wear, just like Jessie. The adults in Casey's life embrace his interests, but Jessie isn't so sure. Boys aren't supposed to wear sparkly, shimmery, glittery things. Then, when older boys at the library tease Casey for wearing 'girl' things, Jessie realizes that Casey has the right to be himself and wear whatever he wants. Why can't both she and Casey love all things shimmery, glittery, and sparkly?"

Teddy's Favorite Toy by Christian Trimmer (Atheneum Books for Young Readers, 2018)

"Teddy has a lot of cool toys. But his very favorite doll has the best manners, the sickest fighting skills, and a fierce sense of style. Then one morning, something truly awful happens. And there's only one woman fierce enough to save the day. Can Teddy's mom reunite Teddy with his favorite toy?"

When Aidan Became a Brother by Kyle Lukoff (Lee & Low Books, 2019)

"When Aidan was born, everyone thought he was a girl. His parents gave him a pretty name, his room looked like a girl's room, and he wore clothes that other girls liked wearing. After he realized he was a trans boy, Aidan and his parents fixed the parts of his life that didn't fit anymore, and he settled happily into his new life. Then Mom and Dad announce that they're going to have another baby, and Aidan wants to do everything he can to make things right for his new sibling from the beginning—from choosing the perfect name to creating a beautiful room to picking out the cutest onesie. But what does 'making things right' actually mean? And what happens if he messes up?"

Nonfiction for Children

It Feels Good to Be Yourself: A Book About Gender Identity by Theresa Thorn (Henry Holt and Co., 2019)

> "Some people are boys. Some people are girls. Some people are both, neither, or somewhere in between. This sweet, straightforward exploration of gender identity will give children a fuller understanding of themselves and others. With child-friendly language and vibrant art, *It Feels Good to Be Yourself* provides young readers and parents alike with the vocabulary to discuss this important topic with sensitivity."

Sex Is a Funny Word: A Book about Bodies, Feelings, and YOU by Cory Silverberg (Triangle Square, 2015)

> "A comic book for kids that includes children and families of all makeups, orientations, and gender identities, *Sex Is a Funny Word* is an essential resource about bodies, gender, and sexuality for children ages 8 to 10 as well as their parents and caregivers. Much more than the 'facts of life' or 'the birds and the bees,' *Sex Is a Funny Word* opens up conversations between young people and their caregivers in a way that allows adults to convey their values and beliefs while providing information about boundaries, safety, and joy."

The Gender Wheel—School Edition: A Story About Bodies and Gender for Every Body by Maya Christina Gonzalez (Reflection Press, 2018)

> "This School Edition takes the original book, *The Gender Wheel* (2017), and puts clothes on all the kids to be more conducive to school environments. It is a powerful opportunity for kids to understand the origins of the current binary gender system, how we can learn from nature to see the truth that has always existed and revision a new story that includes room for all bodies and genders. *The Gender*

Wheel offers a nature-based, holistic non-western framework of gender in a kid-friendly way. Also included are Teacher Tips on how to hold a holistic perspective on gender in the classroom."

They She He Me: Free to Be! by Maya Christina Gonzalez and Matthew SG (Reflection Press, 2017)

"Pronouns serve as a familiar starting point for kids and grown-ups to expand ideas about gender and celebrate personal expression with fun imagery that provides a place to meet and play."

What Makes a Baby by Cory Silverberg (Triangle Square, 2013)

"Geared to readers from preschool to age eight, *What Makes a Baby* is a book for every kind of family and every kind of kid. It is a twenty-first century children's picture book about conception, gestation, and birth, which reflects the reality of our modern time by being inclusive of all kinds of kids, adults, and families, regardless of how many people were involved, their orientation, gender and other identity, or family composition. Just as important, the story doesn't gender people or body parts, so most parents and families will find that it leaves room for them to educate their child without having to erase their own experience."

Who Are You?: The Kid's Guide to Gender Identity by Brook Pessin-Whedbee (Jessica Kingsley Publishers, 2016)

"This brightly illustrated children's book provides a straightforward introduction to gender for anyone aged 5–8. It presents clear and direct language for understanding and talking about how we experience gender: our bodies, our expression and our identity. An interactive three-layered wheel included in the book is a simple, yet powerful, tool to clearly demonstrate the difference between our body, how we express ourselves through our clothes and hobbies, and our gender identity. Ideal for use in the classroom or at home, a short page-by-page guide for adults at the back of the book further explains the key concepts and identifies useful discussion points."

Upper-Elementary Fiction

George by Alex Gino (Scholastic Press, 2015)

"When people look at George, they think they see a boy. But she knows she's not a boy. She knows she's a girl. George thinks she'll have to keep this a secret forever. Then her teacher announces that their class play is going to be *Charlotte's Web*. George really, really, REALLY wants to play Charlotte. But the teacher says she can't even try out for the part . . . because she's a boy. With the help of her best friend, Kelly, George comes up with a plan. Not just so she can be Charlotte—but so everyone can know who she is, once and for all."

Gracefully Grayson by Ami Polonsky (Disney-Hyperion, 2016)

"*What if who you are on the outside doesn't match who you are on the inside?* Grayson Sender has been holding onto a secret for what seems like forever: 'he' is a girl on the inside, stuck in the wrong gender's body. The weight of this secret is crushing, but sharing it would mean facing ridicule, scorn, rejection, or worse. Despite the risks, Grayson's true self itches to break free. Will new strength from an unexpected friendship and a caring teacher's wisdom be enough to help Grayson step into the spotlight she was born to inhabit?"

Lily and Dunkin by Donna Gephart (Yearling, 2018)

"Lily Jo McGrother, born Timothy McGrother, is a girl. But being a girl is not so easy when you look like a boy. Especially when you're in the eighth grade. Dunkin Dorfman, birth name Norbert Dorfman, is dealing with bipolar disorder and has just moved from the New Jersey town he's called home for the past thirteen years. This would be hard enough, but the fact that he is also hiding from a painful secret makes it even worse. One summer morning, Lily Jo McGrother meets Dunkin Dorfman, and their lives forever change."

The Other Boy by M. G. Hennessey (HarperCollins, 2019)

"Twelve-year-old Shane Woods is just a regular boy. He loves pitching for his baseball team, working on his graphic novel, and hanging out with his best friend, Josh. But Shane is keeping something private, something that might make a difference to his friends and teammates, even Josh. And when a classmate threatens to reveal his secret, Shane's whole world comes crashing down. It will take a lot of courage for Shane to ignore the hate and show the world that he's still the same boy he was before. And in the end, those who stand beside him may surprise everyone, including Shane.'

The Witch Boy by Molly Knox Ostertag (Graphix, 2017)

"In thirteen-year-old Aster's family, all the girls are raised to be witches, while boys grow up to be shapeshifters. Anyone who dares cross those lines is exiled. Unfortunately for Aster, he still hasn't shifted . . . and he's still fascinated by witchery, no matter how forbidden it might be. When a mysterious danger threatens the other boys, Aster knows he can help—as a witch. It will take the encouragement of a new friend, the non-magical and non-conforming Charlie, to convince Aster to try practicing his skills. And it will require even more courage to save his family . . . and be truly himself."

Glossary

This glossary is reprinted from the Teaching Transgender Toolkit that was developed by the Transgender Training Institute (TTI). TTI is a trans-owned training and consulting company, providing national trainings and consulting services that are facilitated and informed by transgender and nonbinary individuals, for the benefit of transgender and nonbinary people and communities.

Some terms included in this glossary are not used in this book. In contrast, one term from the book that is not included in this glossary is *medico-legal sex*. As described in chapter 2, "Transgender and Gender-Expansive Children," sex takes on both medical and legal aspects, which are regulated by federal and state-level government entities. As a medico-legal category, the criteria used to define and determine sex can differ based on legal context and not solely on the basis of biology or medical expertise. In the United States, sex is more commonly a medico-legal category than a biological determination. For further information on how our understanding of sex is influenced by social conventions, see Anne Fausto-Sterling's book *Sex/Gender: Biology in a Social World* (New York: Routledge, 2012).

GLOSSARY OF TRANSGENDER TERMS

Transgender Training Institute

This is a glossary of some of the more common terms that are used when discussing transgender identities and experiences. Definitions and preferred terms will vary by location and group.

Affirming: The unequivocal support for an individual person's gender identity or expression, regardless of the biological sex they were assigned at birth; the systematic support to ensure that transgender people and communities are fully represented, included, valued and honored.

Affirming Pronouns: Refers to the most respectful and accurate pronouns for a person, as defined by that person. This is also sometimes referred to as "preferred gender pronouns," although this phrasing is increasingly outdated. To ascertain someone's affirming pronouns, ask: "What are your pronouns?"

Agender: A person who does not identify as having a gender identity that can be categorized as male or female, and sometimes indicates identifying as not having a gender identity.

AG/Aggressive: A term used to describe a female-bodied and identified person who prefers presenting as masculine. This term is most commonly used in urban communities of color.

Biological Sex: A person's combination of genitals, chromosomes, and hormones, usually categorized as "male" or "female" based on visual inspection of genitals via ultrasound or at birth. Many assume that a person's gender identity will be congruent with their sex assignment. Everyone has a biological sex.

Bigender: A person who experiences gender identity as two genders at the same time, or whose gender identity may vary between two genders. These may be masculine and feminine, or could also include non-binary identities.

Butch: A term used to describe a masculine person or gender expression.

Cisgender: (pronounced /sis-gender/): An adjective to describe a person whose gender identity is congruent with (or "matches") the biological sex they were assigned at birth. (Some people abbreviate this as "cis").

Coming Out: The process through which a transgender person acknowledges and explains their gender identity to themselves and others.

(Anti-Transgender) Discrimination: Any of a broad range of actions taken to deny transgender people access to situations/places or to inflict harm upon transgender people. Examples of discrimination include: not hiring a transgender person, threatening a gender non-conforming person's physical safety, denying a transgender person access to services, or reporting someone for using the "wrong" bathroom.

Gender Binary: The idea that gender is strictly an either/or option of male/men/masculine or female/woman/feminine based on sex assigned at birth, rather than a continuum or spectrum of gender identities and expressions. The gender binary is often considered to be limiting and problematic for all people, and especially for those who do not fit neatly into the either/or categories.

Femme: A term used to describe a feminine person or gender expression.

Femme Queen: A term used to describe someone who is male bodied but identifies as and expresses feminine gender. Used primarily in urban communities, particularly in communities of color and ballroom communities.

Gender Conforming: A person whose gender expression is perceived as being consistent with cultural norms expected for that gender. According to these norms, boys/men are or should be masculine, and girls/women are or should be feminine. Not all cisgender people are gender conforming and not all transgender people are gender non-conforming. (For example, a transgender woman may have a very feminine gender expression).

Gender Dysphoria (GD): The formal diagnosis in the *American Psychiatric Association's Diagnostic and Statistical Manual*, Fifth Edition (DSM 5), used by psychologists and physicians to indicate that a person meets the diagnostic criteria to engage in medical transition. In other words, the medical diagnosis for being transgender. Formerly known as Gender Identity Disorder (GID). The inclusion of Gender Dysphoria as a diagnosis in the DSM 5 is controversial in transgender communities because it implies that being transgender is a mental illness rather than a valid identity. On the other hand, since a formal diagnosis is generally required in order to receive or provide treatment in the US, it does provide access to medical care for some people who wouldn't ordinarily be eligible to receive it.

Gender Expression: A person's outward gender presentation, usually comprised of personal style, clothing, hairstyle, makeup, jewelry, vocal inflection and body language. Gender expression is typically categorized as masculine or feminine, less commonly as androgynous. All people express a gender. Gender expression can be congruent with a person's gender identity, but it can also be incongruent if a person does not feel safe or supported, or does not have the resources needed to engage in gender expression that authentically reflects their gender identity.

Genderfluid: A person whose gender identity or expression shifts between masculine and feminine, or falls somewhere along this spectrum.

Gender Identity: A person's deep-seated, internal sense of who they are as a gendered being—specifically, the gender with which they identify themselves. All people have a gender identity.

Gender Marker: The marker (male or female) that appears on a person's identity documents (e.g., birth certificate, driver's license, passport, travel or work visas, green cards, etc.). The gender marker on a transgender person's identity documents will be their sex assigned at birth until they undergo a legal and logistical process to change it, where possible.

Gender Neutral: A term that describes something (sometimes a space, such as a bathroom; or an item, such as a piece of clothing) that is not segregated by sex/gender.

Gender Neutral Language: Language that does not assume or confer gender. For example "person" instead "man" or "woman."

Gender Non-Conforming: A person whose gender expression is perceived as being inconsistent with cultural norms expected for that gender. Specifically, boys/men are not masculine enough or are feminine, while girls/women are not feminine enough or are masculine. Not all transgender people are gender non-conforming, and not all gender non-conforming people identify as transgender. Cisgender people may also be gender non-conforming. Gender non-conformity is often inaccurately confused with sexual orientation.

Genderqueer: A person whose gender identity is neither male nor female, is between or beyond genders, or is some combination of genders.

Intersex: An umbrella term that describes a person born with sex characteristics (e.g. genetic, genital, sexual/reproductive or hormonal configurations) that do not fit typical binary notions of male or female bodies. The term describes a wide range of natural variations in human bodies. Intersex is frequently confused with transgender, but the two are completely distinct and generally unconnected. A more familiar term, hermaphrodite, is considered outdated and offensive.

LGBTQ: An acronym commonly used to refer to Lesbian, Gay, Bisexual, Transgender, Queer and/or Questioning individuals and communities. LGBTQ is often erroneously used as a synonym for "non-heterosexual," which incorrectly implies that transgender is a sexual orientation.

Medical Transition: A long-term series of medical interventions that utilizes hormonal treatments and/or surgical interventions to change a person's body to be more congruent with their gender identity. Medical transition is the approved medical treatment for Gender Dysphoria.

Microaggressions: Small, individual acts of hostility or derision toward transgender or gender non-conforming people, which can sometimes be unintentional. Examples of microaggressions include: use of non-affirming name or pronouns, derogatory language, asking inappropriate or offensive questions, and exhibiting looks that reveal distaste or confusion.

Non-Binary: A continuum or spectrum of gender identities and expressions, often based on the rejection of the gender binary's assumption that gender is strictly an either/or option of male/men/masculine or female/woman/feminine based on sex assigned at birth. Words that people may use to express their non-binary gender identity include "agender," "bigender," "genderqueer," "genderfluid," and "pangender."

Pangender: A person who identifies as all genders.

(Anti-Transgender) Prejudice: An individual's negative attitudes, beliefs, or reactions to transgender people. Examples of anti-transgender prejudice include: believing that transgender people are mentally disturbed, being uncomfortable sharing space with a transgender person, or thinking that transgender people should not be allowed to use public bathrooms.

Pubertal Suppression: A low-risk medical process that "pauses" the hormonal changes that activate puberty in young adolescents. The result is a purposeful delay of the development of secondary sex characteristics (e.g. breast growth, testicular enlargement, facial hair, body fat redistribution, voice changes, etc.). Suppression allows more time to make decisions about hormonal interventions and can prevent the increased dysphoria that often accompanies puberty for transgender youth.

Questioning: A person who is exploring or questioning their gender identity or expression. Some may later identify as transgender or gender non-conforming, while others may not. Can also refer to someone who is questioning or exploring their sexual orientation.

Same-Gender Loving: A label sometimes used by members of the African-American/Black community to express an alternative sexual orientation without relying on terms and symbols of European descent. The term emerged in the early 1990s with the intention of offering Black women who love women and Black men who love men a voice, a way of identifying and being that resonated with the uniqueness of Black culture. (Sometimes abbreviated "SGL.")

Sex Assigned at Birth: The determination of a person's sex based on the visual appearance of the genitals at birth. The sex someone is labeled at birth.

Sexual Orientation: A person's feelings of attraction (emotional, psychological, physical, and/or sexual) towards other people. A person may be attracted to people of the same sex, to those of the opposite sex, to those of both sexes, or without reference to sex or gender. And some people do not experience primary sexual attraction and may identify as asexual. Sexual orientation is about attraction to other people (external), while gender identity is a deep-seated sense of self (internal). All people have a sexual orientation that is separate from their biological sex, gender identity and gender expression.

Social Transition: A transgender person's process of a creating a life that is congruent with their gender identity, which often includes asking others to use a name, pronoun, or gender that is more congruent with their gender identity. It may also involve a person changing their gender expression to match their gender identity.

Trans: This is sometimes used as an abbreviation for "transgender."

Transgender: An adjective used to describe a person whose gender identity is incongruent with (or does not "match") the biological sex they were assigned at birth. "Transgender" serves an umbrella term to refer to the full range and diversity of identities within transgender communities because it is currently the most widely used and recognized term.

(Transgender) Ally: A cisgender person who supports, affirms, is in solidarity with, or advocates for transgender people.

Transgender men and boys: People who identify as male but were assigned female at birth. Also sometimes referred to as transmen.

Transgender women and girls: People who identify as female but were assigned male at birth. Also sometimes referred to as trans women.

Transexual/Transsexual: This is an older term that has been used to refer to a transgender person who has had hormonal or surgical interventions to change their bodies to be more aligned with their gender identity than the sex that they were assigned at birth. While still used as an identity label by some, "transgender" has generally become the preferred term.

Two Spirit: A term used by Native and Indigenous Peoples to indicate that they embody both a masculine and a feminine spirit. Is sometimes also used to describe Native Peoples of diverse sexual orientations and has nuanced meanings in various indigenous sub-cultures.

Source: *Green, E. R., and L. M. Maurer. The Teaching Transgender Toolkit: A Facilitator's Guide to Increasing Knowledge, Decreasing Prejudice & Building Skills. Ithaca, NY: Planned Parenthood of the Southern Finger Lakes: Out for Health, 2015. ISBN: 978-0-9966783-0-8. Available at www.teachingtransgender.com.*

Notes

FOREWORD

1. See American Civil Liberties Union, *Grimm v. Gloucester School Board*, https://www.aclu.org/cases/grimm-v-gloucester-county-school-board.

CHAPTER 1

1. Numerous scholars have described the need for and efforts to provide preservice and in-service training to teachers on the topic of gender diversity. See Clare Bartholomaeus, Damien W. Riggs, and Yarrow Andrew, "The Capacity of South Australian Primary School Teachers and Pre-Service Teachers to Work with Trans and Gender Diverse Students," *Teaching and Teacher Education* 65 (2017): 127–35; Kim A. Case and S. Colton Meier, "Developing Allies to Transgender and Gender-Nonconforming Youth: Training for Counselors and Educators," *Journal of LGBT Youth* 11, no. 1 (2014): 62–82; Laura-Lee Kearns, Jennifer Mitton-Kukner, and Joanne Tompkins, "Transphobia and Cisgender Privilege: Pre-Service Teachers Recognizing and Challenging Gender Rigidity in Schools," *Canadian Journal of Education/Revue Canadienne de l'éducation* 40, no. 1 (2017): 1–27; Mollie T. McQuillan and Jennifer Leininger, "Supporting Gender-Inclusive Schools: Educators' Beliefs About Gender Diversity Training and Implementation Plans," *Professional Development in Education*, (2020): https://doi.org/10.1080/19415257.2020.1744685; Elizabeth J. Meyer and Bethy Leonardi, "Teachers' Professional Learning to Affirm Transgender, Non-Binary, and Gender-Creative Youth: Experiences and Recommendations from the Field," *Sex Education* 18, no. 4 (2018): 449–63; K. Rands, "Considering Transgender People in Education: A Gender-Complex Approach," *Journal of Teacher Education* 60, no. 4 (2009): 419–31.
2. Payne and Smith describe the "fear" that educators from five different schools experienced when faced with a transgender student. See Elizabethe C. Payne and Melissa J. Smith, "The Big Freak Out: Educator Fear in Response to the

Presence of Transgender Elementary School Students," *Journal of Homosexuality* 61, no. 3 (2014): 399–418.

3. Leonardi and Staley document the ways in which knowledge and information helped administrators engage proactively to implement trans-affirming policy. See Bethy Leonardi and Sara Staley, "What's Involved in 'The Work'? Understanding Administrators' Roles in Bringing Trans-Affirming Policies into Practice," *Gender and Education* 30, no. 6 (2018): 754–73.

4. Allegra R. Gordon and Ilan H. Meyer, "Gender Nonconformity as a Target of Prejudice, Discrimination, and Violence Against LGB Individuals," *Journal of LGBT Health Research* 3, no. 3 (2007): 55–71; Andrea L. Roberts et al., "Childhood Gender Nonconformity: A Risk Indicator for Childhood Abuse and Posttraumatic Stress in Youth," *Pediatrics* 129, no. 3 (2012): 410–17.

5. Joseph G. Kosciw et al., *The 2017 National School Climate Survey: The Experiences of Lesbian, Gay, Bisexual, Transgender, and Queer Youth in Our Nation's Schools* (New York: Gay, Lesbian and Straight Education Network [GLSEN], 2018), 1–193.

6. Sandy E. James et al., *The Report of the 2015 U.S. Transgender Survey* (Washington, DC: National Center for Transgender Equality, 2016), 9, http://www .ustranssurvey.org.

7. The violence that transgender people experience has been well documented. Disaggregated data collected by the National Center for Transgender Equality show that the rates of violence are highest for those with multiple marginalized identities. See James et al., *The Report of the 2015 U.S. Transgender Survey*.

8. Harper B. Keenan, "Unscripting Curriculum: Toward a Critical Trans Pedagogy," *Harvard Educational Review* 87, no. 4 (2017): 542.

9. Prudence Carter describes an "ecology of inequality" that demands a holistic, multifaceted approach to inequity. We must tackle inequality at the macro-, meso-, and micro-levels if we expect to alter existing systems of inequality. See Prudence L. Carter, "The Multidimensional Problems of Educational Inequality Require Multidimensional Solutions," *Educational Studies* 54, no. 1 (2018): 1–16.

10. Florida, Maine, Maryland, Ohio, Pennsylvania, Virginia, and Wisconsin. See *Doe v. Regional School Unit 26*, ME, 2014; *Dodds v US Department of Education*, OH, 2016; *Whitaker v Kenosha USD*, WI, 2017; *A.H. ex rel. Handling v. Minersville Area School District*, PA, 2017; *Evancho v. Pine-Richland School District*, PA, 2017; *Grimm v. Gloucester County School Board*, VA, 2019; *M.A.B. v. Board of Education of Talbot County*, MD, 2018; *Doe v. Boyertown Area School District*, PA, 2018; *Adams v. School Board of St. Johns County*, FL, 2018.

11. In 2016, the Department of Education's Office of Elementary and Secondary Education, in collaboration with the Office of Safe and Healthy Schools,

released a compilation of sample policies and practices from across the United States that demonstrate support for transgender students. Some states and cities that have led the way include California, Massachusetts, Chicago, and New York City. See Ann Whalen and David Esquith, "Examples of Policies and Emerging Practices for Supporting Transgender Students" (US Education Department, Office of Elementary and Secondary Education, May 2016), 1–25, https://www2.ed.gov/about/offices/list/oese /oshs/emergingpractices.pdf.

12. Numerous scholars point to the limits of policy for effecting change, noting that policy is mediated by stakeholders, can reinforce beliefs about gender as a binary, or situate transgender children as a problem. See Lisa W. Loutzenheiser, "'Who Are You Calling a Problem?': Addressing Transphobia and Homophobia Through School Policy," *Critical Studies in Education* 56, no. 1 (2015): 99–115; Cris Mayo, *LGBTQ Youth and Education: Policies and Practices* (New York: Teachers College Press, 2014); Wayne Martino et al., "Mapping Transgender Policyscapes: A Policy Analysis of Transgender Inclusivity in the Education System in Ontario," *Journal of Education Policy* 34, no. 3 (2019): 302–30; Elizabeth J. Meyer and Harper B. Keenan, "Can Policies Help Schools Affirm Gender Diversity? A Policy Archaeology of Transgender-Inclusive Policies in California Schools," *Gender and Education* 30, no. 6 (2018): 736–53.

13. Iconic public figures like Grace Jones, Elton John, Prince, Boy George, Annie Lennox, Lady Gaga, and many others demonstrate the fluidity of gender and inspired cultural trends that often transgress gender norms.

14. For example, some people like the term *nonconforming* to describe gender because it suggests rebellion, disruption, or being a nonconformist. Others describe nonconforming as a deficit perspective because it posits "conforming" behavior as normative and positive, and thus, it positions transgender people as outside the norm and negative.

15. As a general rule, I do not use the term *trans* in this volume. *Trans* is sometimes understood as a simple shortening of the longer term *transgender*. Alternately, *trans* or *trans** (the asterisk corresponds to the wildcard in a database search to convey the expansive nature of transgender identities) can be used to intentionally indicate identities other than gender that disrupt or challenge social norms, such as transsexual or transgressive. Thus, my use of the term *transgender* intentionally signals a focus on gender. That said, it is important to recognize that the patriarchal, cisnormative, heteronormative systems that reinforce and reproduce oppression cannot be disentangled. Thus, the idea of separating gender from other systems of oppression is an artificial exercise that oversimplifies the insidious nature of oppression.

16. The term *deadname* can feel jarring to those unfamiliar with its usage. It may seem exaggerated, macabre, or inappropriate, given that the child is not dead. The severity of the term is a reflection of how strongly transgender people feel about being referred to by their chosen name and the deeply negative reaction they commonly have to the name assigned to them at birth. Numerous researchers have documented the positive benefits of chosen name use for transgender youth. See Amanda M. Pollitt et al., "Predictors and Mental Health Benefits of Chosen Name Use Among Transgender Youth," *Youth & Society*, 2019, 1–22; Stephen T. Russell et al., "Chosen Name Use Is Linked to Reduced Depressive Symptoms, Suicidal Ideation, and Suicidal Behavior Among Transgender Youth," *Journal of Adolescent Health* 63, no. 4 (2018): 503–505; Julia H Sinclair-Palm, "What's in a Name?: Trans Youths' Experiences of Re-Naming" (PhD diss., York University, 2016).

17. It is important to recognize that parents' recommendations were based on their perceptions that their children felt supported in school and based on the conversations they had with their children. My request for study participants primarily went to parents who were affiliated with Camp Aranu'tiq, a summer camp for transgender and nonbinary children age eight to fourteen. I also sent requests to one regional PFLAG group (a national parent support group founded in 1973) and one regional GLSEN group (a pro-LGBTQ educator organization founded in 1990).

18. My decision not to interview children is an imperfect choice between two unsatisfactory options. By relying on adults' interpretations, I may misunderstand or poorly convey the children's true experiences. I also recognize that many researchers effectively account for the power imbalance inherent in interviewing vulnerable children and actively work to prevent potential harm or ameliorate any risk involved. As such, my decision is not meant as a judgment of other researchers who decide to elicit stories directly from children.

19. This high incidence of transracial adoptees is not easily explained. Socioeconomic privilege is one plausible explanation. That is, families with the means to adopt (outside the foster care system) are likely wealthier, better educated, and may have greater access to information about being transgender and, thus, be more likely to be involved in the kinds of social networks that made up the sampling source for this study. Anecdotally, in the larger population of families with transgender children who are active on social media, parents perceive a variety of co-occurrences including what seem to be higher than average rates of adoption, giftedness, and neurodivergence among transgender children. To date, no research is available to substantiate parents' perception except with regard to Autism Spectrum Disorders (ASD). One of the

foremost experts, Dr. Aron Janssen, explains, "Current literature suggests a bidirectional relationship; that is, individuals presenting with gender dysphoria are more likely to have a co-occurring diagnosis of ASD, and individuals presenting with a diagnosis of ASD are more likely to have a co-occurring diagnosis of gender dysphoria . . . individuals with ASDs are approximately seven times more likely to be gender variant than same aged peers" (p. 122). Janssen further explains that no causal relationship has been determined despite some speculation that genetics or prenatal hormones could play a role. In any case, popular wisdom among many affirming families of transgender children is to not ask "why?" but rather to love and appreciate their children for who they are. For more information on the co-occurrence between ASD and gender dysphoria, see works by Aron Janssen, including Aron Janssen, "Gender Dysphoria and Autism Spectrum Disorders," in *Affirmative Mental Health Care for Transgender and Gender Diverse Youth: A Clinical Guide*, ed. Aron Janssen and Scott Leibowitz (New York: Springer International Publishing, 2018), 121–28.

20. In two earlier publications, a different pseudonym was used for Meredith, which is still a pseudonym.

CHAPTER 2

1. The term *non-transgender* may also be used as a synonym for *cisgender* as a way to center transgender experiences and identities. I have chosen to use *cisgender* throughout this volume in an effort to add this term to our collective vocabulary. Just as there are many ways to be transgender, there are also many ways to be cisgender.

2. Jody L Herman et al., *Age of Individuals Who Identify as Transgender in the United States* (Los Angeles: The Williams Institute, 2017).

3. Bianca D. M. Wilson et al., *Characteristics and Mental Health of Gender Nonconforming Adolescents in California* (Los Angeles: The Williams Institute, 2017).

4. Bianca D. M. Wilson and Angeliki A. Kastanis, "Sexual and Gender Minority Disproportionality and Disparities in Child Welfare: A Population-Based Study," *Children and Youth Services Review* 58 (2015): 11–17.

5. Transgender history both intertwines with and is distinct from gay, bisexual, and lesbian history. Despite efforts to dehumanize and erase transgender people, scholars have documented a rich history that includes agency and subjectivity in addition to tragedy. Works by Feinberg and Stryker are considered seminal texts. See Leslie Feinberg, *Transgender Warriors: Making History from Joan of Arc to Dennis Rodman* (Boston: Beacon Press, 1996); Susan Stryker, *Transgender History: The Roots of Today's Revolution*, 2nd ed. (New York: Seal Press, 2017).

6. Beemyn offers suggestions for how high schools might include transgender history in their curriculum. See Genny Beemyn, "Transforming the Curriculum: The Inclusion of the Experiences of Trans People," in *Understanding and Teaching U.S. Lesbian, Gay, Bisexual, and Transgender History*, ed. Leila J. Rupp and Susan K. Freeman, 2nd ed. (Madison: The University of Wisconsin Press, 2017), 112.

7. Author and activist Leslie Feinberg is credited with popularizing the term *transgender* as an umbrella term inclusive of those identities that do not fit neatly within the gender binary of man/woman.

8. Language related to sex, sexuality, and gender is undergoing constant change in keeping with new understandings. Both of these terms, *transsexual* and *sex-reassignment surgery*, have been replaced with more affirming language. Overwhelmingly, *transgender* is now used to refer to individuals whose gender does not align with their sex assigned at birth; however, some individuals identify as transsexual, usually if they have undergone some kind of genital surgery, which is now commonly referred to as *gender affirmation* or *confirmation surgery*.

9. See chapter 2, "Ex-GI Becomes Blonde Beauty," in Joanne J. Meyerowitz, *How Sex Changed* (Cambridge: Harvard University Press, 2009).

10. Accounts differ and Johnson herself offered conflicting information regarding her participation. Numerous books and documentaries detail Marsha P. Johnson's life and legacy. See, for example, the 2012 documentary *Pay It No Mind—The Life and Times of Marsha P. Johnson*, produced by director Michael Kasino, and the 2017 documentary *The Death and Life of Marsha P. Johnson*, in which Victoria Cruz of the Anti-Violence Project investigates Johnson's murder.

11. The 20██ U.S. Transgender Survery is the most comprehensive data currently available and reports survery results from twenty-eight thousand transgender adults in the United States. Tragically, 40 percent of respondents had attempted suicide in their lifetime, compared to only 4.6 percent of the general US population. See Sandy E. James et al., *The Report of the 2015 U.S. Transgender Survey* (Washington, DC: National Center for Transgender Equality, 2016), http://www.ustranssurvey.org.

12. The brief summary included here may not reflect the most current legal developments. Additional information can be found on websites hosted by the American Civil Liberties Union (ACLU) at www.aclu.org and the National Center for Transgender Equality (NCTE) at www.transequality.org.

13. Transgender children who have stepped into the media spotlight include Avery Jackson, whose image was featured on the cover of *National Geographic* (January 2017), and Trinity Neal and Jacob Lemay, whose stories have been

shared across media outlets. See also "The GenderCool Project," n.d., https://gendercool.org/; Ruth Padawer, "What's So Bad About a Boy Who Wants to Wear a Dress?," *New York Times Magazine*, August 8, 2012.

14. Lateshia Beachum, "Transgender Political Candidates Are Increasingly Common. The Money Backing Them Is Not," *Center for Public Integrity*, March 6, 2019, https://publicintegrity.org/federal-politics/elections/transgender-political-candidates-are-increasingly-common-the-money-backing-them-is-not/.

15. According to the Pew Research Center: "As far as what share of Americans say they know a transgender person, 37% say they personally do, including 13% who say they have a close friend or a family member who is transgender (9% say they have a close friend and 6% have a family member who is transgender; respondents were allowed to select more than one answer). About a quarter of Americans (24%) say they have an acquaintance who is transgender, while 7% say they have a transgender co-worker." These data come from the American Trends Panel (ATP), collected between August and September of 2017 from 4,573 respondents. The margin of sampling error for the full sample is 2.4 percentage points. See the Pew Research Center blog post: Anna Brown, "Transgender Issues Sharply Divide Republicans, Democrats," *Pew Research Center* (blog), November 8, 2017, https://www.pewresearch.org/fact-tank/2017/11/08/transgender-issues-divide-republicans-and-democrats/.

16. For further information on the biology of sex and how our understanding is influenced by social conventions, see Anne Fausto-Sterling, *Sex/Gender: Biology in a Social World* (New York: Routledge, 2012).

17. For a detailed infograph depicting sex variations, see Amanda Montañez, "Beyond XX and XY: The Extraordinary Complexity of Sex Determination," *Scientific American*, September 1, 2017, https://doi.org/10.1038/scientificamerican0917-50.

18. In biology a hermaphrodite is an organism that has the reproductive organs associated with both sexes, such that the organism can act as either "male" or "female" in reproduction. In fact, many groups of animals do not have separate sexes. The use of the term *hermaphrodite* for humans is erroneous and usually derogatory. The topic of intersex bodies gained greater visibility and acceptance with the publication of the Pulitzer prize–winning book *Middlesex*, which describes a teen girl who learns that she has XY chromosomes. See Jeffrey Eugenides, *Middlesex* (New York: Picador, 2002).

19. Melanie Blackless et al., "How Sexually Dimorphic Are We? Review and Synthesis," *American Journal of Human Biology* 12, no. 2 (2000): 151–66.

20. Jennifer Conn, Lynn Gillam, and Gerard S. Conway, "Revealing the Diagnosis of Androgen Insensitivity Syndrome in Adulthood," *BMJ Publishing Group* 331, no. 7517 (2005): 628, https://doi.org/10.1136/bmj.331.7517.628.

21. "Intersex Campaign for Equality—Promoting Human Rights and Equality for All Intersex People Through Arts, Education and Action," n.d., https://www.intersexequality.com/; "Intersex Society of North America | A World Free of Shame, Secrecy, and Unwanted Genital Surgery," n.d., http://www.isna.org/.

22. Maria Patiño, an Olympic athlete with androgen insensitivity syndrome, was subjected to both chromosomal and hormonal testing and subsequently barred from competing. See Anne Fausto-Sterling, *Sexing the Body: Gender Politics and the Construction of Sexuality* (New York: Basic Books, 2000). Dutee Chand and Caster Semenya, two women affected by hyperandrogenism, were similarly prohibited from participating in the Olympic games due to their naturally high levels of testosterone, a hormone that is present in all women and men. Dutee Chand's story is presented as part of a multi-episode podcast titled *Radiolab Presents: Gonads*. This series also provides detailed scientific information about sex development in utero and also presents the story of Dana Zzyym, an intersex activist. See *Radiolab Presents: Gonads*, WNYC Studios, (2018), https://www.wnycstudios.org/podcasts/radiolab/projects/radiolab-presents-gonads.

23. Details about the case can be found on the Lambda Legal website. "Zzyym v. Pompeo (Formerly Zzyym v. Tillerson & Zzyym v. Kerry)," Lambda Legal, n.d., https://www.lambdalegal.org/in-court/cases/co_zzyym-v-pompeo.

24. The highly personal nature of gender identity means that people often create the language that seems to best describe their experience. These are only some of the ever-expanding terms currently being used to describe gender identity. Also, over time, some terms fall out of fashion or take on a derogatory tone. For example, some transgender people eschew the terms *FTM* (female to male) and *MTF* (male to female) asserting that they did not change, but rather, their true gender identity was not recognized. For further examinations of queer gender identities, see Lee Airton, *Gender: Your Guide: A Gender-Friendly Primer on What to Know, What to Say, and What to Do in the New Gender Culture* (Avon, MA: Simon and Schuster, 2018); Kate Bornstein, *Gender Outlaw: On Men, Women, and the Rest of Us* (New York: Vintage, 2016); Joan Nestle, Clare Howell, and Riki Wilchins, eds., *GenderQueer: Voices from Beyond the Sexual Binary* (Los Angeles: Alyson Books, 2002).

25. Herman et al., *Age of Individuals Who Identify as Transgender in the United States*. In 2017, when the study was published, 0.6 percent was equivalent to 1.4 million adults. This study employed a fairly narrow definition of transgender rather than a more inclusive "anything except cisgender" approach. The disaggregated data present interesting differences across subgroups. For example, younger adults are more likely to identify as transgender, Hawaii

reports the highest percentage of transgender individuals, and nationwide Whites are more likely to identify as transgender than other racial or cultural groups. Given such demographic variations, it appears that some groups may be more willing to identify as transgender. In turn, the actual number of transgender people across all groups may be underrepresented given the stigma associated with transgender identities.

26. Linda Baumgarten, *What Clothes Reveal: The Language of Clothing in Colonial and Federal America: The Colonial Williamsburg Collection* (New Haven: Yale University Press, 2002).

27. See Butler's seminal work: Judith Butler, *Gender Trouble: Feminism and the Subversion of Identity* (New York: Routledge, 1990).

28. Carol Lynn Martin and Diane N. Ruble, "Patterns of Gender Development," *Annual Review of Psychology* 61, no. 1 (2010): 353–81; Kristina R. Olson, Aidan C. Key, and Nicholas R. Eaton, "Gender Cognition in Transgender Children," *Psychological Science* 26, no. 4 (2015): 467–74.

29. World Health Organization, "Moving One Step Closer to Better Health and Rights for Transgender People," May 17, 2019, http://www.euro.who.int/en /health-topics/health-determinants/gender/news/news/2019/5/moving-one -step-closer-to-better-health-and-rights-for-transgender-people.

30. For a scholarly examination of sexual orientation as situated in the context of lived experience, see Sara Ahmed, *Queer Phenomenology: Orientations, Objects, Others* (Durham: Duke University Press, 2006).

31. The 1980s was also marked by the Acquired Immune Deficiency Syndrome (AIDS) epidemic, which was first detected in the United States in 1981 in New York and California. This contagious illness is transmitted via body fluids and was mistakenly referred to as the *gay-related immune deficiency* following a group of cases among gay men in Southern California. The subsequent vilification of gay people and the high death rates within gay communities contributed to increased activism such as the Gay Men's Health Crisis, which formed in 1982, as well as other activist groups. For more information see "A Timeline of HIV and AIDS," HIV.gov, May 11, 2016, https://www.hiv.gov /hiv-basics/overview/history/hiv-and-aids-timeline.

32. For a more in-depth look at the reasons why some support and some oppose reclaiming the word *queer,* see Robin Brontsema, "A Queer Revolution: Reconceptualizing the Debate Over Linguistic Reclamation," *Colorado Research in Linguistics* 17, no. 1 (2004): 18.

33. The term *two-spirit* is reserved for Native American, First Nations, American Indian, and other Indigenous Peoples. For a critique of queer studies' failure to include the narratives and histories of Native peoples, see Qwo-Li Driskill, "Doubleweaving Two-Spirit Critiques: Building Alliances Between Native

and Queer Studies," *GLQ: A Journal of Lesbian and Gay Studies* 16, no. 1–2 (2010): 69–92. See also Alex Wilson, "N'tacimowin Inna Nah' Our Coming In Stories," *Canadian Woman Studies* 26, no. 3–4 (2008): 193–99.

34. The rich history of LGBTQ+ Americans is worth more extensive examination than is possible in this volume. One resource is the acclaimed text by Bronski, winner of the 2012 Stonewall Book Award: Michael Bronski, *A Queer History of the United States* (Boston, MA: Beacon Press, 2012).

35. See research outcomes from the Trans Youth Project, including Kristina R. Olson et al., "Mental Health of Transgender Children Who Are Supported in Their Identities," *Pediatrics* 137, no. 3 (2016): 1–8.

36. The most up-to-date information can be found at the National Center for Transgender Equality website: https://transequality.org/. MAP, Movement Advancement Project, has interactive maps, tables, and charts with state-level data and state-by-state comparisons. See "Equality Maps: Identity Document Laws and Policies," Movement Advancement Project, http://www .lgbtmap.org//equality-maps/identity_document_laws.

37. The World Professional Association for Transgender Health (WPATH) is an international organization dedicated to developing and promoting standards of care for transgender health, including but not limited to medical transition. See www.wpath.org.

CHAPTER 3

1. Some content from this chapter appears as a journal article. See Melinda M. Mangin, "Transgender Students in Elementary Schools: How Supportive Principals Lead," *Educational Administration Quarterly* 56, no. 2 (2019): 255–88.

2. A large body of research documents the direct and indirect influence that principals have on school functioning. See, for example, Joseph Murphy et al., "Leadership for Learning: A Research-Based Model and Taxonomy of Behaviors," *School Leadership & Management* 27, no. 2 (2007): 179–201.

3. Carolyn J. Riehl, "The Principal's Role in Creating Inclusive Schools for Diverse Students: A Review of Normative, Empirical, and Critical Literature on the Practice of Educational Administration," *Review of Educational Research* 70, no. 1 (2000): 55–81.

4. Most educational leadership programs include at least one course, targeted at learning about "diverse" learners or, more aptly stated, historically underserved and oppressed populations; however, these courses are more likely to attend to racial/ethnic diversity than gender or sexual orientation. Numerous scholars have explained why it is important for school leaders to learn about LGBTQIA people and experiences. See, for example, Hélène Frohard-Dourlent, "'The Student Drives the Car, Right?': Trans Students and

Narratives of Decision-Making in Schools," *Sex Education* 18, no. 4 (2018): 328–44; Michael P. O'Malley and Colleen A. Capper, "A Measure of the Quality of Educational Leadership Programs for Social Justice: Integrating LGBTIQ Identities into Principal Preparation," *Educational Administration Quarterly* 51, no. 2 (2015): 290–330.

5. Elizabethe C. Payne and Melissa J. Smith, "Refusing Relevance: School Administrator Resistance to Offering Professional Development Addressing LGBTQ Issues in Schools," *Educational Administration Quarterly* 54, no. 2 (2018): 183–215; Elizabethe C. Payne and Melissa J. Smith, "The Big Freak Out: Educator Fear in Response to the Presence of Transgender Elementary School Students," *Journal of Homosexuality* 61, no. 3 (2014): 399–418.

6. Amy Ellis Nutt, *Becoming Nicole: The Transformation of an American Family* (New York: Random House, 2016).

7. *Doe v. Regional School Unit 26*, 86 A.3d 600 (ME. 2014).

8. See *Doe v. Regional School Unit 26*, ME, 2014; *Tooley v. Van Buren*, MI, 2015; *Dodds v US Department of Education*, OH, 2016; *Whitaker v Kenosha USD*, WI, 2017; *A.H. ex rel. Handling v. Minersville Area School District*, PA, 2017; *Evancho v. Pine-Richland School District*, PA, 2017; *Grimm v. Gloucester County School Board*, VA, 2018; *M.A.B. v. Board of Education of Talbot County*, MD, 2018; *Doe v. Boyertown Area School District*, PA, 2018; *Adams v. School Board of St. Johns County*, FL, 2018.

9. Bethy Leonardi and Sara Staley, "What's Involved in 'the Work'? Understanding Administrators' Roles in Bringing Trans-Affirming Policies into Practice," *Gender and Education* 30, no. 6 (2018): 754–73.

10. For statistics on the percentage of transgender people in the US, see Jody L. Herman et al., *Age of Individuals Who Identify as Transgender in the United States* (Los Angeles: The Williams Institute, 2017).

11. The Transgender Training Institute provides training and consulting to professionals in a variety of fields including, but not limited to, K–12 schools and universities; medical and health-care providers; counselors and mental health professionals; nonprofit organizations and corporations. More information about the Transgender Training Institute and their programs can be found at https://www.transgendertraininginstitute.com/.

12. For more information on the negative effects of the accountability movement on educators, see Alyson Leah Lavigne, "Exploring the Intended and Unintended Consequences of High-Stakes Teacher Evaluation on Schools, Teachers, and Students," *Teachers College Record* 116, no. 1 (2014): 1–29; Jamy Stillman, "Teacher Learning in an Era of High-Stakes Accountability: Productive Tension and Critical Professional Practice," *Teachers College Record* 113, no. 1 (2011): 133–80.

13. Another example comes from the 2018 midterm elections, when Massachusetts held a state referendum (ballot issue #3) in which transgender people's access to civil rights was put to a vote. Although transgender rights were upheld, the perception that the public can vote on citizens' access to equal rights dehumanizes transgender people and undermines the legitimacy of their identities. Similarly, numerous hate groups endeavor to delegitimize transgender people, often under the guise of being pro-family, pro-women, or scientifically informed. For example, the American College of Pediatricians (ACPeds), a pseudo-medical anti-trans organization, is listed as a hate group by the Southern Poverty Law Center. This organization's name is specifically meant to confuse the public, as ACPeds is easily mistaken for the American Academy of Pediatrics, a legitimate organization that has advocated for transgender children and their medical needs.

14. Frohard-Dourlent, "'The Student Drives the Car, Right?,'" 328–44.

15. To learn more about zero-sum thinking and its effects, see Joanna Różycka-Tran, Paweł Boski, and Bogdan Wojciszke, "Belief in a Zero-Sum Game as a Social Axiom: A 37-Nation Study," *Journal of Cross-Cultural Psychology* 46, no. 4 (2015): 525–48; Pedro A. Noguera, "Racial Politics and the Elusive Quest for Excellence and Equity in Education," *Education and Urban Society* 34, no. 1 (2001): 18–41; Michael I. Norton and Samuel R. Sommers, "Whites See Racism as a Zero-Sum Game That They Are Now Losing," *Perspectives on Psychological Science* 6, no. 3 (2011): 215–18.

16. *Doe v. Boyerton Area School District*, No. 17-3113 (3d Cir., June 26, 2018); *Parents for Privacy v. Dallas School District No. 2*, No. 3:17-cv-01813 (D. Or., July 24, 2018); *Students & Parents for Privacy v. U.S. Department of Education*, No. 16-cv-4945 (N.D. Ill., December 29, 2017); *Cruzan v. Special School District No. 1.*, No. 01-3417 (8th Cir., June 20, 2002).

17. One strategy for helping children deal with questions, teasing, threats, or taunts is the use of role play. In role play, adults present possible scenarios, posing difficult questions or pretending to tease. Children have the opportunity to practice their response.

18. For more information on the importance for school-family collaboration, see Susan Auerbach, "Beyond Coffee with the Principal: Toward Leadership for Authentic School–Family Partnerships," *Journal of School Leadership* 20, no. 6 (2010): 728–57; Evanthia N. Patrikakou and Roger P. Weissberg, "School-Family Partnerships to Enhance Children's Social, Emotional and Academic Learning," in *Educating People to Be Emotionally Intelligent*, ed. Reuven Bar-On, J. G. Maree, and Maurice J. Elias (Westport, CT: Greenwood Publishing Group, 2007), 49–61.

19. Bethy Leonardi and Sara Staley, "What's Involved in 'The Work'? Understanding Administrators' Roles in Bringing Trans-Affirming Policies into Practice," *Gender and Education* 30, no. 6 (2018): 754–73.

20. Dr. Kristina Olson is a professor of psychology at the University of Washington and the director of the Social Cognitive Development Lab. Olson directs the longitudinal Trans Youth Project, which is following a cohort of about three hundred children from forty-five US states and several Canadian provinces for twenty years. See Kristina R. Olson et al., "Mental Health of Transgender Children Who Are Supported in Their Identities," *Pediatrics* 137, no. 3 (2016): e20153223.

21. Some school districts also develop their own policies related to gender and transgender students. Chapter 6, "What to Do About Gendered School Spaces?," describes how Greater Prospect School District developed their transgender policy.

22. Under New Jersey statute (*N.J.S.A.* 18A:36-41), the New Jersey Department of Education must provide guidelines for schools concerning the needs of transgender students and assist schools in establishing policies and procedures that ensure a supportive and nondiscriminatory environment for transgender students. See *New Jersey Department of Education, Transgender Student Guidance for School Districts*, October 2018, 2.

23. For example, see Dana L. Mitra, "The Significance of Students: Can Increasing 'Student Voice' in Schools Lead to Gains in Youth Development?," *Teachers College Record* 106, no. 4 (2004): 651–88.

24. For example, see Andrea L. Roberts et al., "Childhood Gender Nonconformity: A Risk Indicator for Childhood Abuse and Posttraumatic Stress in Youth," *Pediatrics* 129, no. 3 (2012): 410–17.

CHAPTER 4

1. These kinds of "savior" stories appeal to the presumed altruism of educators. They can also reinforce power dichotomies and ideologies of whiteness, whereby transgender people and especially transgender People of Color lack agency and are dependent on others for benevolence. Numerous scholars have criticized overreliance on statistics that position gender and sexual minority youth as objects of suffering. See, for example, Lee Airton and Austen Koecher, "How to Hit a Moving Target: 35 Years of Gender and Sexual Diversity in Teacher Education," *Teaching and Teacher Education* 80 (2019): 190–204.

2. Elizabeth J. Meyer, Anika Tilland-Stafford, and Lee Airton, "Transgender and Gender-Creative Students in PK–12 Schools: What We Can Learn from Their Teachers," *Teachers College Record* 118 (2016): 1–50.

3. It is worth noting that the term *poster child* is also commonly associated with fundraising efforts that use the image of a disabled child to elicit pity, such as the March of Dimes fundraising campaign. Thus, this association also suggests that the transgender child may be pathologized in addition to forfeiting their privacy.

4. Canadian education scholar Hélène Frohard-Dourlent makes this point in relationship to secondary students who may assume literal responsibility for teaching their peers and teachers. See Hélène Frohard-Dourlent, "'The Student Drives the Car, Right?': Trans Students and Narratives of Decision-Making in Schools," *Sex Education* 18, no. 4 (2018): 328–44.

5. Elizabethe C. Payne and Melissa J. Smith, "Refusing Relevance: School Administrator Resistance to Offering Professional Development Addressing LGBTQ Issues in Schools," *Educational Administration Quarterly* 54, no. 2 (2018): 183–215.

6. Amy Ellis Nutt, *Becoming Nicole: The Transformation of an American Family* (New York: Random House, 2016).

7. Michael S. Garet et al., "What Makes Professional Development Effective? Results from a National Sample of Teachers," *American Educational Research Journal* 38, no. 4 (2001): 915–45.

8. The distinction I draw here between certified and noncertified staff is imperfect and more appropriate for public school contexts than private schools. In fact, many classroom teachers in private schools are not required to hold a teaching certificate. As such, the distinction I am trying to draw might be thought of as educators with instructional responsibilities and noninstructional. At the same time there are many ways that so-called noninstructional staff serve as instructors, albeit informally. Thus, I have opted to use the terms *certified* and *noncertified* staff. Other characteristics that might differentiate these two broad groups is their union affiliation, if any, as well as their pay scale, whereby noninstructional, noncertified staff have lower salaries than certified instructional staff, or they may be employed as hourly contract employees.

9. Several sources provide evidence that children are unsafe in a wide range of school spaces. See Tracy Vaillancourt et al., "Places to Avoid: Population-Based Study of Student Reports of Unsafe and High Bullying Areas at School," *Canadian Journal of School Psychology* 25, no. 1 (2010): 40–54. The 2017 GLSEN National School Climate Survey further documents that 56.3 percent of transgender students avoid locker rooms, 64.1 percent avoid physical education class, and 80 percent avoid bathrooms. These students report feeling unsafe or uncomfortable in these spaces. See Joseph G. Kosciw et al., *The 2017 National School Climate Survey: The Experiences of Lesbian,*

Gay, Bisexual, Transgender, and Queer Youth in Our Nation's Schools (New York: Gay, Lesbian and Straight Education Network [GLSEN], 2018), 1–193.
10. See Anne Williford, "Intervening in Bullying: Differences Across Elementary School Staff Members in Attitudes, Perceptions, and Self-Efficacy Beliefs," *Children & Schools* 37, no. 3 (2015): 175–84.
11. "The Family Educational Rights and Privacy Act (FERPA) is a federal law that affords parents the right to have access to their children's education records, the right to seek to have the records amended, and the right to have some control over the disclosure of personally identifiable information from the education records. When a student turns 18 years old, or enters a postsecondary institution at any age, the rights under FERPA transfer from the parents to the student. The FERPA statute is found at 20 U.S.C. § 1232g and the FERPA regulations are found at 34 CFR Part 99." US Department of Education, retrieved from https://studentprivacy.ed.gov/faq/what-ferpa.
12. This YouTube video currently has more than eight million views. In 2016 the Whittington family published "Raising Ryland," which explains how they came to support and affirm their son. See Hillary Whittington, *Raising Ryland: Our Story of Parenting a Transgender Child with No Strings Attached* (New York: William Morrow Paperbacks, 2016).
13. Despite the widespread belief that coming out—disclosing one's queer identity—is a freeing process that demonstrates self-acceptance, it is not always liberatory, and queer-identified individuals can be both self-accepting and "closeted," or nondisclosed, which can have more to do with privacy than self-loathing. Also, invisibility can create opportunities to influence people who might otherwise be unwilling to listen to LGBTQ-affirming viewpoints. As such, being nondisclosed can be as empowering as being out. Edward Brockenbrough explains that for some Black queer male teachers, the desire to maintain racial connectedness may be more important than queer visibility. See Edward Brockenbrough, "Agency and Abjection in the Closet: The Voices (and Silences) of Black Queer Male Teachers," *International Journal of Qualitative Studies in Education* 25, no. 6 (2012): 741–65; Edward Brockenbrough, "Queer of Color Agency in Educational Contexts: Analytic Frameworks from a Queer of Color Critique," *Educational Studies* 51, no. 1 (2015): 28–44.
14. Lori Duron, *Raising My Rainbow: Adventures in Raising a Fabulous, Gender Creative Son* (New York: Broadway Books, 2013).
15. These authors offer a compelling description of a "pedagogy of exposure," its limits, and negative effects. In contrast, they also describe a "culture of conversation," which may offer potential for transforming educational settings into more affirming environments. See Elizabeth J. Meyer and Bethy

Leonardi, "Teachers' Professional Learning to Affirm Transgender, Non-Binary, and Gender-Creative Youth: Experiences and Recommendations from the Field," *Sex Education* 18, no. 4 (2018): 449–63.

16. Numerous authors describe the unintended negative effects of training programs that provide shallow opportunities to learn about transgender identities. See Eli R. Green, "Shifting Paradigms: Moving Beyond 'Trans 101' in Sexuality Education," *American Journal of Sexuality Education* 5, no. 1 (2010): 1–16; Robert A. Marx, Leah Marion Roberts, and Carol T. Nixon, "When Care and Concern Are Not Enough: School Personnel's Development as Allies for Trans and Gender Non-Conforming Students," *Social Sciences* 6, no. 1 (2017): 1–16.

CHAPTER 5

1. Afsaneh Moradian, *Jamie Is Jamie: A Book About Being Yourself and Playing Your Way* (Minneapolis, MN: Free Spirit Publishing, 2018).

2. Education scholar Lee Shulman first developed the concept of pedagogical content knowledge, and education researchers across content areas and educational domains elaborated on this concept extensively.

3. Jonathan Cohen, "Social, Emotional, Ethical, and Academic Education: Creating a Climate for Learning, Participation in Democracy, and Well-Being," *Harvard Educational Review* 76, no. 2 (2006): 201–37; Maurice J. Elias, "What If the Doors of Every Schoolhouse Opened to Social-Emotional Learning Tomorrow: Reflections on How to Feasibly Scale Up High-Quality SEL," *Educational Psychologist* 54, no. 3 (2019): 233–45.

4. Karen F. Osterman, "Students' Need for Belonging in the School Community," *Review of Educational Research* 70, no. 3 (2000): 343.

5. Osterman, "Students' Need for Belonging in the School Community," 343.

6. In her 2019 book, Bettina Love describes how our education system communicates that dark children do not matter. Rather than reforming our current system, she calls for a dismantling that includes civic engagement and intersectional justice. See Bettina Love, *We Want to Do More Than Survive: Abolitionist Teaching and the Pursuit of Educational Freedom* (Boston: Beacon Press, 2019).

7. For a helpful introduction to inclusive education that promotes equity and sees possibility in difference, see Diana Lawrence-Brown and Mara Sapon-Shevin, *Condition Critical—Key Principles for Equitable and Inclusive Education* (New York: Teachers College Press, 2015).2015

8. To reduce gender bias, it is not enough to create a gender-blind or gender-free classroom environment. Ignoring gender is likely to reinforce rather than eliminate inequity. See Rands for a discussion of how to provide preservice

education that is gender-sensitive and gender complex: K. Rands, "Considering Transgender People in Education: A Gender-Complex Approach," *Journal of Teacher Education* 60, no. 4 (2009): 419–31.

9. Toward the end of fifth grade, Max adopted a new name, Meredith, and female pronouns.

10. For an example of gender policing in secondary school, see C. J. Pascoe, *Dude, You're a Fag: Masculinity and Sexuality in High School* (Berkeley, CA: University of California Press, 2011).

11. Harper B. Keenan, "Unscripting Curriculum: Toward a Critical Trans Pedagogy," *Harvard Educational Review* 87, no. 4 (2017): 538–56.

12. In her study of Australian teenagers, Ullman found that teachers' positivity regarding diverse gender expression resulted in a positive correlation with students' well-being including having higher academic self-concept, being more confident and motivated learners, and increasing school-based morale. See Jacqueline Ullman, "Teacher Positivity Towards Gender Diversity: Exploring Relationships and School Outcomes for Transgender and Gender-Diverse Students," *Sex Education* 17, no. 3 (2017): 276–89.

13. More broadly, critiques of children's literature include examinations of representation across categories of race, class, culture, language, sexuality, ability, illness, and religion. Further, it is worth noting that, in much of this body of literature, gender and sex are conflated. Authors commonly use *female/male* to describe gender when *girl/boy* are more appropriate terms. In the case of animals, who do not have gender, the use of *male* and *female* is appropriate; however, the characteristics ascribed to those animals are actually gender stereotypes. Generally speaking, the conflation of sex and gender underscores the notion that both sex and gender are assigned at birth with the presumption that they will align and with the erroneous belief that genitalia determine sex/gender. See chapter 2, "Transgender and Gender-Expansive Children," for further explanation.

14. Male animals are central in 23 percent of books, and female animals are central in 7.5 percent of books, as described in Janice McCabe et al., "Gender in Twentieth-Century Children's Books: Patterns of Disparity in Titles and Central Characters," *Gender and Society* 25, no. 2 (2011): 197–226.

15. Mykol C. Hamilton et al., "Gender Stereotyping and Under-Representation of Female Characters in 200 Popular Children's Picture Books: A Twenty-First Century Update," *Sex Roles* 55, no. 11 (2006): 757–65.

16. Thomas Crisp et al., "What's on Our Bookshelves? The Diversity of Children's Literature in Early Childhood Classroom Libraries," *Journal of Children's Literature* 42, no. 2 (2016): 29–42.

17. Crisp et al., "What's on Our Bookshelves?," 29–42.

18. *About Cris* is a self-published work by Nina Benedetto that can be found at www.wonderwisdombooks.com.

19. English is not the only discipline where LGBTQ understanding can be integrated into the curriculum. An example from middle school mathematics involves sixth- and seventh-grade students engaging with data from GLSEN's National School Climate Survey and learning to conduct their own surveys. See Rands, "Supporting Transgender and Gender-Nonconforming Youth," 106–26.

20. In this activity, the teacher references James Charles, a popular vlogger and internet personality, who gained popularity as a teen posting make-up tutorials on YouTube beginning in 2015. In 2016 Charles became the first male ambassador for CoverGirl and, in 2019, boasted more than 16 million followers. Shortly thereafter, Charles was beset by scandal, accused of making a transphobic remark and involved in a public feud with fellow make-up artist, Tati Westbrook. The teacher's classroom activity predates this public controversy.

21. Welcoming Schools, a professional development program created by the Human Rights Campaign, has a similar lesson plan. See their website: welcomingschools.org.

22. In addition to pathologizing gender, institutions of science and medicine have been used to justify race-based and ability-based oppression. For example, the medicalization of race and related efforts to "scientifically" prove a hierarchy of races has been used to justify the dehumanization and abuse of Black and Brown bodies within and outside medical contexts. See chapter 2, "Transgender and Gender-Expansive Children," for a more in-depth discussion of how the fields of medicine and psychology, and in particular the *Diagnostic and Statistical Manual of Mental Disorders* created by the American Psychiatric Association, pathologize transgender people and gatekeep access to health care.

23. See, for example, Kristina R. Olson, Aidan C. Key, and Nicholas R. Eaton, "Gender Cognition in Transgender Children," *Psychological Science* 26, no. 4 (2015): 467–74.

24. Kristina R. Olson et al., "Mental Health of Transgender Children Who Are Supported in Their Identities," *Pediatrics* 137, no. 3 (2016).

25. Diane Ehrensaft, *The Gender Creative Child: Pathways for Nurturing and Supporting Children Who Live Outside Gender Boxes* (New York: The Experiment Publishing, 2016).

26. Colt Keo-Meier and Diane Ehrensaft, eds., *The Gender Affirmative Model: An Interdisciplinary Approach to Supporting Transgender and Gender Expansive Children* (Washington, DC: American Psychological Association, 2018).

27. A study of 129 transgender youth from three cities in the United States found that, for youth who elected to use a chosen name, chosen name usage was associated with large reductions in negative health outcomes. See Amanda

M. Pollitt et al., "Predictors and Mental Health Benefits of Chosen Name Use Among Transgender Youth," *Youth & Society* (2019): 1–22.

28. This conclusion corroborates the findings from other research showing teachers need to be "exposed" to a transgender child before the idea of transgender education feels relevant or they take steps to provide a more gender-inclusive classroom environment. See Elizabeth J. Meyer, Anika Tilland-Stafford, and Lee Airton, "Transgender and Gender-Creative Students in PK–12 Schools: What We Can Learn from Their Teachers," *Teachers College Record* 118 (2016): 1–51; Elizabeth J. Meyer and Bethy Leonardi, "Teachers' Professional Learning to Affirm Transgender, Non-Binary, and Gender-Creative Youth: Experiences and Recommendations from the Field," *Sex Education* 18, no. 4 (2018): 449–63.

29. As trans education scholar Harper B. Keenan stated, "In classrooms I was *taught* to hate my genderqueerness. I was *taught* to hate myself." Keenan, "Unscripting Curriculum," 542.

30. Kevin Kumashiro's work is instructive for helping us imagine the kind of social justice education and activist teaching that can facilitate meaningful change. See Kevin K. Kumashiro, *Against Common Sense: Teaching and Learning Toward Social Justice*, 3rd ed. (New York: Routledge, 2015).

CHAPTER 6

1. Justin Richardson and Peter Parnell, *And Tango Makes Three* (New York: Simon and Schuster, 2005).

2. The notion of space can be a literal physical space as well as an abstract construct. Both these uses of the term are relevant to schools. For a theoretical exploration of space, see the seminal works of Tuan: Yi-Fu Tuan, *Space and Place: The Perspective of Experience* (Minneapolis: University of Minnesota Press, 1977); Yi-Fu Tuan, "Space and Place: Humanistic Perspective," in *Philosophy in Geography*, ed. Stephen Gale and Gunnar Olsson, Theory and Decision Library (Dordrecht: Springer Netherlands, 1979), 387–427.1977

3. It is worth noting that "Colonial Day" curriculum and school events present other concerns beyond gender. Too often, the narrative associated with Colonial history ignores the genocidal practices associated with White settler colonialism and the devastating effects on Native Americans.

4. For interesting insights into bathroom politics, see Sheila L. Cavanagh, *Queering Bathrooms: Gender, Sexuality, and the Hygienic Imagination* (Toronto: University of Toronto Press, 2010); Olga Gershenson and Barbara Penner, *Ladies and Gents: Public Toilets and Gender* (Philadelphia: Temple University Press, 2009); Harvey Molotch and Laura Noren, *Toilet: Public Restrooms and the Politics of Sharing* (New York: NYU Press, 2010).

5. Just as being transgender is not a disability, critical disability activists would similarly state that disability is an ableist construction that is perpetuated through narratives that pathologize difference. See Michael Oliver, *Politics of Disablement* (London: Macmillan Education, 1990); Michael Oliver and Colin Barnes, *The New Politics of Disablement* (London: Macmillan Education, 2012).

6. Sandy E. James et al., *The Report of the 2015 U.S. Transgender Survey* (Washington, DC: National Center for Transgender Equality, 2016), http://www.ustranssurvey.org.

7. A common narrative that has been popularized in the media is the notion of being "born in the wrong body." While it is true that some transgender people seek to align their body with conventional views of what a male or female body should look like, many transgender people assert that their dysphoria is less a result of their body and more a consequence of others' reactions to their body and the need to conform to societal expectations. In contrast to the "born in the wrong body" narrative, some transgender activists have sought to reinforce the notion that, for example, if you are a boy, you have a boy's body regardless of the physical anatomy associated with that body. This body-positive approach can help some transgender people make peace with the body they have.

8. Sometimes the term *stealth* is used to describe transgender people who do not disclose their transgender identity. This term is increasingly perceived as problematic because of its association with sneakiness or dishonesty. Two alternate terms that can be used are *private* or *nondisclosed*.

9. The National Center for Transgender Equality tracks legal rulings related to an array of issues affecting transgender people including discrimination in the areas of education, health, and employment. Consult their website for updated information. See also National Center for Transgender Equality, *Federal Case Law on Transgender People and Discrimination* (Washington, DC: Author, 2018), https://transequality.org/federal-case-law-on-transgender-people-anddiscrimination.

10. A longer excerpt, which contains this quote, is presented in chapter 3, "The Role of Supportive Principals," as part of a discussion of principals' efforts to meet each student's unique needs.

11. In the field of design, universal design is a broad concept that focuses on maximizing product and facility usage by the greatest range of people outside those who might be considered average or typical users, including people of different ages, genders, languages, statures, abilities, etc. Accessible design is mandated in legislation that protects the rights of people with disabilities to access public facilities and services, specifically, in the Americans with

Disabilities Act and in a 1998 amendment to Section 508 of the Rehabilitation Act of 1973, which created standards for information technology
accessibility.

12. The winning design for Sloan's 2018 Restroom of the Future, by Lida Lewis,
specifically addressed the need to create gender-inclusive bathrooms. See
Janelle Penny, "Designing Inclusive and Gender-Neutral Restrooms," *interi-
ors+sources*, May 20, 2019, https://www.interiorsandsources.com/article
-details/articleid/22601/title/gender-neutral-restrooms. Additional information about inclusive public restrooms can be found at the website *Stalled!*:
https://www.stalled.online/.

13. For updates to the international plumbing codes, see the website sponsored
by the International Code Council (ICC): "International Plumbing Code
(IPC) Home Page," *ICC* (blog), January 6, 2015, https://www.iccsafe.org
/content/international-plumbing-code-ipc-home-page/.

CHAPTER 7

1. Spade describes pinkwashing as "a way for activists to talk about how LGBT
legal equality is being used to legitimize and expand the apparatuses of state
violence" (p. 140). He further explains that the original usage comes from
Palestinian queer and trans activists to describe Israel's campaign to position
themselves as human rights champions due to their gay-friendly politics,
while simultaneously occupying Palestine through violent means. See Dean
Spade, *Normal Life: Administrative Violence, Critical Trans Politics, and the
Limits of Law*, 2nd ed. (Durham: Duke University Press, 2015).

2. Organizational theorists refer to these two approaches as *first order* and *second
order change.*

3. Adrienne Rich, *Blood, Bread, and Poetry: Selected Prose 1979–1985* (New York:
W. W. Norton & Company, 1986), 119.

4. One example provided by the *Oxford English Dictionary* (OED) is "Everyone
loves his mother," which conveys a different meaning from "Everyone loves
their mother." Singular *they* can also be helpful when the intention is to con-
ceal someone's gender and, thus, afford greater anonymity. The OED traces
written examples of singular *they* to 1375. The OED also explains that, until
the 1600s, *you* was exclusively plural and *thou* was singular. These changes
over time demonstrate the evolution of language as well as the appropriateness
of singular *they* in modern English. See "A Brief History of Singular 'They,'"
Oxford English Dictionary, September 4, 2018, https://public.oed.com/blog
/a-brief-history-of-singular-they/.

5. These are not the only possible nonbinary pronouns, and new variations
continue to emerge as our language evolves to capture a wider range of

experiences and expressions. One way to practice a new set of pronouns is to talk about the person out loud, when you are alone, using the new pronouns. This approach is helpful if someone you knew previously changes their pronouns or if you meet a new person whose pronouns are unfamiliar to you. Regular practice can facilitate the use of new language. Failing to practice new pronouns and making repeated mistakes are hurtful even if the intentions are not malicious. The Trans Student Educational Resources website has a helpful infograph to guide pronoun usage at https://www.transstudent.org /pronouns101.

6. Elizabeth J. Meyer and colleagues use the term *sacrificial lamb* to refer to transgender and gender-creative children who relinquish their privacy in an effort to bring attention to the need for more gender-inclusive practices in schools. See Elizabeth J. Meyer, Anika Tilland-Stafford, and Lee Airton, "Transgender and Gender-Creative Students in PK–12 Schools: What We Can Learn from Their Teachers," *Teachers College Record* (2016): 17.

7. Julia Serano, *Whipping Girl: A Transsexual Woman on Sexism and the Scapegoating of Femininity* (Berkeley, CA: Seal Press, 2016), 63.

8. Shana Agid and Erica Rand, "Introduction: Beyond the Special Guest—Teaching 'Trans' Now," *Radical Teacher* 92, no. 1 (2011): 5–9.

9. These questions are adapted from Erica Rand, who asks her college-level students to engage in critical self-reflection about gender. See Erica Rand, "So Unbelievably Real: Stone Butch Blues and the Fictional Special Guest," *Radical Teacher* 92, no. 1 (2011): 38.

10. Numerous scholars have written about the role of education policy in facilitating gender equity. See Lisa W. Loutzenheiser, "'Who Are You Calling a Problem?': Addressing Transphobia and Homophobia Through School Policy," *Critical Studies in Education* 56, no. 1 (2015): 99–115; Wayne Martino et al., "Mapping Transgender Policyscapes: A Policy Analysis of Transgender Inclusivity in the Education System in Ontario," *Journal of Education Policy* 34, no. 3 (2019): 302–30; Cris Mayo, *LGBTQ Youth and Education: Policies and Practices* (New York: Teachers College Press, 2014); Elizabeth J. Meyer and Harper B. Keenan, "Can Policies Help Schools Affirm Gender Diversity? A Policy Archaeology of Transgender-Inclusive Policies in California Schools," *Gender and Education* 30, no. 6 (2018): 736–53.

11. In 2016, the Department of Education's Office of Elementary and Secondary Education, in collaboration with the Office of Safe and Healthy Schools, released a compilation of sample policies and practices from across the United States that demonstrate support for transgender students. Some states and major cities that have led the way include California, Massachusetts, Chicago, and New York City. See Ann Whalen and David Esquith, "Examples

of Policies and Emerging Practices for Supporting Transgender Students" (US Education Department, Office of Elementary and Secondary Education, May 2016), https://www2.ed.gov/about/offices/list/oese/oshs/emerging practices.pdf.

12. Title IX of the Education Amendments Act of 1972, 20 U.S.C. §§1681–1688.

13. See *Dodds v US Department of Education*, OH, 2016; *Whitaker v Kenosha USD*, WI, 2017; *A.H. ex rel. Handling v. Minersville Area School District*, PA, 2017; *Grimm v. Gloucester County School Board*, VA, 2018; *M.A.B. v. Board of Education of Talbot County*, MD, 2018; *Doe v. Boyertown Area School District*, PA, 2018; *Adams v. School Board of St. Johns County*, FL, 2018.

14. Lee Gardner, "Why Trans* Students Matter: An Interview with Z Nicolazzo," *Chronicle of Higher Education*, February 23, 2017, https://www.chronicle.com/article/Why-Trans-Students-Matter/239305.

15. Caitlin L. Ryan and Jill M. Hermann-Wilmarth, *Reading the Rainbow: LGBTQ-Inclusive Literacy Instruction in the Elementary Classroom* (New York: Teachers College Press, 2018).

APPENDIX A

1. Mary E. Brenner, "Interviewing in Educational Research," in *Handbook of Complementary Methods in Education Research*, ed. by Judith L. Green, Gregory Camilli, and Patricia B. Elmore (Mahwah, NJ: Lawrence Erlbaum, 2006), 357–70.

2. Michael Quinn Patton, *Qualitative Research & Evaluation Methods: Integrating Theory and Practice*, 4th ed. (Thousand Oaks, CA: Sage Publications, 2014).

Acknowledgments

In the time period that I worked on this book, transgender children were under attack. Not only did the Trump administration launch a full-blown assault on transgender people's rights, but states also worked to deny transgender children access to education and medical care. Each day brought a greater sense of urgency. This book is an expression of my hope that knowledge and compassion can overcome hatred and discrimination. The shortcomings are my own; however, the strengths reflect the intellectual, professional, and personal support I received from countless colleagues, friends, and family members.

I am especially indebted to the educators and families who generously shared their experiences with me. Their stories of love and affirmation point the way forward to a better world for transgender and gender-expansive children. I am equally grateful to the children whose experiences inspired this book. I learned more than I ever could have imagined from transgender children who are living their truth and speaking out about gender injustice. Their bold, and sometimes quiet, acts of self-empowerment will change the world. I hope this book compels more adults to listen and learn from these inspiring children.

This book would not have been possible without support from colleagues who helped me to grow as a scholar, teacher, and researcher. Foremost, I am indebted to my coworkers at the Graduate School of Education at Rutgers University who encouraged me to follow my heart and develop a new line of research. I extend a special thanks to Bill Firestone and Cath Lugg, gracious mentors who raised me from a baby doc student. Their generosity and caring contributed immeasurably to my intellectual and career development. Colleagues too numerous to name, from across many institutions, shared their knowledge and pushed my thinking. Their encouragement made the pressures of academic life just a little easier, and I am particularly grateful to Jill Harrison Berg, Cindy Carver, and Sara Ray Stoelinga. I am also grateful to the Queer Studies Special Interest Group of the American Educational Research Association. In the conservative context of education research, the Queer SIG has continued to fight for visibility, and thus, their efforts helped make space for my scholarship and research. I am especially grateful to Allison Mattheis, Michael Bartone, and Kamden Strunk.

Numerous queer and trans communities welcomed, educated, and inspired me. I am especially indebted to the extended *Camp Aranu'tiq* family: mama bears, dragon dads, counselors extraordinaire, and fierce gender warriors. Most importantly, Nick Teich's activism and love for trans youth motivated me to become the best coconspirator possible. I am also grateful to the folks at PFLAG and *Stepping Stones* in New York City who continue to be a lifeline for so many families. Kalima, Drew, and Judy are rock stars. I owe a big "thank you" to *Camp You Are You* and the parents who created it when the rest of mainstream America was clueless. I am also grateful to all the local, regional, national, and international organizations that are fighting for transgender rights.

I could not have written this book without ongoing support from the Spencer Foundation. A research grant from Spencer enabled me to travel to six states and learn from the dedicated educators whose experiences are presented in this volume. Continued funding, in the form of a conference grant, provided further support for a group of incredible scholars and activists to converge around the topic of transgender students and educators. I am deeply grateful for the opportunity to learn alongside Madelaine Adelman, Judy Alston, Christine Hamlett, Padraig Hurley, Sandy E. James, Kelly Jenkins, Harper Keenan, Joseph Kosciw, Catherine Lugg, Cris Mayo, Lance McCready, Mollie McQuillan, Liz Meyer, Elizabethe Payne, Page Valentine Regan, Robin Roscigno, Susan Stryker, Mario Itzel Suárez, and Nick Teich. These amazing educators contributed to my thinking immeasurably. In addition to funding, the Spencer Foundation afforded greater visibility and long overdue legitimacy to the topic of transgender identities. I extend my deep gratitude to program officers Ryan Gildersleeve, Rhoda Freelon, and Amy Dray, who encouraged me to think bigger, and to Na'ilah Suad Nasir, whose vision for educational equity is changing the field of education research.

Writing a book is a marathon, and many people contributed to my ability to cross the finish line. Although they may not know it, Rebecca Kling and Roland Sintos Coloma gave me the courage to write the first grant proposal. Michael Sadowski had confidence in the topic and my ability to present the findings in book format. An amazing group of reviewers read drafts and provided insightful feedback. Thank you, Megin Charner-Laird, Mitchell Glages-Bombich, Padraig Hurley, Vanessa Ford, Kirkland La Rue, Liz Meyer, and Carolyn Ross. There would be no book without Caroline Chauncey, Editor-in-Chief at Harvard Education Press. She delivered the right level of pressure and support to ensure that this text would become a reality.

The friends I gained on this gender journey are unparalleled in their love, compassion, and activism. It is impossible to list all their names; however, some who held me up and encouraged me at key points include Tracey Armaos, Moriko Nishiura Betz, Margaret Botney, Jennifer Chan, Candice Chaplin, Amy Clark, Susan Francis, Tamar Gendler, Emily Grote, Christy Hegarty, Mica Henderson, Kerry Keenan, Lauren Leahy, Abigail Leibowitz, Mimi Lemay, Grace Mauceri, Vanessa Melchiori, Melissa Moore, Lindsay Morris, Jodie Patterson, Andrea Rashbaum, Angela Rowan, Michael Rowan, Graciela Slesaransky-Poe, Stacia Smith, Jeanne Talbot, Sabrina Tellez-Brennan, Alisa Trachtenberg, Pamela Valentine, and Diana Wilson. Who knew we would be bonded forever in our quest for gender justice? I am equally thankful to friends near and far who tolerated my absences and my work-related monologues; asked how I was doing, especially during the hard times; helped me juggle the personal and the professional; and worried and cared for my children as if they were their own. Thank you, Jackie, Brad, Lydia, John, Pak, Robin, Dana, Jennifer, Jeremy, Micki, and Fede.

Above all, I want to acknowledge my gratitude for my immediate family. I am keenly aware that too many transgender people unnecessarily lose their families of origin. My parents and siblings extended their unconditional love and support, even when they didn't fully understand, which made this journey so much easier. My three children, who invited me on this gender journey, astound me with their integrity and compassion. Tavish, inquisitive artist and deep soul, your adventures are just beginning. Dragon, fierce in name and spirit, your wit and kindness are unparalleled. Tenzin, determined and ingenious, your dedication to justice is inspiring. I know the world is a better place with these three gender warriors among us. My deepest appreciation goes to Timothy Snyder, who won my heart when I was just sixteen. None of this would be possible without him. The life we have built over thirty-plus years is more than I could have dreamed. I am so thankful that he has been by my side for every challenge and every triumph.

About the Author

MELINDA M. MANGIN is an associate professor in the Department of Education Theory, Policy, and Administration in the Graduate School of Education at Rutgers University, where she teaches and conducts research related to teacher leadership and transgender identities in the context of K–12 schools. Dr. Mangin's scholarship is informed by her previous experience as a public high school Spanish teacher in New York City. She is a frequent speaker on the topic of transgender children and teacher leadership, presenting at national conferences as well as at local schools and teacher education preparation programs. Dr. Mangin is a founding member and organizer for Stepping Stones, a New York City, PFLAG-affiliated support group for families of transgender and gender-expansive children. She is the author of "Supporting Transgender and Gender-Expansive Children in School" (*Phi Delta Kappan*, 2018) and "Transgender Students in Elementary Schools: How Supportive Principals Lead" (*Educational Administration Quarterly*, 2019). In addition to her work with transgender communities, Dr. Mangin is a nationally recognized scholar of teacher leadership, the author of a coedited research volume (Teachers College Press, 2008), a coauthored book of case studies (Teachers College Press, 2010), and numerous peer-reviewed journal articles. From 2013 to 2018, she served as associate editor for *Educational Administration Quarterly*. Dr. Mangin is the principal investigator of two projects funded by the Spencer Foundation. *Transforming Public Education: A Research Agenda* is a collaborative project that brings together the expertise of twenty educators and activists for the purpose of improving education research related to transgender students and educators in K–12 schools. The second project, *Transgender Studies in Education: Building a Field of Study,* is a small learning community of education scholars whose collective efforts focus on articulating a vision for the future of educational scholarship informed by transgender experiences and communities.

Index